As We Grow Together:
A Daily Devotional for Expectant Couples

By

Minister

Onedia N. Gage

As We Grow Together:
A Daily Devotional for Expectant Couples

By

Minister

Onedia N. Gage

Other Titles by
Onedia N. Gage

As We Grow Together Daily Devotional for Expectant Couples

As We Grow Together Prayer Journal for Expectant Couples

The Blue Print: Poetry for the Soul

In Purple Ink: Poetry for the Spirit

Living An Authentic Life

The Measure of a Woman: The Details of Her Soul

On This Journey Daily Devotional for Young People

On This Journey Prayer Journal for Young People

Promises, Promises

Yielded and Submitted: A Woman's Journey of a Life Dedicated to God

As We Grow Together

Daily Devotional for Expectant Couples

By

Minister
Onedia N. Gage

As We Grow Together
Daily Devotional for Young People

Purple Ink, Inc. Press

For Information address:
Purple Ink, Inc
P. O. Box 27242
Houston, TX 77227
www.purpleink.net
www.onediagage.com

ISBN: 978-0-9801002-2-8

Printed in United States

7

Dedication

To Hillary and Nehemiah

For teaching me these lessons
And sharing your childhood wisdom with me.

I love you and prayerfully your wisdom will come in
Handy for my grandchildren and great-grandchildren
and all future generations.

God blessed them and said to them, "Be fruitful and increase in number; fill the earth and subdue it."

Genesis 1:28a

You will be with child and give birth to a son, and you are to give Him the name Jesus.

Luke 1:31

Blessed is she who has believed that what the Lord has said to her will be accomplished.

Luke 1:45

To the Couple:

Thank you for selecting **As We Grow Together** as your daily devotional during your pregnancy. You are truly embarking on a blessing. Your pregnancy is a beautifully blessed time in your life. This special time in your life also needs to be a time of prayer, study, mediation, forgiveness and reflection.

The time passes more quickly than you realize. Pregnancy is also God's tool which He uses to teach us that nothing is forever and great things come to those who wait on the Lord. Pregnancy is also His message that He can do great things through us when we are submissive and obedient. And let His will be done in our lives. He has it all planned and timed. He just needs our participation.

God sent His instruction to write this devotional through a great friend. She called me on a Sunday to tell me she was pregnant. At the same time, I was pregnant and another great friend was pregnant, also. She told me that I should write this after I reminded her of On This Journey: A Daily Devotional for Young People. What she didn't know was that He had shown me the vision. She was the confirmation I needed to proceed.

In this devotional, you will investigate who you think you are and discover who will be as a new parent. For those of you thinking: "but I am not a new parent," I beg to differ. You are a new parent each time you parent. My mother was a different parent to me than she was to my sister. In between children, we grow, change, learn and decide to be different parents. So you will parent differently. Lastly, you are new to that little one and that little one is new to you. While experience is the best teacher, most of our experiences demand our change.

Enjoy this time. Use it wisely. Nothing can get time back. I enjoyed all the intimate moments I could with my husband because I knew we would not enjoy that type of time together again ever. Our child changed and impacted the way we spend time together.

May these words bless your pregnancy and the relationship between the two of you. In this devotional, I will often suggest you two are married, because you are. For the duration of the life of the child, you will intersect and be reminded of one another. So if you are not married and don't intend to be, proceed with caution. By the end, you may want to be married, maybe not to him or her, but to someone.

God Bless,

Onedia N. Gage

How to Use this Journal

Dear Reader:

Just a few suggestions:

- ➤ Mark your Bible with the scriptures that we study in the devotional. You may need them later in your life.

- ➤ Feel free to go as you need based on topics.

- ➤ Read the devotional daily. It is helpful for the two of you to both read the devotional. This will serve as discussion topics for you.

- ➤ Pray with your spouse.

- ➤ Pray for your spouse.

- ➤ Pray for your unborn child.

- ➤ Pray for yourself.

- ➤ Journal your pregnancy. There is a companion prayer journal to this devotional.

- ➤ Enjoy your time together.

TABLE OF CONTENTS

WEEK ONE
CHOSEN

Congratulations and blessings! God chose you and your spouse to carry and birth His child. How exciting?! Pregnancy is an awesome time for you and your spouse. I am going to do my best not to simply address this as a woman's devotional. The pregnancy deserves the equal investment of both of you.

Parents are chosen. Count it as the blessing it is and with the reverence it deserves. There are many women who want to be pregnant and can't. This inability plagues them, causes the end of all possibilities to be reached and most options exhausted, including increased emotional anxiety and decreased financial means. There is no explanation needed to explain either event, because both events involve blessings, whether seen or not.

God chose you and your spouse for a time such as this, so we will discuss and discover some of the best uses of this time. We have to be reminded – His plans, thoughts and ways are not ours.

So now that we have accepted God's plan – our pregnancy – we will move forward to uncover the other treasures which accompany this awesome journey of this miracle.

Sunday	He chose you and your spouse to bear a child/children. Many are called, but few are chosen. John 15:16; Luke 1:30; Matthew 22:14
Monday	Children are gifts from God Luke 1:42 (Luke 1)
Tuesday	You and your spouse are made for each other. Genesis 2:22-24; Matthew 19:6
Wednesday	He designed you for a time such as this. Ecclesiastes 3:1, 2a
Thursday	When God is doing His will, expect some storms. Matthew 1:20-21
Friday & Saturday	Expect and prepare for His good and perfect will 1 John 5:14-15; 1 Thessalonians 5:18; Revelation 4:11

Week One – Sunday
He Chose you and Your Spouse To Bear a Child/Children
Matthew 22:14; Luke 1:30; John 15:16

[14]Many are invited, but few are chosen.

Matthew 22:14

When you consider the many people who don't have any children, you understand that your pregnancy is God's choice – not any doing of your own. There are many reasons why God makes the decision of who will have children and when. You are pregnant. God has chosen you for a time such as this. His choice speaks volumes of His role for you and His plans for your life. This is your time to be grateful and thankful and know that your blessings are flowing.

[30]But the angel said to her, Do not be afraid, Mary, you have found favor with God. [37]For nothing is impossible with God." Luke 1:30, 37. It doesn't matter what has happened in your past, God has blessed you and will continue to bless you. You are His prefect creation and He made you in His image. God does not make any mistakes. When the angel proclaims these statements, He has just told Mary that she would give birth to Jesus, and that Elizabeth, her barren relative, was in her sixth month of pregnancy. God will do what He says. Jesus is speaking to His disciples, educating them on Himself, specifically of love, and our relationship to Him and to the Father.

John 15:16 reads "You did not choose me, but I chose you and appointed you to go and bear fruit - fruit that will last. Then the Father will give you whatever you ask in my name." You are pregnant. You are chosen. This is just the beginning of what God will do in your life. You've only just begun.

Week One – Monday
Children Are Gifts From God
Luke 1

[42]In a loud voice she exclaimed: "Blessed are you among women, and blessed is the child you will bear"!

Luke 1:42

Children are not a mistake – spiritually nor scientifically. Children are not accidents. Children are God's plan to fulfill His own promise and purpose. When we behave as if we know this fact, other factors fall into place. I know that when I am discouraged about my life, my decision and my parenting, I realize that my husband and I were chosen for such a responsibility as this. God will not give you anything you can't handle. God will only give you what you can handle. God knows what you can handle. At all times. God selected you as a parent, so using this fact, let's move on to ask what purpose does God have now for you and you spouse.

How do you accept gifts? Do you get flushed with excitement? Do you use the c'est lavie approach? Do you acknowledge gifts as gifts? These are questions that are critical for determining your "gift-receiving" attitude.

When I found out I was pregnant, I said to God, "You chose me?" Motherhood and fatherhood is nothing less than a miracle. God does not bless everyone with children. God sends a clear message when a woman conceives His child. We will discuss stewardship later.

When you get confused and maybe even lose focus, remember many are called, but few are chosen.

Week One – Tuesday
You and Your Spouse Are Made For Each Other
Genesis 2:22-24; Matthew 19:5-6

[22] Then the Lord God made a woman from the rib He had taken out of the man, and He brought her to the man. [23]The man said, "This is now bone of my bones and flesh of my flesh; she shall be called 'woman,' for she was taken out of man." [24]For this reason a man will leave his father and mother and be united to his wife, and they will become one flesh.

Genesis 2:22-24

[6b] "Therefore what God has joined together, let no man separate."

Matthew 19:6

These are some of the most powerful words a married unit will realize. It has nothing to do with how well you relate or how good you look together, but it has everything to do with how God honors marriages. You are made to be together. You are one flesh. One flesh means one body and one mind. Will you differ in opinion? Yes, you will but let's evaluate your objective, your motivation.

Your marriage is designed to be a blessing to both you and others. This pregnancy will be part of this blessing. Before this event blesses others, your marriage blesses others. Giving honest consideration to your surroundings, you will see those blessings and additional opportunities to be a blessing.

This is a time to learn to communicate, reconcile, and compromise. This is a perfect opportunity to grow to agree. No other time is better than now to learn each other – each of you will be married to someone ne; if this is your first or any additional births, most people will agree that birth changes something about you at each one. So this event causes us to move beyond "our box" and move into a "new" place. This is the time to investigate your new thoughts and feelings and fears. Remember, your oneness is the most important factor required for your continued success.

Week One – Wednesday
He Designed You for a Time Such As This
Ecclesiastes 3:1-2a

[1]There is a time for everything, and a season for every activity under heaven: [2] a time to be born
Ecclesiastes 3:1-2a

At the onset of your pregnancy and even your marriage, these events have happened in God's own time. One or the other of you may have wanted to become pregnant earlier or even later, but you are pregnant <u>now</u>. NOW!! Let's spend a moment on that element of time. Now has great significance because you need to be fully engaged in your marriage and pregnancy- now. Time waits for no one. Use each day wisely. No other day looks like this one. The most important thing about now is not taking it for granted. Allow this pregnancy to be great. Don't neglect the moments designed to be beautiful and memorable.

God selected this time for you - spend some time finding out why now. There is a reason. My top five things to do to enjoy your pregnancy:

1. Know that you are beautiful outside – add to the inside. Remember that the baby is part of each emotion you experience.

2. Eat out as often as you can. The service will be better than ever. You won't have these same experiences without hard work after the baby is born.

3. Break out of your routine when you remember. Go to bed early. Sleep late. Do lots of 'out of the normal.' You want to have some practice for the baby's arrival.

4. Get ready to be wowed and surprised. They will do one or both each day.

5. Read all you can. This time in the future will be drastically reduced.

God is ready. So you prepare for some of the best days of your lives.

Week One – Thursday
When God is Doing His Will, Expect Some Storms
Matthew 1:20-21

[20]But after he had considered this, an angel of the Lord appeared to him in a dream and said, "Joseph son of David, do not be afraid to take Mary as your wife, because what is conceived in her is from the Holy Spirit. [21]She will give birth to a son, and you are to give him the name Jesus, because He will save His people from their sins.

Matthew 1:20-21

When Joseph discovered Mary was pregnant but they weren't married, he was disappointed. For some of us, this would've been a storm.

Remember that the tests that arise are designed to develop your testimony.

These storms range from financial difficulties to health disorders which arise during the pregnancy, to delivery complications and everything in between. These storms call for your increased prayer time and increased focus on God. This is a period where you have to be creative in order to fast and pray.

Unfortunately, everyone will not be receptive of your pregnancy. Keep in mind that God appointed you for this assignment. Stay focused and remain calm during the storms and the potential for storms. Grow closer to your mate. Talk more than you ever have. Discuss in detail your hopes, fears and expectations.

God is doing His will through your life and your pregnancy. This is a time to pray fervently and purposely. This is a time to study with zest and zeal. This is a time to grow closer to God.

Week One – Friday
Expect and Prepare for God's Good and Perfect Will
Revelation 4:11; 1 John 5:14-15; 1 Thessalonians 5:18

[14]This is the confidence we have in approaching God: that if we ask anything according to His will, He hears us. [15]And if we know that He hears us—whatever we ask—we know that we have what we asked of Him.

1 John 5:14-15

You have been selected as a parent. It is time for you to prepare for your role. While you can't use these nine months to prepare for his entire lifetime, you can get a great start.

Let's start with your role and responsibilities. During this devotional, we'll walk through God's desire for us as parents. There is, of course, a whole list of things to do as you prepare for the arrival of your loved one. This includes shopping for gadgets, clothing, room décor and furniture and other items. You will look for child care, decide on names, attend showers in preparation for the arrival, attend classes for the birth, and read about parenting. This preparation is critical – no other time will be the same. I spent my nine months reading What to Expect When You Are Pregnant and The Basics of Breastfeeding. I looked for a daycare. I completed one book and started another. I spent days and nights looking for just the right border for her room and all the accessories.

I wish I had spent more time in prayer for our lives current and future. This prayer was not because we needed help in preparation, but because I should've prayed for things and events for which I could not prepare. Our daughter is wonderful and none of my preparation has prepared me for what she does nor any of her many surprises. I can only say that be ready to be surprised and wowed each day.

I have also found that preparation is not for the baby. The preparation is designed to train you to start to act as a parent. I started to transform to a parent as soon as I discovered I was pregnant.

Week One – Saturday
Expect and Prepare for God's Good and Perfect Will
Revelation 4:11; 1 John 5:14-15; 1 Thessalonians 5:18
Part 2

[11] "You are worthy, our Lord and God, to receive glory and honor and power, for You created all things, and by Your will they were created and have their being."

Revelation 4:11

[18] give thanks in all circumstances, for this is God's will for you in Christ Jesus.

1 Thessalonians 5:18

God's good and perfect will needs an audience to function properly. We need to go about our daily lives knowing that God's good and perfect will prevail in situations at all times and we need to expect this.

So how do we give His will our attention, you ask? The first responsibility is to study God's word so that we know our role and responsibilities. The second is to apply what we know and learn to our daily lives. The third is to give our attention to God through prayer and time to the people of the church through ministry.

During these times, realities will be revealed to you about your new life – parenting is a new life – and the new life coming to you. As you expect greatness, you need to be ready to revise your schedule to accommodate her presence. Your preparation is key to the success for you and the new baby.

Part of His good and perfect will is this baby. This gift. You will experience new ones daily through her life. Pattern yourself to see God's presence in your child's life and movement and accomplishments.

Also remember that you are pregnant and soon you will parent – a lifelong journey – which has its own rewards. God has blessed you and found favor with you.

WEEK TWO
LOVE & INTIMACY WITH YOUR SPOUSE

Your marriage relationship is extremely important. This relationship stimulates the life of our child. This relationship is the basis of how the child is raised. If a child sees love and feels loved, then she will love. Children are excellent imitators of their environments.

Love and intimacy with your spouse needs nurturing and cultivating. It deserves your attention. Love and intimacy should be kept as a high level. You each need this love and intimacy. Love and intimacy fuels your marriage. You will need this energy.

One tool we use is The Five Love Languages by Dr. Gary Chapman. Dr. Chapman provides tools and equipment for the renewal, revival and resurgence of love in your marriage. He offers solutions for longtime marital problems and stumbling blocks. I promise you that a great, loving, and intimate relationship makes it easier to make the sacrifices for this baby.

Over the next seven days we will do a review of Dr. Gary Chapman's book with biblical applications for your marriage and your child.

I encourage you to read The Five Love Languages and The Five Love Languages for Children by Dr. Gary Chapman.

Sunday	Love & Intimacy With Your Spouse Song of Solomon 2:10a; 3:4
Monday	Word of Affirmation
Tuesday	Quality Time
Wednesday	Receiving Gifts
Thursday	Acts of Service
Friday	Physical Touch
Saturday	Keep The Love Tank Fulla

Week Two — Sunday
Love & Intimacy With Your Spouse
Song of Solomon 2:10a; 3:4

[10a] My lover is mine and I am his.

Song of Solomon 2:10a

Love and love relations with your spouse need to be kept at an all time high. If you had sex before you were married, then you remember how hot, steamy and seductive your love making was and hopefully it still is. TAKE IT HIGHER!! You need some time alone with your spouse.

1.   Love and intimacy expands exponentially now. Expect your marriage to change for the best. The anticipation, coupled with renewed love and passion, fuels your relationship. You talk about so many new things as you embark on this new dimension of your life.

2.   Children invite you to revisit your love and your intimacy levels. Children are walking bundles of love and there are times it is hard to love them. But now is the time to invest in your loving and intimate relationships.

27

Week Two — Monday
Words of Affirmation

MUDD manufacturers a product they call a complimentary cereal bowl. The cereal bowl has complimentary statements painted on it. "You are handsome." "You are wonderful." At the center of the bowl, where cereal is placed for consumption, it reads "Chicks really dig you." I know two men who have received them. They have blushed incessantly upon receipt.

Everyone flourishes under compliments. Some need words to survive. Let's not get this confused with people who depend on others for their self-worth. You need to compliment your mate and your mate needs to compliment you.

As Dr. Chapman describes, words of affirmation are uplifting and edifying to the recipient. Your words are your investment into your relationship. Your words provide security and comfort to your mate.

Because of the importance of words through this love language, you should do everything you can to avoid criticizing your spouse. Criticism breaks the spirit of those whose love language is words of affirmation.

Dr. Chapman also recommends notes and letters to affirm your mate. He also suggests your personally post yourself a reminder of how important words are. If your language is words, then you should share how your mate can fill your love tank with words.

Week Two — Tuesday
Quality Time

Quality time is the second of the love languages. Dr. Gary Chapman describes fluidly the importance of quality time. This happens to be my love language. One evening during my pregnancy we were out to dinner. A couple spoke to us saying enjoy each moment, each meal at its intended temperature, each late morning and early night. I'm not sure how seriously my husband took the statements, but I could not imagine how accurate they were. Even if your language is not quality time, you should cherish each occasion you are able to share with each other. Not even an extra minute is promised and your love was cultivated over time, whether over a milk shake or in a canoe.

One of the dialects of quality time, Dr. Chapman mentions, is quality conversation. One struggle we have as married couples is quality conversation. Our daily conversations are centered on money; household operations, child-rearing issues and the like. Before marriage and parenthood, we discussed each other, our fears, feelings, and dreams. Your mate still needs that conversation. I know that I still do. I crave my husband's conversation. Keep that alive in your marriage—it will fuel your love and intimacy.

One thing I have learned about keeping my love tank full because of the time I spend with my husband is that a full love tank keeps the love tank of her loved ones full. In other words, when my love tank is empty, I have a hard time spending time with my daughter. When my love tank is full, I can't stop spending time with her. A full love tank for both of you equates to a full love tank for your child(ren).

Week Two — Wednesday
Receiving Gifts

Everyone (almost) likes receiving gifts. Some people, however, need gifts to know they are loved. Spontaneous or planned; simple or extravagant; big or small – it doesn't matter. This love language is not to be misunderstood or confused with buying your mate's affections or love. The gift is an expression the other person's thoughts and demonstrates how much they care.

Dr. Chapman explains that there is also a dialect of this language – physical presence. Your principle presence is your gift to your mate. This should not be confused with quality time. Physical presence actually distinguished itself when one person is experiencing some form of hardship or crisis or emotional experience. The gift of oneself is awesome for another who is grieving or suffering a hardship. The presence of your mate moves you in surprising ways. The gift can definitely be their attention to you and your needs.

With this love language, be sure that you do as much as you can for your mate before the baby arrives. This time now – while you are pregnant – is a special time in your marriage relationship which will never be the same again.

For the person whose love language is gifts, forgetting special days is not okay. For some, our memory may be a little weak, but if your mate's language is gifts then you need to use whatever devices necessary to avoid forgetting. Just remember, there is a little one on the way and they will also hold you accountable for their special days.

Week Two — Thursday
Acts of Service

How does your wife make you feel when she does something for you because you needed help? How does it feel when your husband remembers your requests? If your response is loved, cared for, remembered, or excited, then this is your love language. What people do for you, especially your mate, is more important than anything else that can happen to you.

During your pregnancy (both of you), you need to learn to let people do things for you even if acts of services is not your primary language. As you get closer to term, your chores double; you sleep less and your time is no longer spare. You will need help, sometimes more than other times. Learn to let people help you. Learn to ask.

Acts of service is a form of humility for the contributor and the recipient. My mother and I recently helped a long-time friend do some organization. She was pregnant and she needed some help. She asked me what she could be doing while we worked. I said "rest." Her one year old was asleep. Our husbands were cleaning the kitchen. She had just hosted the baby's birthday party. We were excited to fill her love tank in this manner. She commented that we had lots of energy, but what she didn't know was that I just had enough to help her at that time provided by God. God gives us whatever we need to help each other at that appointed time. I hope what we did helped her and made her future mornings easier.

It is great fulfillment to fill someone else's love tank. I think acts of service are the easiest of the love languages to maintain.

31

Week Two — Friday
Physical Touch

Physical touch during your pregnancy and during your delivery becomes invaluable. Physical touch includes hugs, touches, kisses, massages, and sexual intercourse. After the arrival of our child, physical touch became harder for us, but as soon as we realized that it had diminished, we created an environment in our home where physical touch was reestablished as a priority.

There are times when a simple touch from your spouse will give you just the spark of energy you needed to complete your tasks, including whatever the baby requires of you.

Physical touch also comes in handy in the delivery room. He could massage you and feed you and hold your hand, all of which are designed to provide you comfort and as much relaxation as possible during delivery.

My husband was very attentive in the Lamaze class. He remembered the breathing techniques and the massage techniques. He used them without being asked. When I was in delivery, I forgot the breathing and he demonstrated immediately. His presence and knowledge was invaluable in the delivery room.

My secondary love language is physical touch. This changed from acts of service after we had been married for eighteen months. There is magic and comfort in the hands of our spouses. Uniquely enough, our love languages are the same. It is very interesting to say the least.

Week Two — Saturday
Keep Your Love Tank Full

Your love tank is where your emotional wellness is measured. Dr. Chapman states that keeping the love tank full (p. 23) is essential to your marriage. A full love tank will enhance the health of your marriage. Everyone desires a healthy marriage. A full love tank ensures a healthy and fulfilling marriage.

How to keep your love tank full:

(1)   Use your mate's primary and secondary love languages to meet his/her emotional needs;
(2)   Communicate to your spouse about the level of the love tanks. How is your love tank today? What can I do to fill your love tank?
(3)   Communicate your needs to your mate so that your mate can meet those needs.

As your marriage evolves, your love tank will require different mechanisms to keep it full. However if you recognize a change, then you communicate that change to your mate.

For some, this will seem corny or awkward. This, however, will elevate your marriage. When I ask my husband how is your love tank, I have reinvested in my marriage and in my mate. I have taken time to seek the needs of my husband. His face lights up and he turns towards me and his heart softens then he answers me. This important question doesn't compare to the flat response from "how are you doing?"

I govern myself with the thought of what you sow so shall you reap. I want my love tank full and I want my husband to be active in its fullness. We have promised to edify one another and this edifies.

Just try it and if the climate of your marriage doesn't change for the better, seek other tools which will. I have never heard it not work.

33

WEEK THREE
YOUR ROLE AS WOMAN AND WIFE

God has a job description for us. He clearly defines our role and duties as a woman and a wife. God is quite orderly and He was certain that the woman has a place. He was certain that the wife has a role and duties. Over the next seven days, we will examine our role and responsibilities. For some this will be new – for other a simple refresher or reminder. In either case, our marriages and life will progress much smoother if we learn to function within our role. We don't have a problem with knowing, but we have trouble within the parameters of our role. What do I mean? God designed life to follow certain criteria and guidelines. When we choose to divert from those then we create conflict and confusion. I think that we are God's best creation, and we should act as such.

There are times when it is hard to be a great wife. There are times when it's harder than others to be wise and supportive. But then there are times when it is an awesome experience to be a woman and a wife. You will experience a love of that soon.

Motherhood moves you to reexamine your first roles and responsibilities more carefully. These roles and responsibilities need to be active and functioning as you prepare for your baby. We will investigate the roles, responsibilities, and action plans for achieving success in these.

Sunday	God made woman as a helper to man Genesis 2:20b-25
Monday	(Womanhood defined) A Noble Wife is a Noble Woman First 1 Kings 3:12; Ephesians 4:22-24; 4:32; 5:40; 6:18
Tuesday	The Wife of Noble Character, Part 1 Proverbs 31:10-17
Wednesday	The Wife of Noble Character, Part 2 Proverbs 31:18-31
Thursday	Your Role as Wife Ephesians 5:22-33
Friday	Wives and Our Higher Calling 1 Peter 3:1-7
Saturday	Wives, Some Final Instructions Colossians 3:18; 4:2, 6

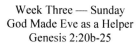

Week Three — Sunday
God Made Eve as a Helper
Genesis 2:20b-25

[20b] But for Adam no suitable helper was found. [22] Then the Lord God made a woman from the rib He had taken out of the man, and He brought her to the man.

Genesis 2:20b, 22

In the grand sequence of events, Eve was created last. The finishing touches and the world's future revolved around a woman. Haughty? No. Responsibility? Yes. God designed women to help man – our husbands. Women are to help men – husbands with God's work.

While women have been blamed for as responsible for the sins of man, mankind and labor pains, we are also known for our successes. We need to remain focused on the ability to achieve success rather than the hurdles.

Helper mean that we assist, not take over; follow, not lead; and submit, rather than control. Do we do all these things all the time? Not really. Are we trying? Everyday.

There are times when I find it hard to help my husband, but I pray for perseverance in my role and responsibility. When I pray, God helps me do my "job."

Something so simple as "helper" is quite complex. God says helper without condition of whether or not we agree or believe. All of his ideas don't excite you or make any sense, but your charge is to help him either bring this to fruition or to see the problem with the plan. All of this through prayer, love and God's guidance.

Sometimes we find it hard to help our husbands, but it is our job. Helping him is our first assignment. God will not honor your prayers if you are not aligned properly with your husband as a helper.

Week Three — Monday
A Noble Wife is a Noble Woman First:
Womanhood Defined
Ephesians 4:22-24; Eph 4:32; 5:10; 6:18; 1 Kings 3:12

[10b] and find out what pleases the Lord.

Ephesians 5:10b

A noble woman aligns herself to God. This noble woman stands for God. She believes in God fully and completely. A noble woman has faith which passes all understanding. A noble woman possesses many wonderful characteristics.

A noble woman knows her first priority is to find what pleases the Lord at all times in <u>all</u> situations. They key here is to desire to know that pleases the Lord and because we desire to know what pleases Him, then we will seek to please Him. He will show us what pleases Him. Eph 4:22-24 [22b] "to put off your old self, which is being complete by its deceitful desires; [23] to be made new in the attitude of your minds."

Our attitude determines how others perceive us, thus helping or hindering our progress. Add to that your attitude impacts your husband's and your child's image – use your attitude wisely. Women have wrath – use it wisely, if at all. God judges us by our attitude as well. Finally, the past which haunts you so much, Noble Woman know that our past transgressions are forgiven and forgotten and act accordingly. Ephesians 6:18: "and pray in the spirit on all occasion with all kinds of prayers and requests." With this in mind, be alert and always keep on praying for all the saints. Pray rather than complain. Pray rather than worry. Pray before quitting. Pray. Pray. Pray.

1Kings 3:12 – I will do what you asked. I will give you a wise and discerning heart, so that there will never have been anyone like you, nor will there ever be. Noble women are extraordinarily unique with wisdom and discernment. God honors what noble women ask for, so ask believing that God hears you.

Ephesians 4:32 – Be kind and compassionate to one another, forgiving each other, just as in Christ. God forgave you.

I learned this scripture during pre-marital counseling with my husband. When I keep this scripture before me then I know I won't need Ephesians 4:31 which reminds us as a noble woman we will get rid of all bitterness, rage, and anger, brawling and slander, along with every form of malice: "A noble woman reminds me to look beyond the flesh and touch the Spirit." Just as a reminder, noble women are sought by all, so when someone crosses your path, seek to meet their needs as a noble woman would.

A noble woman is a servant, not to be served. A noble woman is on assignment from God.

36

Week Three — Tuesday
The Wife of Noble Character – Part 1
Proverbs 31:10-17

[10]A wife of noble character who can find? She is worth far more than rubies.

Proverbs 31:10

Proverbs 31:10-31, the most popular scriptures about a wife, documents the characteristics of a noble charactered wife. These scriptures detail her actions and activities, how her husband and children feel about her. In verses 10-17, she is resourceful, entrepreneurial, creative, earnest, smart, investor and strong physically. She is all those attributes because she is thoughtful and planful. She thinks and plans for the well-being of her family.

For women, timing for planning is crucial. I allocate time to plan for our daily needs and our future. This time provides you an opportunity to budget, plan the family calendars, invest in the family's future (i.e., college fund) and plan my work. Do you have a family mission statement? Does your husband have a copy of the family budget? Do you have a plan for your children's higher education? Do you have the family's vacations planned? Do you own land and other valuables? Do you have too many gadgets (i.e. boats, jet skies) which you do not have time to use? What plans do you have in place for the success of your family? Do you know each of your financial resources are allocated? Do you have business saavy? The answers to these questions constitute a portion of your role as a noble wife. I first read this scripture as a child and I always admitted that I liked this woman and honestly wanted to be her. We all want to be her. We want to find time to be her. I am in prayer for "her" that I submit myself daily to God so that I can be a noble wife. I am tailoring my life and myself so that God can do those things in my life so that I can be a noble wife in my marriage.

Welcome to a photo for the noble wife – go get your mirror. Your desire makes you whole and noble.

Week Three — Wednesday
The Wife of Noble Character – Part 2
Proverbs 31:18-31

[29] "Many women do noble things, but you surpass them all."

Proverbs 31:29

Welcome, wife of noble character. Now that we know that "she" is not imaginary, and we are "her," we can proceed.

The woman is a planner. She works hard and stays up late. She is creative. She is community conscious. She is resourceful. She even sews her sheets. She sews clothes and sells them. Do we have to have all of these attributes? Not the sewing specifically, but resourcefulness is a prerequisite for success.

Verses 26 and 27 are the most important scriptures. A noble wife is wise. Her thoughts are wise. Her actions are wise. She speaks wisdom. Wisdom? How do we gain wisdom? We gain wisdom by asking God. Faithful instruction is on her tongue. Not complaining. Not gossiping. Not ridicule. Not foul language. Wise words and faithful instruction are on her tongue. She uses this wisdom to watch over her household.

Do you remember the Enjole commercial? This is what we are responsible for as wives. Most everything. Just for reminder sake, the commercial features a woman who says "I can bring home the bacon, fry it up in a pan and never let you forget you're a man. Because I'm a woman." This equates to waking up before dawn gathering and preparing for the children, husband and self, going to work, doing all the errands, paying the bills, coming home in traffic, cooking, cleaning, putting everyone to bed (did I mention homework?), making love to your husband, and going to bed well after the news.

A noble woman does all this and more. She also makes time for her dreams, needs and vacation. She allocates time for a quiet moment for her and God to unite daily so that He can refuel her.

A noble woman is you. You do these things. You have these attributes. You are wise.

Week Three — Thursday
Your Role as Wife
Ephesians 5:22-23

[22]Wives, submit to your husbands as to the Lord. [33b]and the wife must respect her husband.

Ephesians 5:22, 33b

Most of us married the man of our dreams or some sort of sweetheart (childhood, high school, or college), but what we had no idea about what submission would mean, at least I didn't. I spend lots of time in prayer on this topic, as do some of you.

I have learned that it means that I have give and compromise <u>especially</u> when I didn't want to. For other of us, submission means we have to turn in our independence card. This was hard to achieve. For some, it means that we had to change our plans to incorporate his plans. However, overall submission means that we submit to God and God will guide, provide and decide. In that same fashion, submit to our husbands. I am learning from my best friend to tell God everything and not to argue or contradict my husband. Let God order His steps and I will be satisfied. Her behavior is the essence of submission.

Submit humbly all your petitions and thanksgiving to God and He promised to handle the rest.

Do you respect your husband? Do you know what it means to respect your husband? It really means to honor him. Honor the decisions you make. As an example, if you agree to a decision that he makes meaning you said okay or you never objected (silent consent), then you should not change the plans unless something unforeseen goes awry. If you have a budget, you should not hide purchases. You should tell him you spent the money, or whatever it was and why. Remember, none of this is because of him, rather it is because of Him.

I will be the first to say sometimes this respect and submission serves up hearty helpings of humility. The key is to remember that God is who is honored, respected, revered and feared when we act appropriately.

The great news is that it is easier when he – your husband – is easy to submit to.

Week Three — Friday
Wives and Our Higher Calling
1 Peter 3:1-7

⁴Instead, it should be that of your inner self, the unfading beauty of a gentle and quiet spirit, which is of great worth in God's sight.

1 Peter 3:4

One of our attributes which defines our worth is a gentle and quiet spirit. Our beauty should be defined by the beauty of the inner self. Is our inner self beautiful? We have a higher calling as wives more so even than a woman. We have our families and husbands reputations in our possession. Our behavior, attitude, and speech communicate volumes to the world about our husbands and homes. Our calling includes guarding our tongue. The very organ which can provide life communicates love and build morals, is the same organ which defeats another's spirit, defiles self-image and disintegrates the function for woman/wife. Wives need to learn to function inside the meekness (Matthew 5:1), the fruits of the Spirit (Galatians 5:22-23) and the beauty of a gentle and quiet spirit.

As a wife, our role is to build. Our title is the first block. Wife caused man to become husband. Children come creating family love blocks. Our blocks then become a structure based on God's design and foundation. We have a calling to build, nurture, uplift, and encourage.

Just a note about his reputation: it is linked to this reputation. Keep a gentle and quiet spirit, especially when it's difficult. God honors your actions.

Last thing: a higher calling requires a response. The calling requires us to abandon the mundane, avoid the mediocre, discount the minute and reject all idleness.

By the very essence of job descriptions, we don't have time for certain things. But most of us want, and quite frankly expect, God's most profound blessings on our marriages, with this pregnancy being an indication of what God will do, so because of our expectations and His promises, we have lots of work to do and a lot of ground to cover. In a short period of time.

Your response to the higher calling needs to be specific, committed, and now.

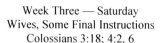

Week Three — Saturday
Wives, Some Final Instructions
Colossians 3:18; 4:2, 6

[18]Wives, submit to your husbands, as is fitting in the Lord.
[2]Devote yourselves to prayer, being watchful and thankful.
[6]Let your conversation be always full of grace, seasoned with salt, so that you may know how to answer everyone.

Colossians 3:18; 4:2, 6

Four scriptures proclaim, "Wives, submit to your husbands (Ephesians 5:22, 24: Colossians 3:18, 1 Peter 3:1). With this many scriptures saying the same message, submission deserves our undivided attention. God honors our submission to our husbands, our gift. If submission challenges you, then fast and pray. God leads, guides, and provides. He will honor your desire, commitment and honesty and He will help you.

Pray. Pray. Pray. The Bible addresses prayer of various levels which all concur: prayer is important. Woman in the Bible have been responsible for praying since Eve. It is our responsibility to pray over our husbands, family, children, and homes.

Our conversations are not always pure, unfortunately. Our conversations are supposed to be full of grace, wisdom, kindness, and love, just to name a few. This sometimes will require prayer. Keep praying until something different happens. God gives us the correct words to speak to and address everyone, but we choose to ignore His words. Keep praying. Your conversations will change.

So wives and expectant mommies, if all else fails remember that your words which are not pure and full of grace can haunt you later. Hillary was eighteen months old and was able to repeat some things. How embarrassed would I be if she repeated something I had said that was less than kind? I keep this thought at the forefront of my mind when I speak. I only want her to know the meek, gentle, and loving words, rather than anything else.

WEEK FOUR
YOUR ROLE AS MAN AND HUSBAND

God has a job description for men. He clearly defines your role as a man and duties of a man, husband, and father. God is quite orderly and He was certain that the man has a place. A significant place: man has a job and is the head of the woman and his home. God's first order of business was to give Adam a job.

Over the next seven days we will examine Adam's job, role, and responsibilities. The Bible clearly articulates God's stance on all matters regarding man and His expectations of man.

Men, and women, too, for that matter, this is a call to action. Man, your role is as difficult as it is rewarding; is as challenging as it is awesome; is as complex as it is delicate; is as confusing as it is honorable. Men, to whom much is given, much is required.

Men, your role is important and extremely valuable. Over the next week, we will uncover tools for your role and responsibilities. We will provide resources for encouragement during your journey as a man and husband. Value exists in your success in your role. Successfully functioning in your role is critical to the growth and advancement of the family. So, we will also provide tools and resources for family success.

You have a hard job, but the rewards are great. Enjoy the journey.

Sunday	God creates man in His own image; Man defined Genesis 1:26-27; 2:7
Monday	God employs man: Man's role Genesis 1:28-30; 2:19-25
Tuesday	"(Adam), Where Are You"? Genesis 3:9-12, 17a
Wednesday	He who findeth a wife findeth a **good** thing. But who are you? Proverbs 18:22 KJV
Thursday	Love your wife: Your role as a husband Ephesians 5:22-23; Colossians 3:19
Friday	Loving Your Wife, Part 2 Ephesians 5:22-23; Colossians 3:19
Saturday	The "Honey-Do" List 1 Peter 3:1-7

Week Four — Sunday
God Creates Man in His Own Image; Man defined
Genesis 1:26, 27; 2:7

[26]Then God said, "Let us make man in our image, in our likeness, and let them rule over the fish of the sea and the birds of the air, over the livestock, over all the earth and over all the creatures that move along the ground.

Genesis 1:26

God creates man daily in his own image. You are expecting and your baby is in God's image. Being created in God's image is quite the compliment, but also carries quite the responsibility.

Because you are created in His image and likeness, you are expected to behave in a certain manner. Some of your character traits should include meekness, kindness, loving, wisdom, forgiving, tender-hearted, patience, long-suffering, peaceful, joy, faith, self-control, goodness, and thoughtfulness. When you are not one of these characteristics, then you are judged. You are looked down upon and find frowns often.

Fair? Probably not. True? Yes. Men are held to a standard defined by God and upheld by Jesus Christ. Possible? Yes. Examples? Love. All men have sinned and fallen short of His glory. So why did God create you in His image if it is virtually impossible to uphold the standard? God created man perfect and free from sin. He only knows to create perfect beings. Adam and Eve sinned and set us up for the rest of our lives. God recognizes your effort to meet the standard. Do you exercise in those areas? When you don't meet the standard, do you repent and ask for forgiveness? Do you study the bible and pray diligently for your wife and family? Do you read about how to be a better husband/man? Do you read about how to understand your wife better? Take time to evaluate what you can do to invest in your wife, marriage, and family. Those are ways you can align yourself to God's image.

43

Week Four — Monday
God Employs Man
Genesis 1:28-30; 2:19-25

[28] God blessed them and said to them, "Be fruitful and increase in number; fill the earth and subdue it. Rule over the fish of the sea and the birds of the air and over every living creature that moves on the ground."

Genesis 1:28

"Rule...." God employed man immediately. Adam had a job. Adam was busy. He was clear about his role. Some men, some of whom are husbands, are confused about their role and their job. How could this be? Our God is not synonymous with confusion.

So what is your job? This is a good time to evaluate your job. Is your job conducive to family life in your new role, as you prepare to father? Are your job requirements flexible for support of the family needs? Are your dreams, desires, plans and favorite pastimes aligned with your job and role as husband and now father?

A sub-brand of your job is to provide. Adam used his job to provide for Eve. In the same fashion, you will provide for your wife. Part of this provision is your benefits at work and how those benefits cover your family and your needs. Do you have paternity leave? What arrangements are needed for time off after the birth? What medical benefits cover the new born and what do you need to do to engage those coverages? Has each details of the hospital been taken care of? Is your hospital bag packed? What is your wife's favorite scripture? Have you attended the Lamaze class? Have you discussed the name options and why? Will your wife breast feed or bottle? How can you help? Are you reading any books about parenting? Adam had it easy – he was in the Garden of Eden with God. His relationship was focused rather than clouded as we are today. However, you have more resources than Adam. You have work to do just like Adam. So let's get to work!

Week Four — Tuesday
Adam, Where Are You?
Genesis 3:9-12, 17a

[11] And He said, "Who told you that you were naked? Have you eaten from the tree that I commanded you not to eat from"?

Genesis 3:11

In verse 9, God asks Adam, "Where are you"? God only asks Adam so that Adam would know where he was. God already knew where Adam and Eve were and what they had done. God was prepared for our disobedience.

Is there a remedy for this? Yes. Using Adam as an example, Adam could have done three things that would have helped change our circumstances. First, Adam could have admitted to God immediately that he had disobeyed, rather than God finding him to reveal the indiscretion. Secondly, Adam could have chosen to obey God. Instead, he knowingly disobeyed God. Lastly, Adam could have owned his mistake, rather Adam blamed the sin on Eve. God chose man to be the leader. Did you choose to be the leader? Do you blame Eve?

The choices you made as a single man and the choices you make as a married man continue to impact your wife and family. Keep this at the forefront of your mind and heart when you are making decisions.

I have found that even if it was my fault or bad judgment, God still holds my husband responsible for the error. God expects husbands to have a daily relationship and communication with Him. If this communication-prayer is happening as it should, Hillory and all husbands can hear God's directions.

Last note – God asked "Adam, who encouraged you to defy me"? That is my paraphrase, but understand that when God said "who," He knew already "who." He asks another questions without waiting for an answer for the first. Who or what overrides God in your life and mind? This is a call to action for us. We need to forsake all others for the Word of Christ. Use God's direction to discern when you are letting "who" separate you from God.

45

Week Four — Wednesday
But Who Are You?
Proverbs 18:22 (KJV)

[22]He who findeth a wife, findeth a good thing.

Proverbs 18:22 (KJV)

When you found your wife, it was the best day of your life. My husband's testimony moves me about him finding me. I am sure that your testimony is just as moving. Have you wondered why He chose to bless you with her? Who are you that God blessed you so? Who are you? I wrote a poem for my husband that I want to share with you.

The Measure of a Man
By Onedia N. Gage

Man,

Do you know who you are?
I asked you a question, Man.
Answer me!
You can't answer me?
That's okay. I'll tell you who you are.

You are my leader, my leadership.
God made you the head and not the tail.

You are my lover.
Christ said love me like He loved the church.
Sacrificially and sanctified.

You make me perfect.

Christ presented the His church without one spot or wrinkle, made it holy and without blemish and whole.

You teach me love.
God shared 1 Corinthians through you and your actions and deeds and words.

You show me forgiveness.
Christ said we shall forgive seventy times seven, without thought or hesitation.
Thank you for forgiving me.

You are my provider.
God made you to meet my needs and be my com forter and be strong for me because I am the weaker vessel.

God is wise having never made on mistake.
He charged you with my care.
He charged you to love me, like on one else is able or gifted or blessed.

You are her father.
Christ said that children are a gift from God.
When He gives you a child, consider yourself blessed.

Your role is as clear as Waterford crystal, while as heavy and as complex.

46

God defined you and you can't change His definition.

I know now you can answer me, but more importantly you can answer for yourself who you are.

I love you because of who you are and your submission to His role.
Forever.

So who are you?

Week Four — Thursday
Your Role as a Husband: Loving Your Wife
Ephesians 5:22-33; Colossians 3:19

[25]Husbands, love your wives, first as Christ loved the church and gave himself up for her. [28b]He who loves his wife as he loves himself. [19]Husbands, love your wives and do not be hard with them.
Ephesians 5:25, 28b; Colossians 3:19

This is a great command and responsibility for you. Love her. Love her unconditionally. Love her without strings attached. Love her when she makes you happy. Love her when she angers you. Love her because she trusts God through you with her life, well-being, spiritual growth and future. Love her through it all, because of it all, in spite of it all, and during it all.

A heart breaking moment happened in my marriage when we had a financial difficulty. My husband was silent. His silence translated into the thinking and really believing that he loved me only when all was well, but when difficulty arose, he didn't love me. It is during our difficult seasons when we are called closer to God and to one another, not farther apart. When difficult times cause separation and silence, in our case, this is not of God. Those circumstances are of the devil and needs to be dismissed immediately. This time above all others you need to reach out for one another. Your bond and relationship, your ability to communicate and love shows God your true heart.

In Week 2, we discussed the five love languages. This should be used as a tool to assist you in loving your wife. If Dr. Chapman does not help you, lean on your understanding through Christ. God will honor your desire to love your wife.

Nothing communicates love to your wife like when you listen and do your best about the details and remembering the special dates of your marriage.

Week Four — Friday
Loving Your Wife, Part 2
Ephesians 5:22-23; Colossians 3:19

[28b]He who loves his wife as he loves himself.

Ephesians 5:28b

There is a study which shows that premature babies grow better when they are held. They thrive because of the touch of those who loved them through touch. I share that because some women need touch and listening like everyone needs air or like you need football.

Genuine love for your wife builds a powerful marriage, which will sustain whatever your marriage has to endure. Your love for your wife insures her security. Her security prompts growth in your marriage. Loving her as God commands assures that she will stand with you forever. The east coast recently sustained a hurricane, Isabel, which was accompanied by winds up to 150 miles per hour. Based on the foundation and strength, some homes and buildings still stand. Unfortunately, others didn't. Winds will come to your marriage. How fast can the winds be before your marriage sustains damage?

Loving your wife is an investment in your marriage. You married her because you love her. Love is an action, not a noun. Your actions speak louder than words. The words you are trying to drown out are in her head when she thinks of all the ways that she wishes you would love her. Ask her what she dreams of, needs, and how she would like to be loved. This conversation will enlighten you beyond your wildest imagination, but will start a new era in your marriage. Love her.

In 1996, John Travolta and Kyra Sedgwick starred in "Phenomenon." John stars as George O'Mally and he falls in love with Lacy, Kyra's character. She makes chairs and because of his love for her, he buys her chairs – all of them. What are your wife's chairs? Let's get closer to home. I'm the author of five books and I know that he loves me, so when he read my second book, I knew how deeply he loved me.

49

Week Four — Saturday
The "Honey-Do" List
1 Peter 3:1-7

[7]Husbands, in the same way be considerate as you live with your wives, and treat them with respect as the weaker partner and as heirs with you of the gracious gift of life, so that nothing hinders your prayers.

1 Peter 3:7

The "Honey-Do" list is your list of chores, tasks and helpful things that you can accomplish which will propel the household forward. I would almost guess that your list never has the following suggestions on them. I have included this list so that you will have a starting point for the love actions I spoke of on Thursday and Friday.

1. Do the entire "Honey-Do" list without excuse, complaint, or frown.
2. Schedule her appointments for her hair, nails, feet, eyebrows, and whatever else she needs.
3. Book her a massage. Surprise her!
4. Send flowers or balloons on the special days and the regular days. Write on the card specifically why. For example: "Thank you for the wonderful meal last night," or "Thank you for 2,160 days of our wonderful life together."
5. Hire a housekeeper as a gift.
6. Run her bath water. You take care of the children (this is very popular with me).
7. Bring her lunch to work.
8. Send cards telling her you are thinking of her and are truly grateful you are married.
9. Rub her feet. Rub her back. Rub her hair.
10. Drop off and pick up the child(ren) from school or daycare.
11. Treat her with more value. Ask her how she is doing and really listen.

The "Honey-Do" list will show you what your wife really needs. These actions give you an idea of what it takes to be her. This should give you an opportunity to see the world from her perspective. These actions show her that you love her.

50

WEEK FIVE
YOUR ROLE AS MOTHER

Motherhood is an awesome gift. Your life will never be the same and it is no longer your own. Motherhood is also a tremendous gift and responsibility. Nothing is quite so rewarding as motherhood – not even fatherhood can measure up.

I certainly desired a child, but I didn't know I was ready. When we conceived, I was scared because I didn't know if I could do a great job. I had no idea how to do a great job. I had a few good examples, but could I be a mother, ultimately the mother God expected me to be?

In the next seven days, I give my seven stars of motherhood. These are my observations on the foundations of a great motherhood – the tools I've used so far. By the way, most plans you make may not materialize. Don't fear, though, the baby will have clothes to wear home and your husband can go home for the car seat, and without the epidural you planned, the baby will still come and you will still be sane when it's over.

Your role is broad, yet vague; rewarding, yet difficult; inspiring, yet revealing; powerful and life-altering. I do know this in her first 18 months, I have learned more than all of my life. She teaches me something new daily and surprises me daily, as well.

Motherhood is a journey, rather than destination. My last points are (1) maintain your sense of humor; (2) call your mother or mother-figure daily, and (3) your only real job is to feed her. No matter what happens, Hillary eats, is warm, has clothes and shoes, and I hold her and hug her so that she feels my love in her language.

Sunday	Your Self-Portrait: What Do You See? Psalms 139:14; Isaiah 55:8
Monday	A Godly Woman Proverbs 31:28
Tuesday	In the Spirit Galatians 5:22-23
Wednesday	Wisdom at Work Proverbs 3:5-6; 31:26
Thursday	Teaching God's Word Matthew 28:20
Friday	Powerful Relationship Builders (so a man thinketh) Exodus 20:12; Matthew 5:5; Ephesians 13:19-20
Saturday	The Reap/Sow Principle 2 Corinthians 9:6

Week Five — Sunday
Your Self-Portrait: What do you see?
Psalms 139:14; Isaiah 55:8

[14]I praise you because I am fearfully and wonderfully made; [8]"For my thoughts are not your thoughts and my ways are not your ways," declares the Lord.

Psalms 139:14; Isaiah 55:8

Many women overcome low self-esteem and others live with a low opinion of themselves daily. There is great news I want to share with you and I want you to share with others: we are fearfully and wonderfully made. God created you and your beauty, inner and outer; He created you in His own image. He created you to serve Him.

We are fearfully and wonderfully made. Some days it's hard to realize or remember but each day, no matter how we feel we need keep this fact at the forefront of our minds.

The following is your to do list:

(1)   Stop criticizing yourself.
(2)   Stop putting yourself down.
(3)   Don't let others refer to you negatively.
(4)   Believe you can do it – <u>anything</u>.
(5)   Know that loving yourself is the least you owe God for loving you first!
(6)   Take time for yourself.
(7)   Care for yourself – spend a little extra time on your appearance when you can especially when you don't feel like it.
(8)   Remember God loves you no matter what
(9)   Remember, the harder it is for you to love yourself, then it's harder to let God love you.
(10)   If you love you, then it's easy for Him to love you.

This is a great time to correct your self image. Whatever it is, it can afford to improve. And you will love the change.

Week Five — Monday
A Godly Woman
Proverbs 31:28

[28]Her children arise and call her blessed; her husband also, and he praises her.

Proverbs 31:28

A woman who fears the Lord is to be treasured. This is the woman all people are drawn to. This woman prays and praises and worships God with her whole heart. She resembles peace and she operates with thanksgiving.

A Godly woman, who can find? I think being a Godly woman is a choice. We choose so many things. We choose to answer His call to Godliness. Sometimes, we choose not to answer His call. That's when the trouble starts.

At any rate, as women we need to choose to be obedient to God's calling. When we exercise in obedience, we exhibit our fear of God. Then we are called blessed. Then He praises us – his wife.

The short list of choices we make to be Godly:

1. Take real quality time and study God's word.
2. Meditate regularly.
3. Pray faithfully.
4. Love your child/children.
5. Concentrate on your womanhood – what God has assigned to you.
6. Plan for your family.
7. Seek wise counsel. Titus 2.
8. Remain faithful no matter what happens.
9. Remain gracious.
10. Stay your course.

Nothing warms my heart more than when my daughter smiles at me. She delights in seeing me when I pick her up from school or when I come home. I delight in her, too. Her smile blesses me. It lifts my spirit and encourages me to continue being the mother and improving my motherhood.

Week Five — Tuesday
In The Spirit
Galatians 5:22-23 (KJV)

[22]But the fruit of the Spirit is love, joy, peace, long suffering gentleness, goodness, faith, [23]meekness, temperance; against such things there is no law.

Galatians 5:22-23 (KJV)

When I read these scriptures for the first time I said, "Ah-ha." These scriptures are important because these attributes are important to God.

Fruit is grown on a tree. This fruit is matured, or grown, by the Spirit. This fruit is born of the Spirit. The Holy Spirit is the spirit the scripture references.

For most of us, only one or two of these attributes are harder to achieve than the rest. For some, we may be having problems in all areas. We recommend that you work on one attribute at a time until you have them functioning well in your life. Functioning well in the fruits of the Spirit stimulates the growth and health of your child. When you are loving, kind and faithful, your child will be loving, kind and faithful as well. Further, children emulate and imitate our mannerisms. They inherit, if you will, our actions and attitudes.

Second to God being pleased with you, our behavior should match the attributes of the fruits because your children are watching. My mother was bundled up with excitement when I shared with her we were pregnant. She then said the apple doesn't fall far from the tree. So when Hillary doesn't stop until she can do something and see it to completion like when she wants to screw the top on the sippy cup or tie her own shoes. Any of these actions make me laugh because she will be just like me.

This insures that I will love, so she will love. I will be joyous, so she will know joy. I will be peaceful and a peacemaker, so she will know peace. I will suffer long so she will know that long suffering is part of God's will. I will be gentle and exercise goodness so that she will be gentle and know goodness. I am faithful because I want her to be faithful. I wanted to be meek my whole life so that I can be her example of meekness. Temperance requires diligent prayer and my temperance has certainly expanded so that she will be calm in the face of adversity and her enemy. They are who they see.

54

Week Five — Wednesday
Wisdom At Work
Proverbs 3:5-6; 31:26

[5]Trust in the Lord with all your heart and lean not on your own understanding; [6]In all your ways acknowledge Him and He will direct your path. [26]She speaks with wisdom, and faithful instruction is on her tongue.

Proverbs 3:5-6; 31:26

The three scriptures call us to action. As women and now motherhood, God designed us to freely lean on Him and trust Him. By creation, we pray more, are more emotional and are mostly more likely to deepen our dependency on God more quickly than our spouses. While this may not hold true in all situations, the real learning is I deepened my relationship with God as a result of Hillary's birth. I knew I needed God more than ever when He blessed me with the responsibility of Hillary. Verse five spoke to me loudly because this baby was a new realm for me. Motherhood requires knowledge and wisdom, neither of which I thought I possessed. If He commands us not to lean on our own understanding about average or daily events, then you should not be surprised that this new event would require to fully lean on Him for your understanding lacks comprehension.

When Hillary was four weeks old, I was still trying to get her to latch on to my breast. I was pumping the milk but it wasn't the same. I was home alone. I was tired because I hadn't been sleeping well, if at all. I cried in frustration, loudly. I then cried to God that He would hear my cry and offer me some portion of peace. These three scriptures combined led to a better day and a better understanding of my role as a mother.

His gift of peace offered me relaxation, increased milk supply and ended my frustration. We deserve to lean on Him – He invited us to release our "stuff" to Him and trust him for everything.

Week Five — Thursday
Teaching God's Word
Matthew 28:20

[20]"and teaching them to obey everything I have commanded you. And surely I am with you always, to the very end of the age."

Matthew 28:20

Your role as mother includes teacher. You are her first teacher. You are her sole source for certain information at least for a particular period of time. You teach her manners, mannerisms, attitudes, points of view and other things through everything you say and do. Even though you may not personally teach her everything, YOU ARE RESPONSIBLE for what she does and does not know. YOU ARE RESPONSIBLE!

You also are her mentor. She patterns her life after yours for the most part, but this requires that you are able and available for that mentoring process. You model the behavior and lifestyle you hope she will adopt and emulate.

Teaching God's word to your child might sound like a great responsibility, but the first step is reading to her while she is still in your womb. Reading Bible stories and scriptures starts you on a great path. This teaches the baby reading, the Word and a love for God's word. When we find something hard, usually it's something we don't do very well or understand. This is your opportunity and head start to study more and prepare to answer the questions your little one will pose.

As you prepare, gather some tools to help you teach. Preparation insures your success.

Teaching requires a lot but teaching is only a by-product of parenting. Love is the hardest concept to teach. They have to see, feel and live with love to fully learn to love.

Week Five — Friday
Powerful Relationship Builders
Exodus 20:12; Matthew 5:5; Ephesians 3:19-20

[12]Honor your father and your mother, so that you may live long in the land the Lord your God is giving you. [5]Blessed are the meek for they shall inherit the earth. [19]and to know this love that surpasses knowledge – that you may be filled to the measure of all the fullness of God. [20]Now to Him who is able to do immeasurably more than all we ask or imagine, according to His power at work on us.

Exodus 20:12; Matthew 5:5; Ephesians 3:19-20

I define honor as love, obey and respect for your mother and father. To honor your parents should be a given. Keep in mind that all of your teachings and wisdom came from them in some fashion. Further and perhaps, more importantly, honor is given to them not only when they are great and deserve honor but when we don't think they deserve it, we owe it because God said so. Do unto your parents as you would have your children do unto you.

If I think I am a warrior, then I am a warrior. If I think I am more than a conqueror, then I am more than a conqueror. Whatever I think that I am, that is what I am. So what do you think for yourself and of yourself? Do you think and feel in the positive or the negative? What you have within you comes out when you are parenting.

Meekness needs to be cultivated. Meekness is a gift to others. I want to be meek, modest and mild, while my power and aggression live in meek love. Meekness combines humble love, a quiet spirit, and a genuine heart. Can you be meek? Do you want to be meek? What's the value of meekness?

As we conclude today of the powerful relationship builders, we will conclude with the power of God, the best relationship builder. In Ephesians 3:19-20, Paul describes God's love as love with such a full content that once He fills you with love it will be beyond your measure. We often box up God's love by our own definition, but our box is only big enough to keep a hamster alive. However, His love does not live in a box of any size. Now, He further reminds us that He also does other awesome acts that we don't see or understand. We live under the impression that we can imagine the highest that is possible but He has power that is at work in us. He gave us an imagination and the ability to ask but He also does so much more. We build powerful relationships because we are powerful and so are our relationships.

Week Five — Saturday
The Reap/Sow Principle
2 Corinthians 9:6

[6]Remember this: Whoever sows sparingly will also reap sparingly, and whoever sows generously will also reap generously.

2 Corinthians 9:6

As a mother, I have reflected and asked my mother many days how was I as a baby, a toddler. So Hillary is clearly a reflection of me, because you reap what you sow.

Fast forward or skip to the future. Truth: You reap what you sow. If you sow love in her life by hugs, kisses, time spent, gifts and encouraging words, then you will reap love in one or more of those same ways. When you teach hospitality and etiquette, then you reap hospitable and mannerable children.

Consider this fact as well, sow what you loved most about your life and your family. These lessons and values offer your child a similar family and value foundation. Further, sow in him what you lacked or what you missed. If you wanted more time with your parents, then you spend more quality time with your child. Since you wished that your parents were more active in your education, be more active in your child's education.

If you sow in your daughter's life those things you desired, then you reap the benefits of your daughter as well as yourself.

A final note: try to avoid living your dreams through him in the material or social activity realms. We all strive to develop well-rounded children we are proud of. Just be cautious of the cost.

WEEK SIX
YOUR ROLE AS FATHER

Dad. Father. Daddy. Pop-Pa. Whatever your child calls you, you are responsible for their growth, for their love tanks; for their knowledge and their behavior. Girls love you. Boys reverence you. They grow to understand you as their role model and example for their lives and leadership.

Being a dad has changed since you were a child. Your role at home will be different from that of your dad. Your dad may have never done the laundry or change a diaper, but you will probably do the laundry, change a diaper or whatever your family needs of you to support the family. You need to evaluate what your family needs and fill that need. These needs will be new for you to fill but valuable to your family.

Further, you need to ask your wife what her expectations are. Actively listening to her and taking notice of her expectations and needs will certainly insure the growth and success of your family. I shared with my husband that I needed his help. I defined help as prayer daily, studying daily and weekly, talking to me as I need, taking responsibility for taking Hillary to and from daycare, and several more items. Initially, his increased responsibilities seemed like a lot of work for him. With all that he was responsible for, he wondered what I was doing. So he asked. I shared with him what my duties are; he realized that he did less but his role was equally as important and it benefitted me and the family. Knowing that makes him understand the importance of his role and duties.

Fathers, your family needs your undivided attention. They also need your investment.

Dads, you are important to the total success. BE PRESENT.

Sunday	Your wisdom counts James 1:5; Proverbs 3:1-2, 7
Monday	Actions Speak Louder than Words Deuteronomy 9:18; 1 Corinthians 13:11; Ephesians 4:31; Proverbs 31:28
Tuesday	Actions Speak Louder than Words, Pt. 2 1 Samuel 13:14; 16:7; Psalm 51:10; Proverbs 27:19
Wednesday	Disciplinarian Proverbs 3:11-12; 13:24
Thursday	Provocation Ephesians 6:14; Colossians 3:21
Friday	Patience (Anger) Ephesians 4:2-3
Saturday	Love Ephesians 5:1-2

Week Six — Sunday
Your Wisdom Counts
James 1:5; Proverbs 3:1-2, 7

[5]If any of you lacks wisdom, he should ask God, who gives generously to all without finding fault, and it will be given to him.
[1]My son, do not forget my teaching, but keep my commands in your heart, [2]for they will prolong your life for many years and bring you prosperity. [7]Do not be wise in your own eyes, fear the Lord and shun evil.

James 1:5; Proverbs 3:1-2, 7

Your role as dad and husband requires your wisdom. As the head of our homes, you decide on our life, often with our input. But God holds you accountable for our provisions, well-being, and all things that concern us, the family. You, as father and husband, need to be wise. Do you have wisdom? Are you wise? Do you seek wise counsel? What is the wisdom test?

(1)   Do you pray before you decide on anything?
(2)   Do you seek your wife's prayers on your thoughts?
(3)   Do you study God's word for answers and solutions to your needs?
(4)   Do you seek wise counsel through the wise persons who surround you?
(5)   Do you communicate with your spouse your findings?
(6)   Do you move strategically or with anxiety?
(7)   Do you study and research all means for completion of your needs and projects?

Being wise requires growth. You need to recognize that God is at work at all times. This fact requires that you understand this demands that your anxiety is misplaced and unwise. Wisdom is no respecter of age. Learning births wisdom. Be present and available to God for His direction and guidance.

Be wise.

Week Six — Monday
Actions Speak Louder Than Words
Deuteronomy 9:18; 1 Corinthians 13:11; Ephesians 4:31; Proverbs 31:28

[18]Then once again I fell prostrate before the Lord for forty days and forty nights; I ate no bread and drank no water because of all the sin you had committed, doing what was evil in the Lord's sight and so provoking Him to anger. "When I was a child, I talked like a child, I thought like a child, I reasoned like a child. When I became a man, I put childish ways behind me.
[31]Get rid of all bitterness, rage and anger, brawling and slander, along with every form of malice.
[28]Her children arise and call her blessed; her husband also, and he praises her.

Deuteronomy 9:18; 1 Corinthians 13:11; Ephesians 4:31; Proverbs 31:28

Prayer
Our children need to see us pray and in prayer. When they witness our prayer time, then they learn to pray. I learned to pray in church, and I teach by praying in front of others. Further, my husband became more confident with prayer when he witnessed my fervent prayers. Allow God to work through with your prayers. Your family will follow suit if you let God be your guide. A father's prayers are particularly impactful and inspiring to the family and important for the family's growth and well-being. I learned fasting at church, as well. I experienced an entire life change the very first occasion I fasted. When you lead by example through fasting and prayer, you as the father set your family up for enormous blessings. Your family discovers who you are when you pray. Don't be ashamed.

Maturity
You are the adult, no longer the child. Behave as such. I grew up with friends whose parents are drunk when they come home or are awakened to drunk parents arriving home. Let the "failure" of your parents be your growth point. Acting mature encompasses mature decisions financially as well. Remember, your role as parent demands that your financial savvy take several steps up to meet the needs of your family. One more thought: I manage a retail store, so I hire quite a few people in this small town and its surrounding area. One day this customer was dropping in the store and she was behaving horribly. She threw some shoes down and demanded one of the associates pick them up for her. She was yelling at the cashwrap. Let's just say that it wasn't a great experience. Six months later, without knowing it, I hired her son. Even after his employment, she continued her behavior. Now he's ashamed.

Women
Your children will treat people, especially women the same as you do. Be kind and compassionate and sensitive to your wife and daughters. Observe and ask questions. Invest in their inner self. The information you gain will carry you far.

Week Six — Tuesday
Actions Speak Louder Than Words, Pt. 2
1 Samuel 13:14; 16:7; Psalm 51:10; Proverbs 27:19

[14]But now your kingdom will not endure; the Lord has sought out a man after his own heart and appointed him leader of his people, because you have not kept the Lord's command.
[7b]The Lord does not look at the things man looks at. Man looks at the outward appearance, but the Lord looks at the heart."
[10]Create in me a pure heart, O God, and renew a steadfast spirit within me.
[19]As water reflects a fact, so a man's heart reflects a man.

1 Samuel 13:14; 16:7; Psalm 51:10; Proverbs 27:19

These four scriptures are awesome. They address what really is important: Your heart. A father's heart is important for the livelihood of your family. Your heart is a reflection of your motives. You are the head of the home. God holds you responsible and accountable for the course you lead your family. Because of that whatever choices you make impact the generations of your children and your children's children. You have to make sound decisions and have great judgement. Further, your prayer life is critical to your family's success as well.

God listens to your heart. God monitors your heart. God is more than fair. He looks for the good within you as well as He judges the impure motives of your heart.

How do you keep a pure heart? How many times have we asked that question? Prayer keeps a pure heart. God also monitors your intentions. In this day, pure hearts may be hard to find a mentor to cultivate. However, pure hearts are required by God. A pure heart attracts God and compels Him to exert His utmost compassion on you. This compassion is important for your family. The Bible recounts several stories of God's wrath on the family and land when a man is functioning with an impure heart. Take heed to those Biblical examples, so that you make decisions with the purest heart.

Above all, your family deserves a pure heart – yours.

Week Six — Wednesday
Disciplinarian
Proverbs 3:11-12; 13:24

[11]My son, do not despise the Lord's discipline and do not resent his rebuke, [12]because the Lord disciplines those he loves, as a father the son he delights in. [24]He who spares the rod hates his son, but he who loves him is careful to discipline him.

Proverbs 3:11-12; 13:24

God disciplines us because He loves us. You discipline your child because of love, not because of hatred, malice, jealousy or exhaustion. Discipline may be hard for you initially. Sometimes you may have a hard time deciding when to discipline or how to discipline. The important point is to discipline.

Discipline is not popular by any means. The grandparents are not your greatest supporters, but you have to remain firm. You have to decide to discipline your child and be firm in your decisions. Further, be firm with your relatives and friends about your disciplinarian decisions. You may need to discuss with your non-supporters how their lack of support affects you. Let them use this time to understand your motives and responsibility as a parent. This may seem strange because sometimes you have to talk to your own parents about this.

Lastly, God instructs you to discipline His gift. He blessed you with the child and He issued the instructions for appropriate discipline. He disciplines us with love and grace and mercy. We need to do our portion for the good of the life of your child. Further, when we are obedient, we are lifted spiritually.

Yes, it's hard to discipline, but it's harder for God – don't you think?

Week Six — Thursday
Provocation
Ephesians 6:4; Colossians 3:21

[4]Fathers, do not exasperate your children; instead, bring them up in the training and instruction of the Lord.
[21]Fathers, do not embitter your children, or they will become discouraged.

Ephesians 6:4; Colossians 3:21

While this scripture states "fathers," let's apply this word to mothers as well. The world emotionally batters our children. At home they need, expect, hope for and should receive love. This love is represented through discipline, instruction, praise, encouragements and protection. As parents, we strive for the best of ourselves and our children. This can only be achieved with all the components working simultaneously.

As a parent we have to decide to strike a balance with our children. Discipline does not have to resemble a drill sergeant. While praise does not mean overlooking their shortcomings or disobedience.

The training and instruction of the Lord includes asking them about their whereabouts, meeting and interacting about their friends, hugging, checking their homework and administering discipline as necessary.

One last thing, parents: decide to share with your child. Share your life with your child. Past, present and future. I don't know much about my mother's past and I wish I knew more. Keep your life focused such that your child is the main part, not the afterthought. Finally, prepare for her future thoughtfully and purposefully. I use one filter to decide to include something on my agenda: what are the provisions for Hillary. After that I set limits on how many events/occasions where there are no provisions for Hillary.

Children thrive on praise. Most of us will have to add to our daily routine, but you won't be disappointed that you did.

Week Six — Friday
Patience/Anger
Ephesians 4:2-3

[2]Be completely humble and gentle; be patient, bearing with one another in love. [3]Make every effort to keep the unity of the Spirit through the bond of peace.

Ephesians 4:2-3

Children require patience. Yours and their own. Their nature is inquisition; they are also observers. They are imitators. They do what they see. They say what they hear. They are your reflection. The apple does not fall far from the tree, but even if it rolled down the hill, it would still be an apple—your apple.

Your second charge is loving one another through difficulties. Bearing with one another requires constant communication with God. This includes disagreements and miscommunications. Bearing with one another means forgiving, praying for, loving and persevering with one another. It means weathering the storm with one another. It means parenting with one another. Just as a reminder, this also means that you will support each other's decisions.

Lastly, "make every effort" demands your full attention, demands your 110% especially when you don't feel like doing it. "Put your best foot forward" – an old cliché, yet applicable to this scripture. Our charge is to keep the unity of the Spirit. Our duty offers us the results through the bond of peace. What is peace to you and your family? Once you gather up your peaceful experience, then focus on the actions which lead to the results of peace. Nothing you have is worth more than God's gift of peace. God provides peace to those who seek peace and who strive to maintain peaceful lives. Further, God honors those who protect the peace which exists around them. When we protect the peace, we show God we understand and appreciate the value of His peace.

Week Six — Saturday
Love
Ephesians 5:1-2

[1]Be imitators of God, therefore, as dearly loved children [2]and live a life of love, just as Christ loved us and gave himself up for us as a fragrant offering and sacrifice to God.

Ephesians 5:1-2

When neither of you has had a full night's rest for the fifth night in a row and nothing has gone as planned, you still love your spouse. Also, you still love the baby, because at the end of each day, when she's asleep and you stare at her, you know that you will give all you have and commit all of your energy to her.

Living a life of love as a father defines sacrifice and defies all understanding. The lengths you will go and heights you will climb are immeasurable at this moment. Your life changes each day she grows. You demonstrate love through your actions. When you hug her, she learns to hug. When you tell her you love her, she learns to feel love. I could go on with these examples, but those two prove my point of the importance of your love's impact on the emotional health of your child.

Although society does not demand a loving man, God strongly demands a loving man. God set the ultimate example through Jesus and John 3:16. Could you be God? Could you be Jesus? Could God have trusted you like He trusted Abraham when He asked him to sacrifice his son? The answers are likely no to all the questions, so the next question is can He depend on you to love His gift like He does? The answer needs to be a resounding yes. Children are gifts – not inconveniences, not an interruption to your life or anything negative that discounts them as the gift they are.

Love the baby as the gift they are. God expects it and we want to discontinue disappointing Him.

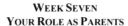

WEEK SEVEN
YOUR ROLE AS PARENTS

Proverbs 4 discusses wisdom at length. God expects parents to gain wisdom and information through experience and reading. God also expects us to pray for wisdom.

God clearly explains our role and fully expects that we will carry out that role completely to His specifications. Parenthood is a gift and should not be treated as a burden. As parents, we are to offer God-given instruction to our children and lead by example. Use this time to clearly define your expectations of yourselves. Many times we have said, "I will never do . . ." or "I will always do . . ." Those statements, while at the time genuine, are poorly timed for first-time parents. First-time parents lack the necessary experience to anticipate the reality of the situations which will arise.

Use this time to unite intimately with God and one another. Let, allow, permit, surrender to God to cover your anxiety, meet all your needs and cover your fears. God had a pre-developed plan; allow Him to show you His plan and use you to bring His well developed plan to fruition.

Parents have very specific instructions from God. Parenting is not easy. We are stewards over the child and we are accountable to God for their lives. Parenthood is an awesome responsibility. Parenthood surpasses all other lifetime milestones. Parenthood should be cherished and for the gift that it is. Use this time to make a commitment to your God-given role.

Sunday	Parenting and Our Christian Lives Ephesians 4:17-32
Monday	Our Timing Ecclesiastes 3:1-8
Tuesday	Faithfulness Hebrews 11
Wednesday	Marriage – Honorable Hebrews 13:4
Thursday	God's Blessed Assurance Hebrews 13:5
Friday	Peaceful Parenting 1 Corinthians 7:15; 14:33
Saturday	Peaceful Parents Philippians 4:7

Week Seven — Sunday
Parenting and Our Christian Lives
Ephesians 4:17-32

[32]Be kind and compassionate to one another, forgiving each other, just as in Christ God forgave you.

Ephesians 4:32

Of the much and faithful instructions given by Paul, these qualify for parents especially. The cliché the apple doesn't fall from the tree is a true assumption for most of us. My mother is an only child, therefore not really able to share because she never had to. I grew up twelve years from the nearest sibling and so I wasn't forced to share either. So it stands to reason, that if I don't change some history, my daughter will not share either. So it goes with other aspects of life that our lifestyles will translate and impact our children's lives.

Verse 32, kindness, compassion and forgiveness are each critical for a child to reflect the same. These are traits we are expected to model if we expect our children to know these qualities.

Verses 22-24, you are new in Christ and you are new being. You are expected to act "new," by completely dismissing the "old." This "newness" involves each aspect of life – your friends, your attitude, your behavior, your decisions, how you treat your family, and on and on. Our Christian lives are important to ourselves and the future of our families.

In short, verse 32 is an example of love: Kindness, compassion and forgiveness are all attributes of love. They don't exist without love and conversely you don't love anyone to whom you are not kind, nor compassionate and unforgiving. These are all characteristics that we need to offer each day to our spouses and family and children.

Week Seven — Monday
Our Timing
Ecclesiastes 3:1-8

[1]There is a time for everything, and a season for every activity under heaven.

Ecclesiastes 3:1

As I shared, I started this during our first pregnancy. When we started trying for the second pregnancy, we didn't conceive as quickly as we thought we would. Question: Why? Answer: God's timing. There are a million reasons why God's timing is correct and my timing is simply a preference.

When you study, please read the rest of the verses. They reinforce the ultimate impact of God's timing. When we surrender ourselves to God's timing that is best for us. We are able to release all our anxiety because the person who truly has our best interest in mind is God. He knows completely what our future holds and exactly how we will handle that. While that's great news for us, it also means work for us, as well. Preparation is required for us to have great responses. Intuition doesn't come to an unprepared mind. Reading, praying and studying prepares us for the expected and the unexpected.

We usually fear the unexpected. But the unexpected is why God is the expert. He determined our level of tolerance and ability to stretch long before our births. He does the same for our unborn children. He knows when the best time for the baby to arrive is – the doctor and the calendar are just guessing. So expect with great anticipation, yet no anxiety because He is in charge and has it all under control despite our plans or efforts to assist Him.

When we function in His timing, we live wisely.

Week Seven — Tuesday
Faithfulness is Crucial
Hebrews 11

[1]Now faith is being sure of what we hope for and certain of what we do not see.

Hebrews 11:1

Faith is a prerequisite for parenting. If you don't believe that fact, ask your parents. Verse one is evidence of each of our lives. Let me explain: thirty years ago, ultrasound didn't exist. Now that it does exist, we can check the health, gender, position, and other factors of the baby(ies). Thirty years ago, parents had to believe that the baby was going to be healthy but any health issues visible to an ultrasound now were left to faith then. As parents, we did the requested ultrasounds; however, we don't choose to know the gender.

That example seems simple, yet it relates to everything else as well. When we are growing up, our parents have to have faith that we are going to grow up the way they prayed we would. They had faith that we would. They were sure of the results they hoped for and certain that what they do not see would come into fruition.

Faithfulness is crucial to parenting. Successful parenting requires faith. Everyday. All of the time. In your most glorious day and in your darkest hour. As parents we inspire our children through our own attitude about ourselves, them and life in general. In order to inspire your child, faith is required. You have to believe the information you share and the image you portray.

Often faith could be hard but not impossible. In all of our lives we may think that faith is defined differently, however they are all the same. It doesn't matter the socioeconomic backgrounds or ethnic backgrounds or anything else. What does matter is that we each believe that we love our child more than the next parents. What matters more is that we want them to love God more than anything. Faith is required to want them to love God more than anything. Everything else we want from them is certainly secondary.

Week Seven — Wednesday
Marriage – Honorable
Hebrews 13:4

[4]Marriage should be honored by all, and the marriage bed kept pure, for God will judge the adulterer and all the sexually immoral.

Hebrews 13:4

What does our marriage have to do with the type of parents we'll be? Some people don't realize how your current lifestyle impacts your parenting lifestyle. As parents, you'll be required to change certain aspects of your life to meet the needs of your children.

This would be a great time to introduce some marriage "game rules" if you will. Rules such as we will never argue in front of the children, we will never include the children in our disputes, we will reallocate how we spend our time, can be instituted immediately and easily and with great reasoning. I have learned that what children see at home is what they learn to expect in the world. My husband and I decided that the values we wanted out daughter to know she would learn at home. We teach love and care at home, so she goes out into the world and loves people with hugs, kisses, greetings and other such gestures. She waves and speaks and hugs strangers. She doesn't ask for our approval. She may learn hurt and hate but she won't learn them at home.

Deciding and teaching are easy. Children crave our attention, love and time. You have been chosen to be parents, so God entrusts you to do that with honor. This honor starts with the two of you. God guides the rest.

Week Seven — Thursday
God's Blessed Assurance
Hebrews 13:5

[5]Keep your lives free from the love of money and be content with what you have, because God has said, "Never will I leave you; never will I forsake you."

Hebrew 13:5

When we decide that we will submit to God's timing and get ready for the first child, we really don't know how much they can cost. And does it really matter? When it's time for the second and all subsequent, we have a much better idea of all the costs, that is.

There also comes a time when we decide to stop having children because we can't afford them. Daycare costs are huge. I do agree. Other items cost, too. But we say to God is that 'Your gift is not great enough for You to provide what we need and for You to overcome those obstacles.' I struggle daily (maybe not that often) with is two children my decision or God's decision. I feel that common sense should set it and I should stop having children when I have exhausted my budget and I have implemented all possible sacrifices.

Arguments erupt on this topic regularly in marriages. The solution is prayer and trust, rather than logic, reason, common sense and selfishness.

On a final note, God has an override button. Don't laugh—it's true. Have you ever seen your plans turned around and usually the completely opposite of what you originally planned? How about couples on birth control who have children? What about couples who want children, are not on birth control and have never been pregnant? God has an override button. What He designs and plans, not one of us can change.

72

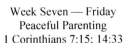

Week Seven — Friday
Peaceful Parenting
1 Corinthians 7:15; 14:33

[15b]God has called us to live in peace. [33]For god is not a God of disorder but of peace.

1 Corinthians 7:15; 14:33

Peaceful parenting means we parent using only Biblical principles, we stand firm in God's plans, and we remain parents, rather than friends. Referencing several scriptures, we find that we are not to provoke our children, we are to give them wise instruction and we are to avoid ungodly influences over our lives.

We <u>must</u> study the word so that we can do these things. We <u>must</u> pray to stand firm on our decisions based on God's plans.

Peace comes and exists when we know for certain that we have done His work and at our best. Maybe this seems vague, however, the truth is He chose you as a parent – you didn't make this decision for yourself. Because He chose you He equipped you. Sometimes it's hard to believe or understand, but it's certainly true.

Peaceful parenting means explaining, talking and listening until she hears you. You are on watch for the fruit God will produce from you and your child. We can't afford to miss the fruit or delay the fruit because we chose discord over peace. Yes, peace is your choice. Peace is His provision and your choice. The fact that He has the plan is reason enough to accept the peace. We don't have to create or execute the plan – that's the great news.

Peaceful parenting is available to each of us. Peace requires our participation and acceptance. Peaceful parenting influences peaceful children.

Week Seven — Saturday
Peaceful Parents
Philippians 4:7

[7]And the peace of God, which transcends all understanding, will guard your hearts and your minds in Christ Jesus.

Philippians 4:7

God's peace – above and beyond all that we can imagine or conceive or understand – is available. He offers us access, unlimited access, to His peace. Just like salvation, peace is free. Your children learn peace from you, as with other characteristics. Experiencing God's peace requires your focus on God and His will.

Being peaceful also means that we have a spirit of peace, rather than dissension and discord. Peaceful persons love harmony. They avoid conflict at all costs. Are you that person? If you are, your child will likely be the same. When I realized that our child is like holding up a mirror, I then turned up my best characteristics and avoided my worst. I want them to have the best of me. I want to be a delight to them, just like I want them to be a delight to me.

Yes, peace is your decision, a decision you make consciously and deliberately to experience, to be guided and live in His peace. Having peace, being peaceful and being drawn into peace is your decision. You decide actively to seek God for His peace. Peace doesn't just happen. You decide and receive His peace.

Your joy will be made new and complete when you receive His peace. Your joy will be full and overflowing when you live in His peace. Your children will live in your peace and they will be introduced to a lifestyle designed by God.

WEEK EIGHT
YOUR PARENTS

Your example of relationship is critical for your success as a parent. Your relationship with your parents dictates your own relationship with your child as a parent. Are we doomed? Certainly not. Quite the contrary. You define your relationship based on what you experienced. You have a chance to change what happened as a parent based on what you experienced from your parents.

Now the important piece of your relationship with the parents is your own behavior. Your behavior has to be focused on God's word – not what your parents did or didn't do. I know initially this will be hard for some of us. However, don't despair, you too can forgive them and overcome your issues, as well as change your behavior to inspire a change in them. At the least, you will be able to reconcile yourself so you are able to parent without hindrance.

Be ever reminded we will be different parents from our parents and our parents' parents. We have extremely different resources and equally different responsibilities from our parents. Also, for me I have different parental goals and desires. As a new parent, we have a chance to develop our parental wish list – the ideas and decisions we will execute as parents, which are not subject to anyone's approval but God's. My priority is communication. Historically, parents don't talk about issues or share family historical information. Most of this information would be instrumental in making better decisions as teens and adults. I want our children as prepared as possible for as many health and financial issues as possible. Those are two areas where I personally struggle.

Sunday	Honor Your Parents Exodus 20:12
Monday	Cursed Deuteronomy 27:16
Tuesday	Death Leviticus 20:9
Wednesday	Forgiveness Matthew 6:14-15; 18:22
Thursday	Sow & Reap Galatians 6:7
Friday	Leave & Cleave Genesis 2:24
Saturday	Follow Instructions Proverbs 1:8

Week Eight — Sunday
Honor Your Parents
Exodus 20:12

[12]Honor your father and your mother, so that you may live long in the land the Lord your God is giving you.

Exodus 20:12

Respect. Revere. Admire. Compliment. Love. Obey. Listen. Honor. Honor your parents. Just as you were chosen, so were they. This is God's commandment. His plans include them and they are just as accountable to Him as you are for parenting.

For some this is harder than for others, starting with their own parents. So how do we honor parents when they have been hard to love, for whatever reason? First, let's start with "because God said so." If we are obedient, then we can depend on Him doing the work. When we are obedient, then He will do the work. Second, we need to evaluate the type of child we are. Be honest with yourself and then confess to your parent. This confession should stimulate quite a bit of dialogue. Thirdly, evaluate the fairness of your expectations. What do you expect and do they know it? You might also want to share how you developed those expectations. Lastly, seek to understand their point of view. In all situations, desire to understand their needs and issues as well as joys and victories.

I want my mother and I to communicate more and on a better level. So I am practicing each day to do so. She makes it hard sometimes but she is still my mother. This is not the time to invoke the sow/reap principle.

Often honoring them can be overwhelming but is what God commands and our consequences seem more severe than theirs for not being as honorable as we hoped.

On the other hand, it is essential that we learn from their examples so that our children want to honor us as well.

Week Eight — Monday
Cursed
Deuteronomy 27:16

[16]"Cursed is the man who dishonors his father or his mother."

Deuteronomy 27:16

Building great relationships is a skill that I try to employ daily. The Bible says for us to be peacemakers. Similarly we want to be peaceful and peacemakers – peace ambassadors. Why is this my role, you may ask? Because if I can behave according to His will then I can stand upright rather than having to continue to ask for forgiveness for being absolutely wrong and knowing that I am wrong.

I want and will do all things possible to have a great relationship with my children because I yearn for that. In order to have that great relationship, then I have to be great parent. Always. Not only when I feel like it. I have to be focused on parenting at all times.

Parenting is hard and it requires all of us. We have to engage our children – that is how great parenting is from the eye of the child. Our material desires don't measure up to our time we give them. Our daughter wants us to watch her videos with her. She wants to sit in my lap when I sit down. She doesn't care about my day at work, nor the money I spend on her clothes. She wants and values our time together. I want to make very effort to ensure that she knows that I want to spend time with her too.

A few years ago there was an email that I was sent about a boy who asked his dad how much he made an hour. The dad answered and the boy left. Later, he returned with $20 and said, "Dad, can I buy an hour of your time?"

This makes me ask am I behaving in a dishonorable manner such that later my child would dishonor me?

Week Eight — Tuesday
Death
Leviticus 20:9

[9]If anyone curses his father or mother, he must be put to death. He has cursed his father or his mother, and his blood will be on his own head.

Leviticus 20:9

God is protective of parents. Why shouldn't He be? He chose us and we should be treated with love, honor and respect. Using the mirror, how are we going to raise our children? What kinds of examples are we going to be before them? Are we encouraging them to hold us accountable for the parents we are? How do they see us treat our parents? Will they measure or judge us on that behavior?

Do we judge our parents on what we see them do or not do? Do we seek to understand their point of view? Or do we simply use our own view?

That is horrible; who would curse their parents? Many people do without even knowing that anything has happened. When we break their hearts through disobedience or out of character behavior, this is an example of them being cursed. How does disobedience measure up to cursed? When we are disobedient, our behavior communicates to God that we don't love Him (John 14:15). Is that a curse to God? Why sure it is. Cursed is not simply the worst that could happen like theft or abuse, but it is the small things that cause them the most grief.

We are not likely to be put to the same death as in Leviticus but God's wrath and judgement can be the same or tailored to get our attention.

I want to live long, prosperous days so I strive to be as pleasant and honorable as possible to my mother. More importantly, I yearn for a particular relationship with my children. That relationship is my motivation to do the right thing.

Establish your motivation for parenting and live by those rules.

Week Eight — Wednesday
Forgiveness
Matthew 6:14-15; 18:22

[14]For if you forgive men when they sin against you, your heavenly Father will also forgive you. [15]But if you do not forgive men their sins, your Father will not forgive your sins. [22]Jesus answered, "I tell you, not seven times, but seventy-seven times."

Matthew 6:14-15; 18:22

Parents have to be forgiven, too. We want our children to forgive us. We should openly forgive our parents. Yes, even for never hearing from them again. And for never spending any time with us, even though they were somewhere trying to provide for us. Especially, when they love our siblings and children more than they seem to love us. FORGIVE THEM. Not forgiving is blocking your blessings and communication with God – not the other way around.

Forgiveness as Jesus would forgive includes for each and every offense, with a willing and open and loving spirit. These are your parents – aren't they worth that? Absolutely, so get started.

Being forgiven starts with forgiving. I need God to hear and answer all of my prayers, especially one of forgiveness. I hinder my prayers when I don't forgive others. One of my best friends invoked the honesty pledge this past year. The honesty pledge is that she would simply tell the truth in an inspirational manner. She wasn't lying before but she may not have been willing to disclose all of her feelings or thoughts previously. What this means now is that she forgives easily. I have adopted the pledge, too. My forgiveness meter has increased as well. I forgive more easily because I am able to address my issues in an upfront manner, leaving people dignified but they know and are aware of what my needs are so that that incident probably won't happen again.

You are the key in forgiveness – of others and yourself. Be proactive.

Week Eight — Thursday
Sow & Reap
Galatians 6:7

[7]Do not be deceived: God cannot be mocked. A man reaps what he sows.

Galatians 6:7

"Do you want to see that again?" If the answer is no then I avoid that behavior. If you plant strawberry seeds, then you expect strawberries when the season arrives, not blueberries.

When we reap what we sow, we have earned that treatment and we deserve what we have received. That is not easy to do but if we do a few things then we will be successful. My mother taught me to think before I speak, don't try to speak while I cry because I can't think and cry, and once those words are out there, they cannot be retrieved. Well while all of this is great information, the golden rule becomes paramount: "Do unto others what you would have them do unto you." Gage's version of the Golden Rule: "treat others better than they treat you." This rule influences hearts, moves people's motivations and changes minds. As we groom children into the great human beings God has destined them to be, these behaviors become crucial to their development and growth.

They learn most things they know by watching us. So when you check your behavior, what do they see? How do they interpret those actions? How do they respond to what they see? How does it impact their lives? How likely are they to adopt the behavior if it is unfavorable? How do you explain and correct your behavior?

At last, you decide daily your behavior and how you will demonstrate life to your child.

Remember, reaping can be great so sow with care.

Week Eight — Friday
Leave and Cleave
Genesis 2:24

[24]For this reason a man will leave his father and mother and be united to his wife, and they will become one flesh.

Genesis 2:24

One flesh is achieved through communication and commitment with your spouse. Our children depend on our unity and closeness for their stability and decision making and overall outlook on life. Their spirits and souls feed off of ours. So it is reasonable to suggest (and there is support for this statement) that if we are not in accord, then our children will be nervous, disoriented and lack coordination mentally.

As married couples, we have to make a conscious choice to consult our spouses and employ discretion and discernment about what we share with our parents, family and others. This is also essential for the growth of our children. Our example of marriage is the longest lasting example they will have. We have to exhibit all of these principles and exercise them well in order to positively influence their lives, both now and in the future. For this reason, when we exhibit marital discretion, you also set an example of how communication in your household can be handled.

Has your child or yourself ever been the source of "private" information for your parents which you or your parents had no intention of telling them at this time? This was a life lesson well learned and well earned for many of us. Understanding how to capture that information in house is invaluable. The household value on being committed to keeping the family information in-the-house is a lesson that will lead them into successful lives and marriages. It's not about secrets from the rest of the family – it is about timing certain family details. The best factor that develops is equal trust among the family.

Week Eight — Saturday
Follow Instructions
Proverbs 1:8

[8]Listen, my son, to your father's instruction and do not forsake your mother's teaching.

Proverbs 1:8

About the time we decide that we should've been listening it's time to speak. This is a powerful lesson because we have to speak on issues we have previously tried to avoid, discount and ignore. We need those lessons now to give to our own children in hopes that we are more impactful on them than our parents were on us with valuable life lessons we'll need when we least expect it.

When we reflect on the value of listening to our parents, then we elevate our parental value as well. This is a great time to employ those "brilliant" strategies that we think are so much better than our parents' approach. At any rate, our parents' knowledge needs to be replicated as often as possible. With much anticipation, hopefully our parents' wisdom is derived from their parents and learning that their parents were right too. Now, this profoundly wise counsel that has been generated over several generations has a chance to mature a small being into a great person with just a small bit of care.

We each know that there were things that we missed great opportunities to achieve because we didn't listen and we missed the mark on our listening skills. As new parents we have a chance to recapture that chance through our own children and by recognizing the error in our own ways. God honors our commitment to get it right with our children. He also honors our personal change through our parents.

WEEK NINE
COMMUNICATION WITH YOUR SPOUSE

Did you marry your spouse because you loved to talk to them? Do you still love talking to your spouse? Do you talk about the same topics? Do you talk the same length of time to your spouse? Do you look into your spouse's eyes for the deep intimacy you did when you were courting?

Quality communication with your spouse is essential and crucial to a quality marriage and quality parenting. Quality communication requires your attention to details and your consistency, your truth, your memory, your active listening and your unconditional love.

Most times when communication lacks in your marriage, you and your spouse need to investigate the root of the problem. There may be any number of causes but the communication needs to be corrected immediately. Now some couples may never have communication issues. This is definitely a blessing. But for those of us who do or have had these problems we will address how to handle those possible issues this week.

Great communication is the cornerstone of the essential components of a great marriage. Communication requires work on both parties and commitment to success of both parties. Will we be working and committed on the same level at the same time at all times? Well no, but what we are trying to achieve is the working commitment for the goals of a great marriage and great communication:

Sunday	How do you settle disagreements? Ephesians 4:26-27
Monday	Your Spouse's Love Language Ephesians 5:22-33
Tuesday	Your Family's Mission Statement Isaiah 32:8
Wednesday	The plan for the child's care Proverbs 20:18a
Thursday	Are we on the same page? 2 Corinthians 13:11b, c
Friday	You and Your Spouse's Communication: What, When & Where? Ephesians 4:32, 1 Peter 3:8-9
Saturday	You and Your Spouse Communicate: How and Why? Ephesians 4:32, 1 Peter 3:8-9

Week Nine — Sunday
How Do You Settle Disagreements?
Ephesians 4:26-27

[26]"In your anger do not sin": Do not let the sun go down while you are still angry, [27]and do not give the devil a foothold.

Ephesians 4:26-27

This is my guiding scripture. We make mistakes when we are angry. Our thought process is cluttered when we are angry. We cannot focus on the main issue but during our anger we potentially create other issues. This is what we want to avoid – creating additional issues.

Many married couples develop "argument" or "angry" rules, such as "we won't go to bed angry" or "we discuss our issues within one hour" or "we discuss our issues after the children go to bed." Whichever rule sheet you develop is fine but please develop some guidelines. These guidelines will create, stimulate and maintain your commitment to honestly and openly address your issue.

May I also suggest that your rules include listening completely to the other person before speaking and while not anticipating what they will say or developing your response before they are complete.

Remember that the person with whom you are angry is your mate, your one flesh. Fight fair. When the fairness dwindles, be prepared to challenge the fairness with the root of the problem – not your reaction to this "new" issue. Remind your husband when you have a disagreement that this internal disagreement is still a team function. We are the team. Team is defined as people striving for the same objectives. Teams generally wear the same uniform and colors, etc., so it stands to reason that you desire mostly similar things. When it doesn't look good, simply remind him that your jerseys match and the back of them have your last name on the back. He should relax and realize that at the end of it all, you love him and will not intentionally hurt or harm him.

In the defense of all humans, we often have to be defensive in the world, workplace and otherwise. Remember to keep your home safe, secure and sacred against those outside forces. Prayer is critical for this to work.

84

Week Nine — Monday
Your Spouse's Love Language
Ephesians 5:22-33

[28]In the same way, husbands ought to love their wives as their own bodies. He who loves his wife loves himself.

Ephesians 5:28

Define love. Share your definition with your spouse. And vice versa. Sometimes we forget or the definition changes or expands. We need to routinely check the status of our spouse's love tank. As well as the status of their own emotional, mental and physical well beings. As a side bar, my husband attended as many doctor's appointments as he was able. Likewise I scheduled my appointments such that they are conducive to his schedule and thus convenient for him. Those types of events are acts of love. It required effort to schedule them so he could attend. His involvement reminded me of his love. My effort reminded him of my love.

What can you do daily to fill the other person's tank? Do you want to be in a loving position with your spouse? If so, then you do the extras and the little details that fill that love tank.

The Bible doesn't command that wives love their husbands, only to respect him. But we should strive for the love. Likewise, husbands often have to stretch to love at the biblically-ordered Christ-defined level of love. This not impossible, though. As a husband, you can love at this level with intention and effort. When you truly love your wife, life is so much more fulfilling starting with your relationship with God elevates.

You may wonder how loving your wife fully and deeply moves you closer to Christ. It's actually exactly the reverse yet cyclical. As you both are more intimate with Christ, the closer you become to one another. This is known as the triangular relationship, where God is at the top point and you and you spouse are on either points at the bottom. As you progress up the sides of the triangle towards God, then you shorten the distance between you two.

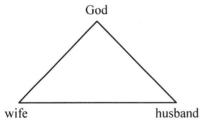

So the love language is important and keeping a gauge on the love tank is mentally important. If your gas tank in your car is low, then you go to a gas station and fill up. If your love tank is empty or not full, then you seek your spouse for a filling encounter.

You will seek immediate results as well as you will reap immediate benefits.

Week Nine — Tuesday
Your Family's Mission Statement
Isaiah 32:8

[8]But the noble man makes noble plans, and by noble deeds he stands.

Isaiah 32:8

Your family needs a mission statement. A mission statement provides guidance for your family's direction. The mission statement influences your decisions and all of your plans. When you first developed our statement, it may be difficult to remember that it exists. Eventually, you will both be able to refer to it and use it for the purpose it was designed. Initially, the importance was vague to both of you but when you post the statement, your attitude changes to more serious and committed to the statement and its content.

Your mission statement should include your goals, your values, the time you are committed to spend together, and other important details on which your family is based and how you define your family and future. Be specific as possible as you write your statement. Your husband may want your families to spend certain holidays together and to travel on a family vacation together once a year.
You may want to have a Sunday dinner where you sit together and without the television. You have to work together to make these items work for the family. These specifics also define the expectations held by one or both members of the family and marriage. These types of specifics open the lines of communication for you and your spouse.

The Franklin Covey Planner gives a format for developing a mission statement if you need assistance. We have included our statement for your reference. The statement becomes the written statement reflecting your family's foundation. This becomes important for the growth and future of your family. If the whole statement is too much, start small with one important factor.

The mission statement also facilitates how you raise your children. Eventually you pass this statement along.

Week Nine — Wednesday
The Plan for the Child's Care
Proverbs 20:18a

[18a] Make plans by seeking advice.

Proverbs 20:18a

I remember my first child care search. I came home and announced impractically to my husband our baby wasn't going to day care because I was so frustrated. They were too expensive, too far, too dirty, etc. I was so disappointed in what I saw; maybe because my expectations were too high or misplaced. The next day my husband came home and said that he had a potential day care and we would go visit it tomorrow. We did and the center was great. We left a deposit and my baby would be cared for there.

You and your spouse need to, no <u>must</u> agree, on where your child spends their 10 hour days. Yes, your child has the potential to spend 10 hours per day in day care while you work. You pay someone else to spend more time with your child than you will awake in any given day. For my children's ten hours, it has to be the best. The best we can manage and afford.

Seek the counsel of those around you. Make some serious decisions coupled by sacrifice and faith. One of our friends quit working so that she could stay home. I don't know what that took financially or her own personal sacrifice (not only giving up daily adult conversation). It was a decision they made together that no one but them has to understand.

Use this time to liquidate any unnecessary debt. Without this debt it is easier to make other decisions.

Excellent child care is not necessarily the most expensive. We were paying $180 per week at a well-known center. I came to pick up Hillary and she was soaking wet in urine. I changed her school by Friday. I have to be able to focus at work knowing that she is completely taken care of.

This is a critical decision in the life of your family. Seek the state's agency on approved centers so you know the history of the centers you may select. This decision is a profound one – one which is extremely impacting and sometimes difficult to change.

Last bit of advice: each person needs to commit to honestly communicating his and her feelings. If you won't want to stay home, then say that. If you don't want someone to be in your home, then say that. In the end, your honesty is more valuable than wondering if you'll hurt your spouse's feelings. This decision is serious and should be made with as much objectivity as possible.

Week Nine — Thursday
Are We on the Same Page?
2 Corinthians 13:11b, c

[11b, c]Aim for perfection, listen to my appeal, be of one mind, live in peace. And the God of love and peace will be with you.

2 Corinthians 13:11b, c

"Be of one mind." When we were married, we became one flesh. We also need to be of one mind. There have been some areas where my husband and I were not on the same page because we had never discussed a particular issue. In the area of children, you need to discuss all aspects. My husband announced one day in a group of our friends that he wanted our children to stay at home and me with them. Then at a later date, similar group, he announced that he didn't want his children to stay at home. We had never discussed these points before his announcements. While that may not have been fair or wise, it was clear we weren't on the same page.

Get on the same page on as many issues as you can as soon as you can. Raising children and all related aspects require the parents to be of one mind and on the same page. Raising children is an assignment from God. We need to understand our roles and fulfill that role. There are aspects of successful parenting that can be at risk without that oneness. This is a perfect time to discuss these areas that gives you the greatest concerns. We all have some preconceived ideas about how we will parent and what we will expect as we parent. Start at that point of expectation, then go from there to discover all of the expectations. Each parent will discover new expectations and parenting aspects they previously were unaware. Parenting expectation conversations reveal this unawareness. As one example, my husband doesn't think that our children should have their own telephone. I think they should. The important fact about this particular example is that the phone as we know it today is on its way to extinction. Does it matter that we are not on the same page for that now? No. In ten years when this matters, we'll be discussing another aspect of communication, rather than a simple phone. However, if we are at this point about education then we are needing to address that aspect immediately.

So, examine the long-reaching effects before wasting valuable time on non-time sensitive issues.

Week Nine — Friday
You and Your Spouse's Communication: What, When and Where?
Ephesians 4:32; 1 Peter 3:8-9

What are we talking about? When are we talking about it? Where are we talking about our issues/concerns? There is a guideline by which to establish some family communication guidelines. We have developed what we have over Hillary's growth, not really establishing any hard-fast guidelines. Since then we have developed some rules:

(1) We don't disagree in front of the children.
(2) We don't complete any conflicting issues in front of them.
(3) We don't say <u>anything</u> harsh to one another. Ephesians 4:32.
(4) We respect one another for our opinions.
(5) We don't discuss issues initially with others or in front of others. (I really get concerned when I hear issues/concerns for the first time.)
(6) We discuss most issues in our bedroom by default, not by design.
(7) We discuss issues as they present themselves with the same sense of urgency as the issue is urgent.

Your rules will be developed based on your personal style, your parents, family and some societal influences. My mother-in-law stated that she took her problems into her bedroom, never raised their voices and never in front of their children. She was my husband's example for how he leads us. My family on the other hand had no male leadership. His short stay in my home was clouded by his violent activities against my mother. Obviously, I decided that will not be my life or lifestyle. For some women, this is when you will be challenged in the area of submission. Submit to your husband. Submit to God always. This covers the potential for when you don't agree with your husband.

Husbands, lead with Christ's love. The cyclical effect described in Ephesians 5 allows each of you to do your jobs.

Week Nine — Saturday
You and Your Spouse Communicate: How and Why
Ephesians 4:32; 1 Peter 3:8-9

[32]Be kind and compassionate to one another, forgiving each other, just as in Christ God forgave you. [8]Finally, all of you, live in harmony with one another; be sympathetic, love as brothers, be compassionate and humble. [9]Do not repay evil with evil or insult with insult, but with blessings, because to this you were called so that you may inherit a blessing.

Ephesians 4:32; 1 Peter 3:8-9

How and why. Always easier said than done. Make the scripture personal. Am I kind and compassionate to him, forgiving him, like Christ forgives me? Do I live harmoniously with him (not picking even one argument); am I sympathetic, loving and humble? Do I respond well when he upsets or offends me or do I decide to offend or upset him as payback? When he does offend or upset me, do I honestly share those details with him and truly forgive him when this has been resolved? Each person has to be accountable for his and her own behavior. I have listed those questions because we each need to examine ourselves for how we treat our spouses and how we behave with our spouses.

Just remember that this is your God-given mate. How you treat her will be judged by God. I have never understood relationships where the spouse treats others better than their spouses. You are married. You are one with that person. Ephesians 5:2 reads "In this same way, husbands ought to love their wives as their own bodies. He who loves his wife loves himself." This applies to wives too. Ephesians 5:22-32 addresses how we are to treat each other as spouses.

How: with the same love you married each other.
Why: because God said so and because you should want to.

The normal reasons why communication fails during a certain period of your marriage is one of your love tanks are near empty and you love language is not being addressed. When we all review the conditions of our courtship and marriages, you will realize that you need to reintroduce those elements to meet your spouse's needs. As a result your needs will be met.

WEEK TEN
YOUR COMMUNICATION WITH GOD
YOUR INDIVIDUAL AND COLLECTIVE PRAYER TIME WITH GOD

I read in a book that if I depended on my husband to be my prayer partner, I would be disappointed. I was disappointed that the book stated that. I realize that the expectation of being my prayer partner is high but I didn't start the expectation. God expected my husband to pray with and for us, first. Then I just used His idea because I liked it. Prayer time with your spouse is truly special and important. I have learned some unique facts that I heard for the first time in front of God. It is awesome to pray with your spouse. It is awesome how close you two can become. It is amazing to watch God in your life and marriage because of your prayers. Prayer with God is essential for the growth between us and Him. Our prayer time should be consistent. Select a specific time of day. Select a place where you and God can commune without interruption.

Prayer is your time to gain complete clarity on your direction. "In all thy ways acknowledge Him and He will direct thy paths." Proverbs 3:6. Seeking God's direction, seeking His face, seeking His voice = humbling ourselves to acknowledge His sovereignty through prayer. Prayer is when you reach solitude, peace, rest and you can leave your burdens with God knowing they will be taken care of.

Finally, prayer is our tool by which we can access His power. His power is very important for us to have. His power is what moves us from our current status of Christianity to new levels where we begin to really experience God and His promises.

Dedicate time to access His power – it's the best investment of your time.

Sunday	Prayer time with God as a Family Isaiah 56:7d
Monday	Reading/Studying God's word as a Family Joshua 1:8, 24:15
Tuesday	Prayer time individually 1 Thessalonians 5:17
Wednesday	Study time individually 2 Timothy 2:15
Thursday	How will your child know God – What will you do for your child? Proverbs 22:6
Friday	Prayer Acts: Teaching your child to pray Matthew 6:9-13
Saturday	Prayer Acts: Teaching your child to pray, part 2 Mark 11:24

Week Ten — Sunday
Prayer Time with God as Family
Isaiah 56:7d

[7d]For my house will be called a house of prayer for all nations.

Isaiah 56:7d

There needs to be a time when you pray as a family. Yes, it is essential, helpful and powerful. Yes, it is unpopular yet we as people we ask a lot of God. He requires those requests be made in a particular manner – one of which is family prayer.

The most valuable lesson we teach our children is how to pray. We must set the example. We must be leaders in prayer. As the husband, family prayer demands your leadership, your attention, your time and your initiative. Quality prayer time demands that the husband prays for the family and calls the family together for prayer.

What can be accomplished as a family who prays together:

1. God experiences the intimacy He desires and deserves.
2. God is honored by the togetherness of the family during prayer. This unity transcends to other areas of the family's existence.
3. We allow God to do His work.
4. We learn what each family member needs.
5. We exhibit that we are truly focused on God.
6. God can talk to us collectively.
7. He can hear from us as a family.
8. We can see the evidence of God's work and blessings through His actions as a result of our prayers.
9. God experiences our commitment to Him through our prayers.
10. God experiences our love for Him.

This time is important to facilitate our growth toward God. As we grow closer to God, then we grow closer as a family. Prayer is the greatest facilitator of this growth.

Week Ten — Monday
Reading/Studying God's Word as a Family
Joshua 1:8; 24:15

[8]Meditate on it day and night, so that you may be careful to do everything written in it. Then you will be prosperous and successful. [15]Then choose for yourselves this day whom you will serve: But as for me and my household we will serve the Lord.

Joshua 1:8; 24:15

Our pastor says regularly that we should know scriptures so that when the enemy presents itself, we will be armed with God's word and not the world's words. I agree wholeheartedly. We have to read and study to absorb that in our spirits. We have to do more than hearing scripture at church or on tape or in passing. We have to actually read, recite, reread, and write, understand, apply and adapt the scripture to our lives for the scripture to remain in our mind, heart and spirit. At church, we recite the scripture each Sunday for one year. This practice has been effective for our members remembering scripture, especially our young people.

Developing a study and reading plan is the first step for achieving the goal. Your plan could also progress in phases. For example, phase one may mean you read for fifteen minutes twice daily for thirty days. At thirty days, phase two starts, extends the time to thirty minutes twice daily. At the end of thirty days, phase three starts with using two or more versions to read the same scriptures. Developing a plan is quite important so that you can accomplish your goals. Without a plan, you may wander away from achieving anything.

Last thing: be realistic with your plan. Habits form in twenty-one days. So if 30 days is too long, then at least twenty-one should establish a great habit for reading and studying. Another idea you may want to consider is writing scriptures on index cards you want to remember and reading it aloud daily, until you have it memorized.

Try these suggestions for your plan. In just a few days you may be surprised of your progress.

*As a part of your plan, each family member can be responsible for a different chapter of the book you are reading. They also may have a day to lead the discussion of the verses you've read. This participation encourages ownership of the study.

Week Ten — Tuesday
Prayer Time Individually
1 Thessalonians 5:17

[17]Pray continually.

1 Thessalonians 5:17

To pray continually means a continuous focus on God. Praying also means your thoughts as well as your verbal prayers. I find myself asking in my thoughts for any relief that I stand in need of. For instance, when I am overwhelmed or frustrated, I mentally ask God for something to work for me right now. In my prayers, both verbal and non-verbal, God knows that I depend on Him for all aspects of my life.

Prayer provides power and peace. Prayer deserves your time – completely devoted to prayer. The hardest aspect of prayer is finding time to pray. I have established some prayer guidelines that may assist to establish this time.

Prayer Guidelines:

(1)   Pray at the same time each day
(2)   Make a prayer list – what are you believing God for?
(3)   Tell your spouse and closest friend or family member or someone else who can hold you accountable for keeping your prayer commitment.
(4)   Pick a scripture that identifies where you are in your life and pray that scripture for a week or two or until you have (memorized) adapted the scripture to your life and layered them into your spirit. When you pray God's scriptures back to Him, miraculous movement happens within your life because of God's blessings and your new attitude about your situation.
(5)   Believe what I ask when I pray.
(6)   Leave your worries, burdens and troubles with God when you pray.
(7)   Be committed to prayer with God. It's your own personal time to have God's attention – undivided.

Week Ten — Wednesday
Study Time Individually
2 Timothy 2:15

[15]Do your best to present yourself to God as an approved, a workman who does not need to be ashamed and who correctly handles the word of truth.

2 Timothy 2:15

In order to "directly handle the word of truth," we must study that word, know that word, love that word. Our credibility as a Christian depends on our ability to know God's word. Knowing His word requires our time to study. On yesterday, I suggested a plan that insures your study time becomes a focus in your family life. Your individual time is just as important. A similar plan to the one suggested on Tuesday insures a great study life.

As a part of your plan, you may also consider a study and accountability partner. This person has similar goals and can support you in reaching your goals. This person may also engage in discussion of what you are reading. It is important to remember that an accountability relationship is a two-sided relationship where you both bring some leadership to the study. Further, you have similar goals. These propel into achieving your mutual goals with ease, sooner and with a greater sense of accomplishment. The scripture calls us to be "a workman who does not need to be ashamed." This is encouragement for indulging in deep and thoughtful study for we know that knowing more about God through the study of His word leads us closer to Him. Being closer to Him influences us as the workman He called us to be.

Lastly on study, "do your best to present yourself to God as one approved" demands us to take several actions. We must commit to do our best. No excuses. God requires a tenth, inclusive of our time. A tenth of the day is two hours and twenty-four minutes. If we start with thirty minutes per day, we are still short 56 minutes. We have to build to that. We have to do our best regardless of our circumstances. Secondly, as one approved simply means that we are studying the word, understanding the word, applying the word and then sharing the word. Sharing the word is really important to God. Often we fall short of His goal to share the word, with the ultimate goal of making disciples, which is a command of Christ.

So as you can see, our family and personal study impacts a further goal than that of our own – it potentially affects persons crossing our paths for years to come. That fact further reinforces the importance of our study time.

Take your study time seriously and with the importance intended.

95

Week Ten — Thursday
How Will Your Child Know God? – What Will You Do for Your Child?
Proverbs 22:6

⁶Train a child in the way he should go, and when he is old he will not turn from it.

Proverbs 22:6

As you prepare to parent, you will decide to parent in a certain fashion. These decisions should include how you will share God with your gift from God. Our daughter is smart and usually surprises me with new learnings. My promise is to protect her overall environment so influences which cross her path will not negate our home teachings. She also amazes people with her information bank, memory and her ability to repeat what she hears. We had our baby, Nehemiah, and Hillary stayed with my mother. Between starting a new school and a week with my mother, she came home singing "Jesus Loves Me." It doesn't matter who did it, what matters is that it happened in the important places at a great time.

My husband usually puts our daughter to bed. The nightly routine includes a bedtime story and prayers. Keep in mind that both parents need to be equally driven to teach in this manner. If you are not equally driven, you need to be in agreement about what you want to achieve.

I teach young people and one of my philosophies is that we allow outside influences to teach our children so much. We have to decide not to be popular but to follow Christ. I stand firmly on my convictions that if they can learn the songs on the radio, then they can learn scriptures, attend church and other church functions. As a parent, our decisions last a lifetime, often regardless of how big or small. Just so that you will understand the full impact of your decisions, observe your spouse's behavior. Then if available, observe your in-laws (mom, dad, siblings and grandparents). I am convinced you will find the answers to your questions.

Last note: my husband wanted to know why I wrapped my washed lettuce in a paper towel, then put it in a plastic bag. He didn't ask me. We went to my grandmother's and he saw her do the same thing with the lettuce. We were in the kitchen a time later when he said I know why you do that.

Your actions become that of your children. Or they become the complete opposite. This is the time to decide to make the right decisions so that neither of you will be ashamed of the other's behavior.

Week Ten — Friday
Prayer: ACTS – Teaching Your Child to Pray, Part 1
Matthew 6:9-13

[9]This, then, is how you should pray: "'Our Father in heaven, hallowed be Your name, [10]Your kingdom come, Your will be done on earth as it is in heaven. [11]Give us today our daily bread. [12]Forgive us our debts, as we also have forgiven our debtors. [13]And lead us not into temptation, but deliver from the evil one."

Matthew 6:9-13

This is known as the Lord's Prayer. Many of us learned the King James Version. I did not find the ending I learned in the scriptures I read. "For thine is the Kingdom and the power and the Glory. Amen." I am not really concerned with that ending. I am, however, wondering why more children don't know the Lord's Prayer. When determining how to teach my child to pray, I start here. As you progress, you can add family prayers, family member's names, and any other concerns. "What happened to 'Now I lay me down to sleep'" you may ask. You may introduce whatever prayer you feel most comfortable with. I only advise on the Lord's Prayer because the verse opens with "this, then, is how you should pray:" The preceding scriptures (Matthew 6:5-8) give prayer instructions, all of which we should teach our children. The most important principle of prayer is complete honesty with God and yourself. God already knows what we need and want before we ask (Matthew 6:8).

Teaching them to pray includes establishing a time and place to pray.

So what should we teach:

(1)   Pray daily and continually. (1 Thess. 5:17).
(2)   The Lord's Prayer (Matt. 6:9-13).
(3)   Be honest (Matt. 6:8)
(4)   Don't worry about what to pray (Romans 8:26-27).
(5)   Jesus sets the example of prayer (John 1-7; Mark 6:46, Mark 8:6, Mark 1:35, Luke 22:39-46).
(6)   He makes provisions for prayer (Matt. 18:19-20) and answers (Matt. 7:7-11; John 15:7).

In which order, how much at once and what they will retain in any one setting will be based on you and your children.

Their greatest example of prayer is you. Sometimes they need to see you on your face prostrate before the Lord, praying for your needs. Your personal prayer life is really all the teaching they will need.

Week Ten — Saturday
Prayer: ACTS – Teaching Your Child to Pray, Part 2
Mark 11:24

[24]Therefore I tell you, whatever you ask for in prayer, believe that you have received it, and it will be yours.

Mark 11:24

Faith is critical for prayer to be effective. You have to believe what you ask will be given. You also need to live like you believe what you have asked.

Now, I want to share ACTS of prayer to you for your information. ACTS is an acronym for adoration, confession, thanksgiving and supplication.

Adoration is your attitude about Jesus in your life, your actions and consequently your prayers. This portion of the prayer is where you express your love and praises for Him. "Oh God how I love and adore you. Jesus, I honor and praise You for Your love and care for me."

Confession is your time to confess your sins – specifically those you know and then those you can't remember but did commit. Again, honesty is the best policy. God already knows all of our sins, even before we commit them.

Thanksgiving is your time to give thanks for what God has done, what He will do and for His sovereignty. Thanksgiving is your time to tell God exactly what you expect in your life in the most respectful manner possible.

Supplication is us humbly submitting ourselves to God's will and desires for our lives. Supplication requires admitting that we know He is fully in control and that we admit that we are His vessels to use as He pleases for His good works which He planned in advance (Ephesians 2:10).

These four elements involved in a prayer is a great model for prayer. As I have said before, however, the best model is our commitment to prayer. Our best example is Jesus, then we are the example after Him.

Please avoid the regular human pitfall of wanting to pray like someone else. God wants your best prayers – not someone else's.

As a side bar, as your study increases, your prayers deepen.

98

WEEK ELEVEN
PRAY FOR YOURSELF AND YOUR SPOUSE
THE POWER OF A PRAYING WIFE/HUSBAND
BY STORMIE OMARTIAN
COL. 4:2-6

Your prayer time is essential for your spiritual growth. There is no time more important than your prayer time. Neglect of your prayer time delays your spiritual growth. In your marriage, prayer is doubly important. Prayer is vital. The success of your marriage hinges on your dedicated, committed and faithful prayer life.

God answers prayers with yes, no, and maybe. Keeping focus on God's wills and desires influences your prayer attitude. Prayer changes your circumstances for the better, also known as God's will. I am committed to my prayer life and sometimes it suffers. Busy schedules. Unrealistic expectations. Children. Work. Church Ministry. All things or events that will interrupt your prayer life if you allow them.

I'm sure that you have developed your prayer requests and thanksgivings, so I will share some suggestions and some of my list: healthy marriage, healthy children, time for myself, quality time with my spouse, Godly instruction for my children, type of wife God called me to be, and Keep Him first. Prayer is your lifeline. Prayer is your source of refuge in your good times and bad.

Sometimes it may be hard for you to remember to pray but it is the best source. Lastly, pray for two additional sources: a prayer partner and a wise married woman of God.

Pray. Pray. Pray.

Sunday	Some Prayer Instructions, Part 1 Colossians 4:2-4
Monday	Some Prayer Instructions, Part 2 Colossians 4:5-6
Tuesday	The Power of a Praying Wife: A Personal Testimony
Wednesday	The Power of a Praying Wife: A Personal Plea Ephesians 3:12
Thursday	The Power of a Praying Husband: A Personal Testimony Ephesians 5:28
Friday	The Power of a Praying Husband: A Personal Plea 1 Peter 3:7
Saturday	The Power of Prayer: 12 Reasons to Pray and Fast

Week Eleven — Sunday
Some Prayer Instructions, Part 1
Colossians 4:2-4

[2]Devote yourselves to prayer, being watchful and thankful. [3]And pray for us, too, that God may open a door for our message, so that we may proclaim the mystery of Christ, for which I am in chains. [4]Pray that I may proclaim it clearly, as I should.

Colossians 4:2-4

Paul is in jail for sharing Christ. Paul was committed to Christ in a manner many of us cannot boast, or even whisper. Paul is committed to sharing Christ in an ultimately sacrificial manner – again in ways most of us wouldn't do. Are you willing to travel to foreign lands to share Christ? Are you willing to live with strangers to share Christ? Are you willing to be jailed for Christ? If you are not willing to do these things, we are not Paul and we need to be committed to prayer. Our prayers for ourselves and other Christians who are following God's calling. Our prayers will bring to fruition God's will in our life.

Marriage and parenting are a true testimony of the mystery of Christ. As a reminder, Paul was not married and advised us not to marry. But some of us do marry and parent anyway.

Your commitment to prayer influences your testimony. As well as enhances your marriage. When I pray as I should I feel better about myself and my marriage. When I pray as I ought, I am able to respect my husband in a Godly manner. This is all important because prayer is the solution and the key for your marriage.

The added responsibility of children and all that parenting entails forces you to rely heavily on prayer.

Pray prayers of thanks.
Pray for those who cross your path.
Pray that you are a Godly spouse and effective parent.

Week Eleven — Monday
Some Prayer Instructions, Part 2
Colossians 4:5-6

[5]Be wise in the way you act toward outsiders; make the most of every opportunity. [6]Let your conversation be always full of grace, seasoned with salt, so that you may know how to answer everyone.

Colossians 4:5-6

First, defining outsider is critical. Outsider is everyone but yourself and God. Family and friends judge us first. When we say we are Christian, our inner circle will measure us and our behavior based on their perception of the Bible. Take a deep breath and reread that sentence. Avoid questions like, "how can they judge me," or "they just started reading the Bible." Both of these questions are not okay. Our family use us an example. We need to be that example, thus our testimony to be strong. Be wise. Obviously being wise means that you have to be the Christian you have advertised regardless of what the other person says or does. This allows us to make the most of every opportunity with every person we encounter, starting with our loved one.

Gage's rule of love: don't love outsiders more than you love those at your home.

The tongue and the ear are profoundly powerful. What the tongue delivers is life or death. What the tongue expresses can be wonderful or horrible. The effects can be the same on the ear. The tongue delivers what the ear receives, then from the ear to the soul and spirit.

How your tongue impacts someone's soul is our responsibility to guard with extreme care. Self-control is a display of wisdom. Add this to your prayer list. Nothing is more sobering than your three-year old repeating something you never intended for her to hear. As a parent, you decide and discern the information given in any format to your child.

Be protective of his ears. He deserves the very best.

Week Eleven — Tuesday
The Power of a Praying Wife: A Personal Testimony
By Stormie Omartian

The Power of a Praying Wife is indeed powerful. Mrs. Omartian imparts wisdom that is truly marriage-impacting. I read PPW as a single woman because a male friend recommended it. I thought when I started that will be a quick, easy read and all will be well with the world. I began reading and her words changed my entire view on marriage and my role as a spouse. As I read I truly had to consider my position on marriage. I had to decide on how I was going to handle my own issues. Most importantly, how was I going to handle the unknown issues that would arise. The answer is presented clearly: PRAY. Pray often and sacrificially.

One of the biggest corrections I had to make was I was under the impression "he" would be changing. God's challenges is for me to change with God's help, I will do God's will in my marriage. The other point is that I have to do the right thing even if "he" doesn't and especially when he doesn't.

After I read through page 49, I put the book down and thought about whether or not I wanted to do those things. Then I had to decide that I was willing to say, "Lord, change me." When I decided that I could do it, then God sent my husband when I wasn't doing anything out of the ordinary.

Last word, God sends valuable information in a variety of avenues. Be on the lookout for Christ-directed information. Remember, His word guides. God's word is directional and correctional, not of "feel good."

Week Eleven — Wednesday
The Power of a Praying Wife: A Personal Plea
Ephesians 3:12

[12]In Him and through faith in Him we may approach God with freedom and confidence.

Ephesians 3:12

As a wife, I want to submit to you my personal plea and commitment. I need to read the entire book each year. I need portions as needed based on our current situation. Rereading the material does two things: (1) I am reminded of the information which I need, and (2) I will have a new perspective on the same material. Often God shows us new measures with the same previously read material. Perhaps we weren't receptive to this the first time or we needed the other information more.

God sends us what we need at exactly the time we need it. Be careful not to challenge God. Hebrews advises us not to give up. Keep praying and wait on God's response. Remember, as you wait, keep working, keep doing what God called you to do. Keep doing what God tells. This is how we exhibit our faithfulness. God measures our faithfulness by our perseverance and steadfastness. Sometimes it's hard to be the wife. No matter what happens or doesn't, you are still the wife. You are still to respect Him by respecting him. Even when he is not obedient to Him.

In my former career, I was a retail store manager. This position offered me the opportunity to meet and even hire and supervise many people. One of the assistant managers was complaining about her husband. They were newlyweds. At this point, they had traveled because of his career so she had started once again in another small town. I asked her why she was complaining, so she explained. I replied that he was acting like a husband. If I closed my eyes, she sounded like any other wife. I then told her not to act like the husband. Some time later, she didn't do something similar to what she had complained about her husband. I looked at her and said stop acting like the husband. She simply smiled. That statement became the theme. It doesn't mean that we are better. It does mean that we are consistent. We are the helper. We are the wife.

Week Eleven — Thursday
The Power of a Praying Husband: A Personal Testimony
By Stormie Omartian
Ephesians 5:28

[28]In this same way, husbands ought to love their wives as their own bodies. He who loves his wife loves himself.

Ephesians 5:28

This book outlines some similar principles as the PPW but focused on help and tools for husbands. We didn't read the other's book. Mrs. Omartian equips husbands with tools for a prayerful marriage.

I highly recommend this book. The book is a reality check for your role as a husband as it relates to your duties. The best thing is that husbands are offered encouragement for an investment in his marriage in a unique way. "How could you say that? Prayer is not unique." It is unique to pray for your marriage and especially your spouse, particularly when there's nothing wrong.

Prayer is practical. The results are immediate because of how you will when you pray for your spouse not because God answers them immediately. Prayer appreciates your relationship similar to how real estate appreciates. Prayer increases the value of you marriage. Prayer enhances your relationship with God, thus also enhancing the marriage relationship. Remember the triangle:

God

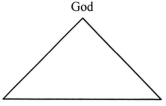

As you _ you er to God, you two w spouse · to each other. Not the reverse. Prayer is critical to this growth.

Prayer humbles you before God and your spouse. I realized that when my husband prays for me and our needs and our family, I love him more. I am a better wife.

Prayer provides power. This power is the fuel to your marriage. Your marriage requires prayer, similarly your car needs fuel.

Pray for your wife, privately and in her presence.

Week Eleven — Friday
The Power of a Praying Husband: A Personal Testimony
1 Peter 3:7

⁷Husbands, in the same way be considerate as you live with your wives, and treat them with respect as the weaker partner and as heirs with you of the gracious gift of life, so that nothing will hinder your prayers.

1 Peter 3:7

One more plea I didn't mention before, please pass on this blessing. I have given away and repurchased more of these books than I can count. They were a gift to us and we give them as gifts to others.

I know when my husband has and has not prayed for me. I can tell by my demeanor. I can tell by everything we do and don't do.

I appreciate his prayers because it means he loves me. I also like the prayer rituals we do. We hold hands when we pray over dinner, even in public. We hold hands when there is prayer. When we touch and agree, God grants our prayers.

I know that I'll manage when he doesn't, but I know we do best when he does. I measure his investment in the marriage by his prayers, communication and his level of detail for the issues and events in our marriage. His prayers feed his own spirit and energizes him to excellence as a man of God and consequently as a husband. Prayer is the lifeline between he and God so that he receives his daily empowerment to be the man God called him to be.

It is highly suggested that your husband's prayer life be maintained by praying several times a day. He is your husband. You both have other responsibilities and you have children.

A regular man would falter. A spirit-filled man has a power source regulated by God, not man, which will never fail him.

Husbands, your prayers are the most critical.

Please pray diligently daily.

Week Eleven — Saturday
The Power of Prayer
12 Reasons to Pray and Fast

12.   Prayer is your time to confess with God our sins. He already knows but when we confess, it cleanses and the guilt is eliminated. It is when God forgives us. 2 Ch. 7:14.

11.   Prayer is our time to spend time in the awesome presence of God. It is a private, sacred time where God can talk to us and we can tell Him everything, particularly the desires of our hearts. Eph. 6:18.

10.   Prayer is a time where we can listen to God. I have decided that while I don't listen in proportion to how much I tell God, eventually He will help me to listen more.

9.   Prayer is a time when we intercede for others. God calls us to intercede for others, especially when they ask us. Intercessory prayer is crucial to the needs of others. James 5:16; Job 42:8.

8.   Prayer and fasting are companions for spiritual well-being and successful spiritual warfare. Prayer doesn't always accompany fasting, but fasting is always accompanied with prayer. I cannot fast without prayer. Matt. 26:36-46.

7.   Fasting eliminates the spiritual space between you and God. We are most at one with Him when fasting. When you eliminate as many objects in your life as possible and focus totally on Him, your relationship increases by leaps and bounds. When I fast, I sacrifice food, television, frivolous conversation and leisure activities in various increments. While you are pregnant, fasting from food is not an option. However, totally eliminating fast food, chips and similarly non-healthy foods from your diet is wise. Matt. 4:1-11.

6.   Jesus fasted. As usual, His life as an example overwhelms me, but offers me a clear understanding for what I need to do so that my relationship with God is all that it can be. Matt. 4:5.

5.   Prayer provides us the peace we continually search for and request. Phil. 4:7.

4.   Prayer is where you are freed from your burdens. He said that He would give us rest for those burdened and heavy laden. Matt. 11:28.

3.   Prayer is the communication of our faith. We communicate our belief in God and His sovereignty through our prayers.

2.   Fasting communicates our seriousness for our relationship with God. He provides us some specific instructions on how to fast, and when it is appropriate. Matt. 6:16-18.

1.   Jesus taught us how to pray. God answers us when we pray. Prayer is our lifeline to God. Prayer is crucial to our relationship with God. He calls us to pray. Matt. 6:5-15.

WEEK TWELVE
PRAYER AS A PARENT
THE POWER OF A PRAYING PARENT
BY STORMIE OMARTIAN

As parents, we have been gifted. God doesn't allow everyone to be parents. Not even our friends who we feel deserve to be parents. Why we don't know but it's really not up to us. We are gifted as parents. We are parenting someone who God has also bestowed with gifts. We are parenting the next Christians, the next teachers, attorneys, judges, pastors, the next president, senators, congresspersons, governor. We are trusted with God's messengers. Just imagine what it was like to be Mary, mother of Jesus. Could you have done it? At 12, Jesus was teaching at the synagogue.

Prayer facilitates our conversation with God about what He wants us to do as parents and what He wants us to know about our children. One of my dear friends worked from home when she had her first child. She stopped working after the second child was born. She struggled with the choice but knows it's what God wants her to do. On the other hand, I left my job 3 months before my son was born. I started a home based business after he was born. Then after he turned one, I sought full-time employment while still engaged in my writing, home based business and mothering two and of course, my husband, not to mention my church and my duties there.

Pray over your children. Their well-being is in your hands. We are responsible for them – for the rest of their lives. Prayer is powerful for all that we desire our children to be and to have and to know. Prayer is powerful. I cannot repeat myself enough. Prayer changes attitudes, minds and actions. Keep praying.

Sunday	Praying for Our Children: the Depth of Your Prayer Psalm 6:9
Monday	Praying for Our Children: the Width of Your Prayer Ephesians 6:18
Tuesday	Praying for Our Children: the Territory of Your Prayer Philippians 4:6
Wednesday	Praying for Our Children: the Impact of Your Prayer Matthew 11:25
Thursday	Praying for Our Children: the Best Way to Pray Matthew 26:39
Friday	Praying for Our Children: YOU 2 Thessalonians 1:11-12
Saturday	Praying for Our Children: My Personal Testimony

Week Twelve — Sunday
Praying for Our Children
Prayer defined – The Depth of Your Prayer
Psalm 6:9

[9]The Lord has heard my cry for mercy; the Lord accepts my prayer.

Psalm 6:9

What is prayer? Prayer is the discussion with God of our desires, fears, dreams and our children's health, welfare and love. Prayer is our frank conversation with God with the assistance of the Holy Spirit. Prayer is submission to God of all of what burdens us.

Prayer is a gift and a blessing. God shows His compassion because of prayer. He offers the opportunity to share what He already knows and He doesn't laugh. He listens intently and He hears us, especially when we rejoice, praise, worship and cry.

God offers His peace because of prayer. Prayer is our job for our children. Prayer is our investment in their lives. Prayer exhibits our concerns for our children.

Is it hard to pray for our children? For some it could be but for most prayer is a staple. Prayer exhibits love and faith. Prayer enriches our children's lives. Prayer also guards our children's hearts.

Mrs. Stormie Omartian dedicates several chapters to the importance of parents praying for our children. The power of prayer is phenomenal for God's desired results, saves heartbreak, and alleviates pain.

God expects us to pray for our children.

What should we pray when we pray for our children:

    (1)   health
    (2)   love
    (3)   Godly influence
    (4)   education
    (5)   God's favor

These requests seem simple and they are. However, God can do His best work with the most simple requests.

108

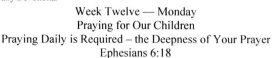

Week Twelve — Monday
Praying for Our Children
Praying Daily is Required – the Deepness of Your Prayer
Ephesians 6:18

[18]And pray in the Spirit on all occasions with all kinds of prayers and requests. With this in mind, be alert and always keep on praying for all the saints.

Ephesians 6:18

Daily prayer is the children's daily bread. Prayer feeds their spirits. Your prayers need to cover their travel, safety, the teacher, the food, retention of information, a strong thirst for knowledge, their relationships and general health. Your daily prayer is your personal labor of love. When you put your prayers out to the Lord, He hears your petitions for your child. He honors your commitment as a parent to prayer.

Our children also have to pray daily. It is the most beautiful sound to hear my daughter pray. She started at age 2. She now prays over each meal and before bed. Next I will teach her to pray in the morning before starting her day. This is one of the most important treasures we can teach our children – prayer. We taught our daughter the Lord's Prayer.

Another very powerful experience is when your child hears you pray – both of you, together. So much power exists when children see their parents pray. Through witnessing you pray, they experience the power of prayer first hand in a phenomenal manner. When they are in your presence as you pray, they learn how to pray as well. Your credibility is concrete when they witness you pray. Later in life you will need to access this already established credibility. When you instruct or advise them in the area of prayer in relation to God answering prayers, they will not question your word.

Prayer is the area we cannot leave to chance, church, God or any other outside influences. When they know that prayer is the access card to God and the solution to the issues, problems and confusion in their lives, they will know what to do when they are distressed and when trouble attempts to set up residence.

Teach them to pray.

Week Twelve — Tuesday
Praying for Our Children
The Territory of Your Prayer
Philippians 4:6

⁶Do not be anxious about anything, but in everything, by prayer and petition, with thanksgiving, present your requests to God.

Philippians 4:6

The territory of our prayers is all inclusive. Pray over everything in their lives and your lives. Pray over the areas that you most fear. Pray for the issues that you experienced as a child and young adult. Pray for wisdom and behavior. Pray for their health, dating habits. Pray for the absence of controlled substances and alcohol. Pray for Christian friends and mentors.

Pray for their education. Pray for their dreams. Pray for their future. Pray for their goals. Pray for their faith. Pray for their mission. Pray for their focus.

Pray for their soul. Pray for their spirit. Pray for the persons who will cross their paths. Pray for the people who will invest in their lives. Pray for their spouses and spouses' in-laws. Pray for their purity.

When I use my surreal vision for my family's life, I find myself looking at the children at each of their schools wondering will this be a person that my child marries. I think about where my child's spouse is. I consider their upbringing and well-being. I consider that they are Christian. This seem too distant? It may seem so, but keep in mind we have 17 years to do what God tells us to do, making an impression on them on their lives as God instructs. Seventeen years is not a long time. I don't know when my children will marry but I know that if I follow the Instruction Book, I will have a greater influence than I would otherwise have if I don't pray.

Last note on the territory of your prayers. There are families who experience turmoil because the child met someone (usually an adult) on the internet. They meet. He assaults her (a minor). Your innocent child, your baby, no longer innocent, violated.

Pray for their communication. Pray for their security. Pray for their discernment and yours.

Pray.

Week Twelve — Wednesday
Praying for Our Children
The Impact of Your Prayers
Matthew 11:25

[25]At that time Jesus said, "I praise You, Father, Lord of heaven and earth, because you have hidden these things from the wise and learned, and revealed them to little children.

Matthew 11:25

Why do we pray? We can't afford not to. When I watch the news, I realize that my children's lives depend on my prayers. My fervent prayers. The news greatly distresses me. The news is 35 minutes of death, violence and bleak visions of life.

We pray to prepare their hearts. We pray that information they receive is aligned with God's will. We compete with entities we may never know of while parenting our children. This type of competition includes a dozen other influences. We don't always know the depth of that competition or the range of that competitive influence. Just imagine the events that have happened to children you know or maybe even yourself. Do you know anyone who is addicted to drugs? Had a baby out of wedlock? Has an incurable disease related to sexual relations? Attempted suicide? Succeeded?

I do. These events challenge, stretch and divide families daily. I was never even approached to try drugs. I never had to say no – I was never asked. I was never in an environment where I had to decide. God can keep our children from these events and issues when we pray.

My mother and I talk about this from time to time. I remind her that her challenges as a parent are not the magnitude of others. I remind her of His blessing and His keeping power. Look over your life and think of the life-altering events and the challenges. Examine these events for their impact. Think about the tools which enable you to make great or poor decisions. This wisdom and knowledge is what you will pass on to your children.

The impact of your prayers is far reaching. The effects of your prayers last the rest of their lives.

Week Twelve — Thursday
Praying for Our Children
The Best Way to Pray
Matthew 26:39

[39]Going a little farther, He fell with His face to the ground and prayed, "My Father, if it is possible, may this cup be taken from Me. Yet not as I will, but as You will."

Matthew 26:39

Jesus teaches us to pray, via example and instruction. Jesus taught us to pray the Lord's Prayer. Technically the Lord's Prayer doesn't cover our specific needs but it covers a multitude of needs we have if we don't know how to pray.

The Holy Spirit assists with what to pray when we don't know what or how to pray. The Holy Spirit intercedes on our behalf.

The Rules of Prayer:

(1)	God is waiting on us	(6)	Believe
(2)	Honesty required	(7)	Leave your concerns w/God
(3)	Confession	(8)	Let Him do His will
(4)	Share the desires of your heart	(9)	As a family, when available
(5)	Consistency	(10)	Do the practical, pray for the unknown

Jesus knew that He would spend a finite time frame on this earth, so He exhibited practical application of God's word and instruction. God prayed for Jesus. Jesus prayed to God. He prayed for most things, but didn't ask should He cure the sick, heal the leper, or raise Lazarus from the dead. He did the practical. He prayed not to be sacrificed for our sins. He prayed for strength while He fasted. Jesus' example applies to our lives. I don't need to pray about how late should she be allowed to stay out with her friends, should she drive at 16, 17 or 18, can he play football. These are practical, common sense decisions that we as parents are equipped to make alone. I will pray for guidance for her good decision-making while she is in college, for her spirit of discernment to choose her friends wisely and keeping her away from drugs, alcohol and sex.

Do the practical, pray for the unknown.

Week Twelve — Friday
Praying for Our Children
The Most Important Petitioner for Your Child: YOU
2 Thessalonians 1:11-12

[11]With this in mind, we constantly pray for you, that our God may count you worthy of His calling, and that by His power He may fulfill every good purpose of yours and every act prompted by your faith. [12]We pray this is so that the name of our Lord Jesus may be gloried in you, and you in Him, according to the grace of our God and the Lord Jesus Christ.

2 Thessalonians 1:11-12

We, by far, are the most important petitioners for our children. No one can pray for my children like I can – not in my place, in addition to my prayers. My mother, mother and father in law, grandparents, aunts, uncles, cousins and friends should all pray. Their prayers are important and contribute to their lives. However, none of these prayers replace my prayers or my husband's. I remind my mother that her perceived troubles with us doesn't match what others have endured.

What does a parent pray so that when a college student doesn't go to a toga party nude under the sheet? Which prayer covers not attempting/committing suicide? What prayers keep him from raping someone or her from being raped? What prayers keeps her focuses in school? What prayers insure his success on the team? Which prayers lock in their health? What prayer inspires leadership within them that is so natural you almost transition because you were busy praying and praising?

Not one prayer in particular does any of these things. It is a combination of all of our prayers, followed up by communication, love and God's will and grace.

In the twenty-first century it is hard to raise the children my grandmother parented, however, I have announced my village concept desire. I want the whole family's experience and input in my children's life so I make fewer mistakes, wise choices, and more diverse experiences as a result. I led a sheltered life and I understood. I want the sheltered with a bonus life for my children.

The prayers that count the most are – OURS.

A right or wrong prayer: NO.

Who prays: US.

When do we pray: Continually.

What do we pray: God's will in combination with the desires of my heart.

How do we pray: fervently and frequently.

Why do we pray: Because our complete love for Him through our love for them speaks volumes and in volumes.

Where do we pray: privately and in their presence.

113

Week Twelve — Saturday
Praying for Our Children
Power of a Praying Parent – A Personal Testimony
by Stormie Omartian

First, I am a fan of Stormie Omartian and her works. As you remember from earlier weeks, I shared with you the impact of her books. I really hope that you will read her <u>Power of a Praying Parent</u>.

I have shared some of my personal experience, which I feel were greatly impacted by a strong prayer influence. There have been times when I have shared with my mother instances when prayer was effective for my safety and well-being. My mom and I compare notes about our perceptions of my childhood.

I know that my prayers have been answered in so many areas for my children in areas of health, education and security. In praying for them, I have also gained wisdom for decisions and choices I make in my daily life which directly and indirectly affect them and their futures.

I am accountable to them for praying. My daughter developed the knowledge to hold us accountable for our actions and words, likewise our prayers. The first time she told me that God was her friend, I found myself more accountable to her and God. Praying for them signifies that I am their biggest fan. My support strengthens their self-esteem which leads them closer to God.

Finally, as a praying parent, God uses this time to reveal to us the answers to the uncertainties we experience as parents. We need to use this time to explore for more wisdom in those areas we need clarity. This is also the best time to increase communication with your spouse.

Prayer can lead you two closer as you grow closer to God. This time needs to be consistent, comprehensive, and collective.

Praying for our children is our biggest and best investment in their lives.

WEEK THIRTEEN
PRAYERS FOR YOUR CHILDREN

In several weeks, we have alluded to prayer for your children, so we will identify some specific areas of prayer. These areas are a simple sample of the depth and breadth of your prayer life. Prayer is required for successful parenting as God defines.

Prayer is the most powerful investment in their lives. Prayer also allows you to get what you need to run the parenting marathon. So by all means, pray for yourself, your spouse, your marriage, your life, your family and everything else that concerns you. We live because God supplies life. He provides us a platform for prayer. He expects us to request what we need, and the desires of our heart. This is the definition of comprehensive prayer.

Spend some time examining your current prayer life. Think about ways to extend your prayer life, depth and breadth. Reading about prayer helps develop a passionate prayer life. Joining a prayer ministry fuels your prayer life. These three methods can catapult your prayer life several levels.

My personal method to hold me accountable and to move my prayer life to a higher level are eyes – her eyes and his eyes. Those two pair of eyes are all that I need to move the needle in my prayer life. Sometimes when I have fallen from my prayer life, one of them looks at me and causes me to start to pray on the spot, with my eyes open, holding one of them because they need my prayers and my commitment to God. My personal banner for God shows when I least expect it and when I need it most. They cannot read the word for themselves yet so they need me reading, fasting and praying as their intercessor.

I am their prayer warrior. I wrote a poem years ago about a prayer warrior's role. I had no idea then that it would be my role now. I stand against evil and other forces in their place. My prayers now saves me time for later.

> "Mommy?"
> "Yes, Hillary?"
> Hillary: "Is God talking to me?"
> "Yes, Hillary, He is," responds mommy.

Sunday	Praying for her spirituality Galatians 5:22-23
Monday	Praying for his actions. Proverbs 20:11
Tuesday	Praying for his obedience Ephesians 6:1; Colossians 3:20
Wednesday	Praying for her knowledge Deuteronomy 4:9
Thursday	Praying for his respect Leviticus 19:3, 32
Friday	Praying for love for and within him 1 Corinthians 13:2a, 13
Saturday	Praying for her future 1 Corinthians 13:11; Jeremiah 29:11; 3 John 2

Week Thirteen — Sunday
Praying for Her Spirituality
Galatians 5:22-23, 25

[22]But the fruit of the Spirit is love, joy, peace, patience, kindness, goodness, faithfulness, [23]gentleness and self-control. Against such things there is no law. [25]Since we live by the Spirit, let us keep in step with the Spirit.

Galatians 5:22-23, 25

As parents, we have to prioritize our time and protect our time. So when I decide what to pray, the top priority is her spirituality. If her soul and spirit is not on a firm foundation, nothing else matters. So the spirit and the soul rank most important on the prayer list.

You know a tree because of the fruit it bears. Apple trees have apples. Pear trees have pears, etc. So my first order of business to be reflective of the Spirit. I must first be fruit of the Spirit, then I can expect the same from her. Not before. It is rare that a child finds his own way to righteousness, but it has happened. Those areas of the fruit I lack, I pray for improvement in that area first. Next I pray for her full development in all the areas.

The scripture shares that we can never have too much of the fruit. The scripture encourages us to fully develop the fruit because there is no law against the fruit.

Typically, I only hear verses 22 and 23 taught, but I added verse 25 because this scripture encourages our spiritual fitness.

"Let us keep in step with the Spirit" encourages us to align ourselves with the actions the spirit wants us to exhibit.

There are some times when we are greatly aligned and other times when we have missed the mark. The greatest lesson when we are out of step with the Spirit is realigning ourselves immediately through confession, supplication and repentance.

The greatest lesson we can pass on to our children is how to do this with a completely submissive heart. The second lesson is how to keep in step with the Spirit through prayer, study and model behavior.

Pray for her soul and spirituality.

Week Thirteen — Monday
Praying for His Actions
Proverbs 20:11

[11]Even a child is known by his actions, by whether his conduct is pure and right.

Proverbs 20:11

My prayer is for well-behaved, well-mannered children. I pray that my children act as they should and they exhibit behavior becoming. Likewise, I have to be an example of excellent conduct.

My mother reminds me that I talked excessively in class. However, she never remembers being called to school for poor behavior. My husband on the other hand was known for being the class clown. I can only hope for the best.

I often reflect on my high school years and at one time wished I was more popular but after my class reunion I realized that I was well-known but for the right actions. I was never asked to the formals because I didn't do drugs and was not known for sexual activity. I was proud of my reputation when I found out. Now that means I had protected my reputation. I couldn't date the guy I wanted to date, though. At the time, it seemed like an impossible situation. Now I don't regret a moment. That was a valuable lesson – one my mother probably couldn't have verbalized better. I am proud to share this with you and my children. As for the guy I asked to prom and he said no because there would've been no relations, I respect his honesty and thank him. He claimed to have an older date who didn't show. I went with my neighbor. By that time I also had a boyfriend who was working a concert. It was not my ideal prom but it was not the disaster it could've been.

Finally, let our actions be exemplary of who we represent – GOD.

117

Week Thirteen — Tuesday
Praying for His Obedience
Ephesians 6:1; Colossians 3:20

[1]Children, obey your parents in the Lord, for this is right. [20]Children, obey your parents in everything, for this pleases God.

Ephesians 6:1; Colossians 3:20

I can recall countless stories where the ending would have been different had I been obedient. I can conjure about a dozen reasons per occurrence why I should be excused for my disobedience.

I pray my children are different. I pray they are obedient. Their obedience will save us time and money and accidents.

Their obedience earns them some blessings from God.

Their obedience captures God's attention and pleases Him.

Their obedience is a reward for parents. It means you prayed. It doesn't mean you did anything else or anything right.

I often wonder if I had listened to my mother would I be in a different place. The answer is most certainly yes. The difference is would I have gained the same wisdom – maybe. That potential was wrapped in her presentation. My mother detested the question, "why." It is classic generational differences. "Why" was considered disrespectful. The typical response was "because I said so," which selectively went ignored.

As you probably recall, you promised you would be a different parent. Word of caution, do not tolerate disobedience. The long range consequence can cost you unanticipated and unimagined heartache. Expose your "parental differences" in your response while demanding obedience. Parenting differently doesn't mean you yield different results.

I promised I would be a different parent and I am but my mother demanded obedience and I will do the same, not using the same mechanisms however, but I demand obedience.

Week Thirteen — Wednesday
Praying for Her Knowledge
Deuteronomy 4:9

[9]Only be careful, and watch yourselves closely so that you do not forget the things your eyes have seen or let them slip from your heart as long as you live. Teach them to your children and to their children after them.

Deuteronomy 4:9

If you have ever heard the expression "mind like a steel trap," you might have envied it. You wished for more memory, or maybe a better memory. I happen to have that mind like a steel trap. Once information enters my mind, it seldom is forgotten or lost. The gift is my daughter's mind resembles mine closely.

I pray for their knowledge and retention and the ability to apply that knowledge to life's events. There were times when I once wished that my knowledge weren't so comprehensive, however, I realize its blessing and accept it.

My daughter remembers words, events, phone numbers in her short life. Word of caution, I don't tease, play or lie. She remembers conversations that you didn't think she even heard. She is extremely intelligent. With that knowledge, she will hold you accountable. Do not say anything you cannot do. Be truthful when the circumstances change. Treat her with respect.

Hillary had a large vocabulary at age 2. She uses words she learned contextually. Be aware they are listening especially when they don't appear to be.

Last note on knowledge, psychologists have studied that the brain's components come together completely by age 12. Psychologists also say that the personality is formed by age 5. This is your job: feed her or him with knowledge and love. This is your only job. This is not a test. This is the real work. It is the hardest 18 years of your life. Not your own 18, as you previously thought.

Make every day count.

Week Thirteen — Thursday
Praying for His Respect
Leviticus 19:3, 32

[3]Each of you must respect his mother and father, and you must observe my Sabbaths. I am the Lord your God. [32]Rise in the presence of the aged, show respect for the elderly and revere your God. I am the Lord.

Leviticus 19:3, 32

Teaching respect is usually through modeling behavior, rather than from talk. Your actions speak louder and last longer than your words.

You can determine the level of their respect by your own level. If you still say yes ma'am to your mother, then he will say yes ma'am to you. Respect is earned. They are children so your forgiveness meter is not big. Use your need to be forgiven quite sparingly.

Respect them. Listen to them. Give them the time the desire and more than what they deserve.

It is easy to mimic respect if you have grandparents, then you can show your children how to treat your parents as grandparents.

Treat respect as your homage to God. I demand my mother to communicate with me. My daughter demands communication of me. Respect is similar and is facilitated through communication.

Respect includes God, His word, the world, other individuals, life and himself.

Respect shows up in all areas and in all manners. Keep a respectful life and having that life before them will teach how respect is lived.

Week Thirteen — Friday
Praying for Love for and Within Him
1 Corinthians 13: 2a, 13

²but have not love, I am nothing. ¹³And now these three remain: faith, hope and love. But the greatest of these is love.

1 Corinthians 13: 2a, 13

With love, everything is possible. If I want my children to know love and experience love, then I have to show them love and provide them an environment where they experience love. Ultimately, I need to show them God's love and how He is the definer of all love that man has named and renamed. God is the exhibit of love. As I experience His love, I translate that to my family.

Even though we know God's love, we may not always experience that love. I have to do love tank checks frequently to insure that my family's love tank is on full.

The ways children like to love that we may not always be receptive to: hugs, kisses, "play with me," "talk to me," encouragement, praise, time – quality, "I want to sit in your lap," "watch television with me," and the list goes on. My point is that they need to be loved at their volume (how loud) is your love and at their volume (how much love can you give). Children are highly intuitive and equipped with a discerning spirit. They will announce their need for love if you will simply listen. Love even when you discipline.

Ways to quickly empty their love tanks: mommy/daddy doesn't have time (and never make time), wait (and never get around to addressing their request), mommy/daddy has to do "this or that" (is that really more important than her or him?), and the list goes on. Love them so that when they go out into the world, they won't have to use the world's definition and get shortchanged.

Love them because He said so.

121

Week Thirteen — Saturday
Praying for Her Future
1 Corinthians 13:11; Jeremiah 29:11; 3 John 2

[11]When I was a child, I talked like a child, I thought like a child, I reasoned like a child. When I became a man I put away childish ways.
[11]"For I know the plans I have for you," declared the Lord, "plans to prosper you and not to harm you, plans to give you hope and a future.
[2]Dear friend, I pray that you may enjoy good health and that all may go well with you, even as your soul is getting along well.

                                                    1 Corinthians 13:11; Jeremiah 29:11; 3 John 2

Recently I was working on our financial plans and I decided that we needed an increase in our savings. We needed a college savings plan and several other financial vehicles for the children. Then the next words out of my mouth would change my husband's life forever: "we'll need about $25,000 for her wedding and I want to give them the down payment for their home."

Good news: God's plans for my children and my plans may not always match but we are aligned with the magnitude and grandness we both have planned. The bad news is that I can plan and pray, but I can only teach her in a fashion so that our plans can even relate.

My mother probably never imagined that I would be a published author. She may not have even been surprised but this is more than she imagined because last time she checked I was scheduled to be a corporate attorney. Our plans relate: successful individual as defined by Gage, Christian wife, mother of two, Christian minister, published author, successful entrepreneur, triple-degreed, drug-free, and the list could go on.

I know where I would like both of them to attend college. I know that I want them successful, and I have all these plans but she still has to live according to His will. His plans override my wildest dreams.

Final note on success and desired plans; this will only be great if his soul prospers at the same rate. There is a song, an old hymnal, that says "it is well, it is well with my soul." Being a well soul requires close relationship with God. A well soul can then prosper.

I am glad His plans are better than our own, even for myself.

WEEK FOURTEEN
VISION
A GAME PLAN WITH GOD'S LEADERSHIP

Status quo means not exceeding the limits or testing the boundary or going above and beyond to achieve the results. My vision for my family is everything but status quo. Your vision for your family should include strategic plans for fulfilling the purposes God has for us as well as meeting the demands that children bring. This is a great time to investigate your plans for the major benchmarks of her life.

The vision needs to fulfill a purpose. Some events relating to completing the vision will be temporary. A visionary acts without short-sightedness, but rather the long-term effects on some great, yet sacrificial, decisions.

A friend had her son six months after I had Hillary. She took a courageous step in her career and proposed and was approved to work at home. It was important to her that her son be home with her. She made the necessary arrangements for his care when she had away meetings and conferences but most of her work week was with her child at her home. On the other hand I went back to work at my high-profile career, thinking it was important.

Two different decisions. Two families. Two women. I wasn't wrong to return to work but could've made a different decision. Or could I? Different results. What is your vision? What will you do during the different milestones in his life?

Your vision and the related actions starts the legacy you pass on to your children. Because of your choices, you can provide valuable influence to your children while they develop their vision.

The vision you and your spouse share serve critical for the life you now share with a little person. So how will you structure your vision?

What does God have for your vision?

Sunday	Let's Examine the Questions
Monday	Let's Examine the Costs
Tuesday	Personal Testimony – (Hillary)
Wednesday	Personal Testimony – Nehemiah
Thursday	As I Compared Notes
Friday	What is Your Vision Habakkuk 2:2
Saturday	Making It Happen

Week Fourteen — Sunday
Without Vision the People Will Perish
Let's Examine the Questions

After the bliss and excitement wanes and just before (or during) the morning sickness sets in, there are several questions you need to answer:

(1)   What will you name the baby?
(2)   Will you find out the gender during the ultrasound?
(3)   Who will be the child's guardian parents?
(4)   Will you return to work?
(5)   If yes, who will care for your child while you are at work?
(6)   How long will you stay home with the baby? Do you have enough time at work to take off the time you desire?
(7)   Can you work from home? If not full-time, then some days of the week or some half-days?
(8)   Can you and your family afford for you to stay home for 6 months? a year? eighteen months?
(9)   What happens if you are scheduled off 12 weeks and you don't want to return to work?
(10)   How will your life be different with this birth?
(11)   When can you employ some help? Parents? Friends? Housekeeper?
(12)   How will you raise your child?
(13)   Are there any decisions you need to make before the baby arrives?
(14)   How will you decorate the nursery? Will it be complete before the baby arrives?
(15)   Will you breast feed? If not, which formula? Why?
(16)   And other questions which may keep you up at night or wake you very early.

Some of these questions are not critical or life-changing but for those which are, let's examine them. First, pray for wisdom, insight and sound decision-making.

What is your vision?

Week Fourteen — Monday
Let's Examine the Costs

There are costs associated with the life changing event. What are these costs? Starting with question four, "Will you return to work?" If you say no, can you adjust to be without that income? Can you replace that income within four to six months? Can you generate that income from home? Can you live without your benefits? Can your husband's benefits cover the family? Can you be completely out of debt before the baby arrives? Your 401k contributions will stop. Can you increase your husband's contributions to not lose the gains for the retirement plan? After the increased deductions, can you live on the one salary? Can you take an extended leave which secures your position for the length of time you want to stay at home in lieu of leaving completely?

So if you return to work, when will you return? Will you have enough paid and unpaid leave for the length you choose?

Who will keep the baby? Daycare? Home-sitter? Nanny? Have you started the interview process? Do you have the list of questions to ask?

Have you considered all of the options of your career to include those positions which would allow you to work from home?

Have you considered all of the best possible options for your family?

Let's count the costs. The most important costs is what you achieve holding your own baby as often as you can until she is no longer a baby. She won't let you hold her long.

You will never get these days back. Use them wisely.

Week Fourteen — Tuesday
Some Personal Testimony

When we conceived Hillary I had recently accepted a promotion. I thought it was great. I was wrong. I stayed home for eight weeks. We were on the road as soon as I could drive. I recall her giving back her milk as I was trying to get my eyes examined. During those eight weeks, I was lonely and alone. All the arrangements and help I thought I had failed. I had little sleep. It was a notable disaster.

Have a plan with a paid backup. Ask your family and friends. Hope they come. Pay the cook, housekeeper and Doula. Now enough of the pitiful. I didn't investigate the other careers I could've easily transitioned to so that my motherhood could've been easier.

At any rate, I took my baby to a daycare, and being unable to leave because she wouldn't stop crying. I had to call in that day.

What did that change do to her? I don't know but we have communicated about each move. I have promised her little change for a few years where school is concerned.

I have learned that I thought my life could proceed as normal. I was wrong. I try to recover and recapture that time but of course I am unable.

The sacrifice of my baby's time was not worth the "job" I kept and gave the wrong priority to ended when the location closed just after I gave birth to my son.

Establish a vision suitable for your family. One you will be proud to share. I'm not completely ashamed because I know mothers have experienced worse but I certainly want to share my lack of wisdom and how it impacted my family.

Final note: My most upsetting moment was when she took her first steps, I was at work and I couldn't leave. She was walking. I was working. The results of poor choices.

Week Fourteen — Wednesday
Personal Testimony, Part 2

Nehemiah gave me more trouble during the pregnancy than Hillary, but the outcome was different. I stayed home for 18 months with Nehemiah. When I needed temporary care, he went to a home sitter. Simultaneously, I started a new home-based business, and published two new books. Now the home sitter was okay, not exactly the blessing I counted on. He could stay with me because my home-based business allows me the flexibility to keep him with me. Besides I had learned from Hillary the importance of choice. When he took his first 18 steps, I was there to count them and be the mom I imagined.

I am investigating returning to work full-time but only if I am able to put my children first. My children like to socialize so school is good for them. School is great for me because I am a room mom and am really involved in their activities. This is what I wanted as part of my vision.

He will attend school with Hillary when he is 18 months. The school didn't keep infants. I found the value of school versus daycare with Hillary. They will both stay there until first grade. At which point, I will investigate what is best for them, not for my budget. I can always make more money. I won't ever get to educate or love or play in this moment again. A little redemption for a mom.

Week Fourteen — Thursday
As I Compare Notes

At the top of every mother's list is the best for my kids at whatever cost. Then we stamp "SACRIFICE" on each subsequent item on the list.

I referred earlier to a friend who worked from home when she birthed her son. She already had a daughter who was older. Then on the exact day I had Nehemiah she birthed a daughter. She did the impossible – she QUIT her job. She cited the reason of it was best for my family. It was never her initial vision but it's what is best for her family. Could you quit your job? Leave your career?

It is only temporary. When I wrapped my brain and attitude around that fact, not concept, but fact, I could really understand how to move forward and QUIT my job.

We compare notes regularly about how the changes are affecting everyone and it seems to be going well. We agree that we enjoy picking them before rush hour. We like being able to see our children between the six's, not at the six's. I would be stressed out to get the daycare center before too late. I don't want my baby to be last to go home. It gives me my pride to be able to be at her school for school parties and school dinners. I want it to be that way always.

Life is short. Our life is designed to be full and powerful and impacting. We have to live orderly. Activities we participate must align up to the mission statement and vision. Some of it's hard but it's not an option. When I have treated the vision or mission as an option, I have regretted it, immensely, not to mention what it cost me.

Final note: When you do what's best for your children, you find no regrets.

Live a focused and refined life.

128

Week Fourteen — Friday
The Family Vision and the Family Mission Statement
Habakkuk 2:2

²The Lord answered me, "Write the vision."

Habakkuk 2:2

Yes, write the vision so you can measure the situation against the vision. This leaves little to chance. There will be times when you will have to hold your spouse accountable and vice versa. There are times when my friends check my accountability. No, it is not easy but is necessary. Include in your vision, your total vision of their life; what type of care, will they school – public or private, when, where, how will you feed her, and all relevant factors. Revise as needed but keep that working document before you so you remain focused on the vision.

As for the mission statement, we used the Franklin Covey worksheets to develop our statement. It is difficult to take either document and remind your spouse that even his dream that he has had most of his life does not match the mission or vision statements. It's hard to tell your wife that this career doesn't support the mission or vision statements.

Both statements require prayer and time to write and adopt. Set a deadline and meet it. Develop the statements. They really make life easier when you are making decisions for your family.

Both statements and even the need for the statements will be challenged from time to time. Stand firm on your decisions and convictions. We are all challenged regularly. I listen respectfully, hear the facts and then share why we have chosen our course of action.

My mother and I always conflict about the children being in daycare than when I switch them to another place. I simply explain that this is better. After the third move, she just listened. She doesn't even question me anymore. It wasn't about being right for me but for the children. The first time though, she challenged my decision and even insisted that change may have been bad and my choice was poor. I had to stand with my decision. She later said she understood. In the future, I shared my concerns earlier than the move. She had a chance to process the situation, then provide her feedback. She felt better and so did I. My decision never changed but the process was smoother.

The grandparents prefer to know the vision, too.

Week Fourteen — Saturday
Making It Happen

As I said earlier, these are the hardest working 18 years of your life. This is a short window which seems so long. You decide on the vision, then you have to develop an action plan.

October of every year, I start to plan next year. I keep great records of doctors' appointments and eye exams. This way I can pencil those in and keep up to date. We plan for about 2-3 weeks, including vacations, birthday celebrations, when to spend the holidays, even the budget for gifts and events. I suggest you do the same.

If this is your first or even your fifth, when you add another person's agenda to your calendar, you just multiplied your workload. You've got to remember more, you've got to do more, you need more, you've got to plan more. It is your smartest move. PLAN. PLAN. PLAN. Executing the plan is its own project. Explain the plan. Share the plan. After those two steps, execution becomes easier.

Now you are accountable for the results of making the vision happen. Your little one(s) is counting on you to deliver the vision.

Remember not to be completely afraid to make mistakes. As young people, they forgive easily if you say "sorry." They forget most of your mistakes, too. So with that said, please don't spend much time on those errors. Do spend time moving toward the vision with love.

Often you will be questioned so it is a good idea for you and your spouse to become more unified than ever. Rare, but possible, the questioner may be your spouse. Remind him/her gently of what the vision was, how the plan was established through the vision and remember to be focused on the end result for which you are striving.

Keep focusing on making it happen.

Keep your word to yourself and your children and your family.

WEEK FIFTEEN
VISION
THE FINANCIAL STRATEGY

Part of your vision will include a new financial strategy. With the birth of a new baby, there will be budget changes. You need to discuss how to plan for the school, diapers, formula, wipes and all other necessities. Most couples are unaware of the costs associated with a baby. We have to consider the costs (Hillary hadn't arrived yet). All costs are not financial though. On my first Mother's Day, my mother asked me why she had to go to daycare and I commented that we couldn't afford for me to stay at home. I asked her if she could stay at home and keep her and she said no. Sometimes the cost is personal sacrifice and are you willing to sacrifice for the good of the children.

From my personal experiences I have decided that I need to be in a financial situation when I have grandchildren to do what I had wanted to happen for me. I don't always think I can afford the "best" option but I really have decided that I can't afford not to choose the "best" option and readjust the budget.

So what will be affected more than your money? Your time. Your leisure activities. Keep that in mind as you plan. Be prepared for the unexpected. I planned to breast feed. It didn't work as long as I wanted it to work. I introduced formula sooner than I planned to my children and to my budget.

Do your research. Ask God. Ask your friends. Develop the plan. Be ready and willing for any changes that may need to occur.

Don't forget to support each other as these life changes occur. You will need more compassion for one another than you ever have. Ephesians 4:32 is a starting point for developing this needed increase of compassion.

Lastly, the budget is not firm. It is a guide. Write it in pencil.

Sunday	Your Attitude About Money Malachi 3:10
Monday	Your New Financial Plan
Tuesday	New Expenses to Expect
Wednesday	Can I Stay at Home
Thursday	The Debt-Free Plan
Friday	Maintain Your Lifestyle Perks
Saturday	Your Insurance Plans

131

Week Fifteen — Sunday
Your Attitude About Money
Malachi 3:10

[10]Bring the whole tithe into the storehouse, that there may be food in my house. Test me in this," says the Lord Almighty, "and see if I will not throw open the floodgates of heaven and pour out so much blessing that you will not have room enough for it."

Malachi 3:10

The attitude you and your spouse share about money need to be similar to insure your ultimate success. For some this will be easy and for others more difficult.

First correction we always need to measure: 10% of what He allows you to have belongs to Him for you to give to Him. The 90% belongs to Him but He lets you keep it to cover your needs and to cover what He calls you to do. Wow! That was a mouthful. Second, money is not the root of evil. Greed for money is not good. Lust for money is sinful. There are other examples, however, money mismanagement is the worst of all evils available. Sometimes I wrestle with this concept. Money management is a Godly principle. Being a great steward of God's money is how He measures the reward process. Great stewardship is a testimony of your commitment to God. Your bank statements and checkbook are evidence of where your treasures are.

Lastly, teaching your children how to handle money is only our job description, not the school, not the church, and not their grandparents. It is about us – the parents. I have used this time to reflect on when I went wrong and I have used this time to "course correct" several issues I experienced.

We have found that having a plan for the money eliminates forgetfulness and whimsical spending. Seek sound, professional financial advice so that you can have a long-term plan you can be proud of and adhere.

I also want to share with you that you need to realize and be realistic about the budgetary changes you experience as a parent. As babies, they arrive with nothing. Through God, we provide their everything. For my husband, the daycare cost overwhelmed him the most. For me, it was the gadgets or accessories if you will.

Be mindful of these areas so that you can address them as they arise with as much grace as possible. This will enhance your attitude about money.

Week Fifteen — Monday
Your New Financial Plan

The family needs a family plan. This new plan will include additional life insurance, medical coverage and expenses (babies go to the doctor 10 times in the next 2 years) barring any illnesses in between regular checkups and immunizations, child care, medicines, formula, clothes and the list goes on and on.

Be realistic. Unrealistic expectations and budgets are the source of much controversy between couples.

Be honest. Not knowing what is really happening, or what to expect with the baby does not make it okay to disregard the need for honesty.

Be flexible. There will be some events which do not go as planned, including the budget.

Be specific. Be clear and concise about your desires for your family. You and your spouse need to openly discuss your desires.

Be swift. Do not procrastinate on your priorities of taking care of these changes.

Be resourceful. Investigate all options your company offers as sources for information and your benefits. You may find your solutions at your office. Investigate the options your friends use for similar issues they face as parents.

Be patient. While you will not be able to solve your situations overnight, you will reach a solution and solve the problem.

Be focused. Don't let non-issues take precedence over priority issues.

Be fair. Take advantage of this time to grow closer to your spouse because of the new information, new decisions and new life you will experience. Start planning early, like now, to achieve the best results. You should have as much as you can have done prior to the baby's arrival.

The family plan is critical for your peace of mind.

Week Fifteen — Tuesday
New Expenses to Expect

New expenses include diapers, wipes, baby wash, baby lotion, baby shampoo, baby oil, formula, cereal, juice, school tuition, clothes, school uniforms, jar baby food, crib, dresser, photos, photo albums, photo frames, doctor's visits, co-pays, medication, vitamins, bedding, room decorations, music DVD's, educational tools, etc. I could make the list longer.

I attempted to breast feed both my children. The breast feeding did work out so I chose the next best feeding method, formula by Similac with the special ingredients of breast milk. Similac Advance retails for $23 per can. My son consumed 32 ounces each day. The can of formula lasted 5 days. I spent $125 each month for 10 months on formula. I had to work that into the budget since I had only penciled it in the figures.

There are many expenses. Decide what is most important. Allocate for the most important items. Stand by your decision. Take action based on that decision.

This is one of the most sacrificial times of your life. When our daughter was born, a cousin stated to my husband that he would have to give up golf. He now has since realized why she said that and that she was right.

Most new parents don't have a complete view of what these new expenses will be. The most important thing is how you handle these expenses.

Listen to what others say. They are speaking with experience, honesty and zeal when they share their stories with the moral to the story. Further, listening now creates an ally for later. . . . balls, toys, rattles, shoes, socks, hair accessories. Oh, I could still go on about the increased expenses.

Week Fifteen — Wednesday
Can I Stay at Home? How Can We Afford for My Wife to Stay Home?

Do you desire to stay with your child(ren)? Do you desire for your wife to be able to stay home? If this is your desire, then you have some preparation to do.

1.   Eliminate debt. Double your payments. Use any bonuses or tax refunds to pay down the debt. Consolidate your bills.

2.   Eliminate the unnecessary. Practice living on one income. The other income is savings.

3.   Examine your lifestyle and spending habits. Determine if any of those aspects need to change. Agree on what will change. Start new so that you can take advantage of saving the money.

4.   Examine the tax issues you will encounter from this change. Examine the healthcare plan and benefit package for any new considerations.

5.   Solicit the support of family, friends or a service for occasional care when you need to run an errand or go to the doctor.

6.   Decide how long you will stay at home. You need a definitive timeframe so that there is no false expectations.

7.   Establish venues for activities. Research the library, zoo, children's museum and other such activities for the hours, cost and special events they have scheduled. Decide what you can afford and what you want to do with your time with the baby.

8.   Don't forget to establish some "you" time. Also establish a date night alone with your spouse.

9.   Keep in touch with the outside world. Human contact is important. Be honest about your needs and your personality.

10.   Keep the options open for change as necessary. If you change your mind about staying at home, go forward with confidence and do what it takes. It takes courage to spend that much time with a small human being. It takes more courage to decide it's not the best for you and your family.

Use these tools to determine what is right for you. I returned to work after staying home eight weeks with my first child. I stayed at home and worked from home for eighteen months with our second.

Week Fifteen — Thursday
The Debt-Free Plan
Lenders and Not Borrowers

I was not smart enough to complete this process prior to our first child. However, try to get this done as soon as possible.

The debt-free plan frees you up to work on the great aspects of marriage and parenting.

Some experts suggest paying off the debt from lowest to highest. Other experts suggest you pay off the highest interest rates first. Whichever method you choose, choose a method and stick to it. This will be extremely rewarding for you. Make a chart of which debt will be paid with how much and by when. Using a chart keeps you on track and committed for the debt-free plan to be a reality.

CUT UP THE CARDS! Keep one for emergency, shred the rest! Keep the one with the lowest interest rate.

David Beck suggests in <u>The Automatic Millionaire</u> that you have your payments made automatically, particularly the mortgage and car payments. These automatic payments will reduce your payment length.

Debt-free is important. It makes peace of mind possible. It keeps arguments to a minimum if not totally eliminated.

Practice paying cash. This was difficult for me initially. Sometimes it is still a work in progress.

Lastly if it looks like debt-free seems really far off, consider earning extra income through an extra job or a home-based business. The home-based business will generate the additional income you need and provide you with some tax benefits.

Can you count down to debt-free?

Week Fifteen — Friday
Maintain Your Lifestyle Perks

My mother advised me when we built our home to not overbuild so that we could still afford a hamburger. Her wisdom about the budget was timely and thoroughly applicable for the new budget.

You still want to be able to have date night. Your quality time with each other is of the utmost importance. Do <u>everything</u> you can to reduce your expenses so that you can still afford date night and the "special" gifts.

After our son was born, I noticed our date nights had become non-existent. I spoke to my husband about it and soon realized that we both had different expectations about date night. He was thinking expensive restaurant. I was thinking we could use one of the three picnic baskets which have never been used. I was hoping we would fill the basket with two salads, bottle waters, strawberries, and M&M's or pound cake. When we had this conversation, he was surprised at my response.

Before the child(ren) you had your pick of your spouse's time. With children, you have to be strategic in your planning of everything from daily dinners to date night to quiet quality time.

Keep in mind that you and your spouse still need each other's voice, touch, time and companionship. We are constantly working on our dialogue, our communication and the quality time we knew during our courtship and first year of marriage. Keep the favorite aspects of your marriage in front of you and your spouse.

Your spouse will appreciate your attention to detail.

Week Fifteen — Saturday
Your Insurance Plans

I spent several weeks analyzing my insurance plans after I had my son. Our auto insurance need to be increased so we increased the coverage, changed companies for a lower rate and found out about all possible discounts. Also at the end of each year between Christmas and New Years, we will take a defensive driving course for $40 each which will save me $200 per year and improve my driving rating for the lowest possible prices.

Next I looked at our life insurance policies. We wanted to have a specific cash value when the children turned 18 years old so we structured the coverage amounts to insure that we had that money available if we needed additional funds for college. We also increased my husband's coverage because we had a new baby. Take time to investigate your policies so that you can achieve maximum coverage and results at the lowest possible cost.

This is also a great time to evaluate your future needs. Decide what changes you'll be making in the next 5-10 years. This information serves useful for great rates now. If you can afford to make those changes now do so. Your savings will certainly be worth it.

You also need to check on you parents' plans. Often we are responsible for their care at some point. Plan with them for their future too.

With your benefit information from your job, make the applicable change as well to add the new baby to your insurance coverage. You might assume that the baby is automatically covered and she is not. You usually have 30 days to add her or the medical bills are redirected to you and are then your full responsibility. Double check with you benefits coordinator to insure the proper enrollment has taken place. Use that time also to cover your Dependent Care Flexible Spending Account options. Get the full benefit of your benefits.

Lastly, read all of your receipts for health care. It is critical you understand these documents and to get help when you don't understand.

Finally, adjust your beneficiaries accordingly to include your new baby.

Congratulations!!

WEEK SIXTEEN
LOVE
GOD'S DEFINITION

The definition of love is so clear that Paul delivers through God's instruction he left no room for dispute or discussion. The definition is absolute and finite and infinite and fluid all at the same time. God has a way with words, doesn't He? Paul shares so well what God gave him.

Our charge is that we do the same. Life just doesn't happen. Our steps are ordered. God has predetermined plans for us. God has the ultimate love. He loves us in so many ways – always better than we love ourselves.

Our challenge is living as these scriptures say. Go to 1 Corinthians 13 and replace "love" with your name. After you replace your name, read the verses slowly and aloud. Did they make you feel different? Did the sound of your voice convict you in your weak areas? When I did this the first time, I cried after the first few verses. I was so convicted by the Holy Spirit that I cried for ten minutes.

Our next step is to access the power of love. Love is powerful enough to change minds, hearts, souls and actions. How we access that power is also ordered by God. We are not strong enough to love correctly on our own. The Holy Spirit provides us the powerful access that we need for loving others as commanded. What does that power look like and feel like? Well, as a parent, it is important that we are in a comfortable love disposition. Your love tank levels will directly impact how you show and share love with your mate and children.

It is when your love tank is nearly empty, completely empty or past empty that your access to the Holy Spirit and His power to access love at its deepest and most meaningful level.

1 Corinthians 13 fully defines love. If we get 25% of the definition correct, then we have really accomplished something.

Sunday	Excellence Defined 1 Corinthians 12:31
Monday	What is Life Without Love 1 Corinthians 13:1-3
Tuesday	Love is a Noun 1 Corinthians 13:4-5
Wednesday	Love is a Verb 1 Corinthians 13:6-7
Thursday	Love Exceeds Our Abilities 1 Corinthians 13:8-10
Friday	Love Exceeds Our Expectations 1 Corinthians 13:11-12
Saturday	The Greatest Characteristic: Love Greater than all Others 1 Corinthians 13:13
Appendix:	When we are love – place your name in the blank

Week Sixteen — Sunday
Excellence Defined
1 Corinthians 12:31

[31]But eagerly desire the greater gifts. And now I will show you the most excellent way.

1 Corinthians 12:31

The "but" implies that we should change our course and we should. Instead of what we currently desire, we should "eagerly desire the greater gifts." Often we are seeking, pursuing and desiring other things other than the greater gifts.

Love is the subject. It is the greater gift. This scripture opens the entry way for an excellent love lesson. Only Paul can present a lesson of this magnitude. God uses the most unlikely candidate to prove and further illuminate who He is.

The deepest expression of life is love. Mastering love is a lifelong journey. In this instance mastering love is living love. Love is a noun, adjective, adverb and verb. Only a few words in the entire world can boast such grammatical designations. For this reason, we know we have to work to experience, achieve, understand and act love.

Love requires attention, planning, intensity, creativity, longevity, patience, knowledge, understanding and most of all prayer. Similar to wisdom, God can equip you to love if you ask. Just like wisdom, love finds only the prepared and mature persons. Love also finds shelter in the softest of hearts and requires strength. Only the strong people love passionately, obediently and completely without fear of judgement.

Excellent love is immeasurable and rewarding, only defined by God, communicated by Paul, lived by Jesus, and fulfilled by us through our obedience.

While we are discussing the excellent love God has for us, we will explore how we can share, receive and experience the excellent love Paul describes.

Week Sixteen — Monday
What is Life Without Love
1 Corinthians 13:1-3

[1]If I speak in the tongues of men and of angels, but have not love, I am only a resounding gong or a clanging cymbal. [2]If I have the gift of prophecy and can fathom all mysteries and all knowledge, and if I have a faith that can move mountains, but have not love, I am nothing. [3]If I give all I possess to the poor and surrender my body to the flames, but have not love, I gain nothing.

1 Corinthians 13:1-3

There are at least 10,000 songs with the word "love" in the lyrics or title. There are thousands of books about love. However the best definition is in the Word of God. So after we read the definition God has designed, we will investigate two questions: (1) how do we experience the love God describes?, and (2) how do we share and teach the love we learn and experience? Life without love as defined in the Bible is empty. First, to experience the truest love is based on our God relationship. God is the only being who is <u>required</u> to love us. That was a powerful mouthful. He designed us to love Him. God is the only being who can and will love us unconditionally and completely. The only way to experience the described love is to experience God.

Experiencing God requires prayer, supplication, obedience, and forgiveness. We've spent some time on several of these topics, however we will spend time on His pure love. All that God asks of us in order to show our love for Him is our obedience.

However, we have done nothing to earn His love. We have done little to keep His love. His love doesn't come with strings, attachments or conditions. His love is more powerful than we know.

When you know and regularly experience God's unconditional love, then you can then begin to share similar love. God's love empowers you to love yourself first which is key to loving others, especially strangers. Then you are able to teach that love to your children through your behavior. Finally, you are able to love God back without Him doing anything additionally. Further, you can then love others using that same model.

We all desire unconditional love with the natural persons we love. Let's model that love so we may experience that love in kind.

Week Sixteen — Tuesday
Love is a Noun
1 Corinthians 13:4-5

[4]Love is patient, love is kind. It does not envy, it does not boast, it is not proud. [5]It is not rude, it is not self-seeking, it is not easily angered, it keeps no record of wrongs.

1 Corinthians 13:4-5

Love is who God is. Love is why He made us. Love is what God made us.

So let's try this contemporary version of this scripture: The Message Bible reads:

> Love never gives up.
> Love cares more for others than for self.
> Love doesn't want what it doesn't have.
> Love doesn't strut,
> Doesn't have a swelled head,
> Doesn't force itself on others,
> Isn't always "me first,"
> Doesn't fly off the handle,
> Doesn't keep score of the sins of others.

Love is a noun. A noun is the subject of a sentence. The subject is what takes the action. There are actions that reflect love. These are actions which demonstrate love. How can we be that noun? We pray and we decide. We are empowered by God to love as He defined.

The Message explains how we are to behave, act and react so that we are love, the noun. Some of the descriptions may seem hard but He does intend for us to be all of those nouns and adjectives at the same time.

All of God's requirements require prayer to achieve and maintain. I pray daily to be the definition of love all at the same time.

The remarkable fact about love is that we are equipped to completely love everyone we know and everyone we will meet.

Love is who we are; why we were created.

Week Sixteen — Wednesday
Love is a Verb
1 Corinthians 13:6-7

⁶Love does not delight in evil, but rejoices with the truth. ⁷It always protects, always trusts, always hopes, always perseveres.

1 Corinthians 13:6-7

The Message continues with:

> Love doesn't revel when others grovel,
> Takes pleasure in the flowering of truth,
> Puts up with everything,
> Trusts God always
> Always looks for the best,
> Never looks back,
> But keeps going to the end.

When I discovered that love was a verb, I changed my attitude and actions. Love is who we are and what we do. Remember that God designed each of us with plans for us before He created us.

Love is not on the 50/50 plan – this is where most relationships go awry. The 50/50 plan is a plan based on each person's actions and whether it meets the other person's criteria. "I don't do _____ because he no longer does _____." Fair on neither account. Is that love? No, so that makes two wrongs.

Love really is doing what you want to or should for someone in spite of what they do, don't do or how they make you feel. Love acts because of rather than in spite of the other person or situation.

Love is the answer to what would Jesus do. Love is the answer to the question how do I know a Christian when I meet or see them?

Love moves mountains, makes miracles, offers compassion, provides comfort and shares with many.

Love heals, invokes peace, changes minds and tenderizes hearts.

Love requires action. A famous artist sang "Love is a Contact Sport." Love transforms who you are into what you do.

As spouses and parents, we love fully and when we do we show others how to love.

Week Sixteen — Thursday
Love Exceeds our Abilities
1 Corinthians 13:8-10

[8]Love never fails. But where there are prophecies, they will cease; where there are tongues, they will be stilled; where there is knowledge, it will pass away. [9]For we know in part and we prophesy in part, [10]but when perfection comes, the imperfect disappears.

1 Corinthians 13:8-10

When you are love and when you love, love never fails. You will not fail when you are love and when you love. Love is always appropriate. When in doubt, love.

Love's power overrides the regular and the mundane, even the factual. Love overcomes fears and stifles falsehoods. Love overwhelms your spirit, contradicts the logical and reunites the broken. Love moves us out of our own way. Love challenges who we want to be versus who we really are. Love challenges our abilities to do everything. Love empowers us to do all things.

Love relocates the boundaries you have established in your mind, soul and heart. These self-inflicted boundaries extend, or in some cases, are eliminated.

Love often is difficult to fully understand. God planned it that way. He is perfection. He is not completely revealed to us, however His love for us is complete and fully sacrificial.

Love forces us to examine our feelings, fears and focus. Love further suggests that we deepen our emotional investments in God, ourselves and others.

We don't love because of choice rather than supply. We have access to an unlimited love supply. We have to access that supply. The supply given by God of course.

When we are faced with love, we are often asked to express ourselves in a manner we are not always comfortable.

We are too weak to love by ourselves but with God we can love openly, comfortably and completely.

Week Sixteen — Friday
Love Exceeds Our Expectations
1 Corinthians 13:11-12

[11]When I was a child, I talked like a child, I thought like a child, I reasoned like a child. When I became a man, I put childish ways behind me. [12]Now we see but a poor reflection as in a mirror; then we shall see face to face. Now I know in part; then I shall know fully, even as I am fully known.

1 Corinthians 13:11-12

Complete love requires maturity, growth and wisdom. We learn how or how not to love from our parents and family. Likewise, we teach our children how to love based on our experiences. Rather we should focus heavily on the Bible's definition and description of love. Our personal definition of love is clouded with hurt, misconception, misperception and conditions. Some of it is good but it is not completely pure.

Love is an ongoing process and journey, rather than destination. Once you experience true and pure love, you will want to always experience that love. With God, you only have to be still to experience that love. With people, you have to do something or some things to experience their conditional love. And the reverse is also true. Ask yourself, what "strings" and "conditions" are attached to my love. We all do but our strings and conditions are not fair because we do not offer disclosure statements. Achieving God's definition of love requires long term commitment, wisdom and patience.

Have you experienced someone's unconditional love? It is overwhelming to see someone's emotional response to you when that love is not returned.

The experience of the love is far reaching and simply exceeds your wildest expectations.

Week Sixteen — Saturday
Greater than All Others
1 Corinthians 13:13

[13]And now these three remain: faith, hope and love. But the greatest of these is love.

1 Corinthians 13:13

We will be known for our love, then faith and lastly, hope. There are certain people you have known or know of that are well-known for how deeply they love. They are always remembered, well-liked, and they keep lots of company. Do you love deeply, freely? Are you loving and kind? Does love find you? Are you optimistic about people? Do you look for the good in people? Do you share love in your touch? Do you forgive first? And often?

Does your definition of love model God's?

Does your behavior model the definition or the world's?

Do young people love you? Do others find peace in your presence? Do you share your wisdom freely? These are some questions we need to examine so that we know how to course correct. Love is not easy. Sometimes it's quite difficult. According to His definition, love covers all offenses. What do you do to show others how to do that? God expects us to mentor others to the great relationship He desires with all of us. How do you do that? To everyone you encounter, even those who do not treat you favorably?

Do you find yourself seeking to love others? Do you love the relatively unloved? Are the unlovable drawn to you? Do people change their behavior to be loved by you? Do you share your love testimony with others? Do you feel that God blesses you based on how you love others?

So love as defined by God is a tall order. He equips us though to do what He asks and expects.

Love is the greatest attribute.

WEEK SEVENTEEN
LOVE: GOD EXHIBITS HIS LOVE

God shows repeatedly that He loves us. He created the world. He created us in His image. He saved us. He gives us gifts. He blesses us beyond belief. He plans for our future.

Daily. He loves us daily – all day long.

How do you know God loves you? How do you tell others that God loves you? Does God's love for you elevate your love for yourself?

Based on all that God does, how will you use His exhibition to develop your own love life which you share with your spouse, family, others, and most importantly, your child? How will you show them discipline? How will they know that you love them?

My daughter knows how I love her when I welcome her to sit in my lap, when I read to her, when she climbs in bed next to me and we watch "Blue's Clues," and when we laugh and smile together. She likes to touch my arm and twirl my hair. She likes to put her head on my shoulder just when I'm "busy."

We are God's children and all we want is His time and His attention. Our children want the same time and attention. I received an email once about a little boy who wanted to spend time with his dad but he was always working. One day after asking the same question and getting the same answer, he asked his dad how much he made an hour at work. His dad responded that he made $20 an hour.

The son went to his room and returned with a $20 bill and handed it to his father, saying now can you spend time with me. Whether this story was true or not I'll never know but the sentiment is happening daily all over the world. How will we allocate time for our gifts – our children – who crave our time and energy? How will they know through the time they spend with you, your views and ideas? How will they know what is right and wrong with your presence? Time with you is valuable and <u>required</u>.

How will you love your child?

How will your child know that you love them?

Sunday	His Love and Our Children John 14:15, 21, 23, 24a
Monday	The Ultimate Gift of Love John 3:16
Tuesday	The Refuge God Provides Psalm 46:1
Wednesday	Our Knowledge of God Psalm 46:10
Thursday	God Forgives Us Psalm 103:3
Friday	Could You Do It?

Psalm 103:10-12

Saturday

For Great is His Love
Psalm 117:2

Week Seventeen — Sunday
His Love and Our Obedience
John 14:15, 21, 23, 24a

[15]If you love me, you will obey what I command. [21]Whoever has my commands and obeys them, he is the one who loves me.
[23]Jesus replied, "If anyone loves me, he will obey my teaching. My father will love him, and we will come to him and make our home with him. [24]He who does not love me will not obey my teaching.

John 14:15, 21, 23, 24a

Obedience is often hard, especially for us as adults. I often pray that God doesn't think I don't love Him when I am disobedient. I think that He is referring to disobedience to His will rather than sin as result of disobedience. Of course, sin saddens God.

Generally speaking, we are obedient but we can be disobedient. Part of the disobedience is not listening, not obeying His will, and blatantly sinning. While He forgives us for all of those acts, we need to focus on obedience daily.

What kind of model of obedience are we as parents? I remind everyone I am in contact with that my daughter is a tape recorder and a mirror, which means she repeats what you say, if it sounds interesting, immediately and remembers it for a while. She is also able to remember where items are which interests her. She is able to repeat actions you take, such as dance moves, driving, the lawn mower and talking on the phone. She learned our phone numbers by listening to me talking on the phone.

Jesus is our example of Christian behavior. We are their example. I regularly check my mannerisms and tone and slang because my daughter models me and repeats what she hears at school, church and anywhere. If you don't want people to know certain things about you, don't show your children, either. Take it one step farther: eliminate that behavior altogether. If you can't show your children, then you shouldn't show anyone.

Jesus further reinforces that love is a verb.

149

Week Seventeen — Monday
The Ultimate Gift of Love
John 3:16

[16]For God so loved the world that He gave His one and only Son, that whoever believes in Him shall not perish but have eternal life.

John 3:16

What if God asked you for your child as a sacrifice to save yourself and the rest of us from death because of our sins even those who hate God and don't believe in Him? Well, that's what happened. In our situation, we would discuss the decision with our spouses, our friends, our family and strangers. God didn't ask anyone anything. God created the very beings that defied Him and disobeyed Him, and plotted and killed His only Son.

I have asked other women why did God choose Mary and not someone else. He could trust her. Based on the lineage and trust, she got picked! How exciting! He couldn't trust me and the rest of us. As a matter of fact, I'm glad He didn't pick me because He wouldn't have to experience my selfishness and doubt and lack of faith.

Mary matured spiritually a lot as Jesus became a man and took on God's assignment for Him. There were numerous events in the Bible which made me ask myself how Mary felt when it happened. As a parent, we experience many emotions when we relate to our children; at birth, birthdays, holidays, etc. Are these emotions similar to what God experiences?

We can't repay Him. We can't match Him. We can't top Him. What we can do is share that same sacrificial love that God has shared so far with us.

In addition, when we share God with our children and they accept Christ, then we are certainly pleasing God and showing Him our love.

He will never ask us to do exactly that but what He does ask of us, He expects us to comply.

He loves us that much. He asks us to love with that same sacrifice.

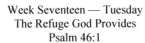

Week Seventeen — Tuesday
The Refuge God Provides
Psalm 46:1

[1]God is our refuge and strength, an ever-present help in trouble.

Psalm 46:1

Refuge is a safe place to cry, laugh, think, pray or whatever reason you would seek solitude. When we seek God for our refuge rather than outside influences, we can fully experience God's fullness and His peace. During this refuge, we can hear Him and spend quality time with Him.

Further God is our strength – who we will lean on in our weakness. When we are at our weak points, God is the strongest in our lives and situations. He offers us Himself to access all that He is. Let's be realistic – we don't trust God always or maybe we don't trust Him on time or soon enough. We often believe we can handle our "stuff," so we do. Then we make such tragic mistakes, so we promptly ask God to fix and intervene on our behalf. Then we want Him to hurry up. His timing never meets our standards. He did promise to be an ever-present help in trouble but that doesn't mean we can trust Him at the eleventh hour.

This scripture implies that we have a consistent and complete relationship with God so that we trust Him with everything. Everything means everything. All means all. So when do we seek His refuge? We should seek His refuge regularly rather than rarely because our circumstances have overcome us.

God's refuge alone is His love in action. His provision of strength is more than enough.

God continues to exhibit his complete and sacrificial love for us. What can we do to show Him that we love Him? What can we do to show Him we love Him?

Trusting Him is a start. Put all your stuff in His hands. Ask for wisdom to know how to hear His voice. Ask for wisdom to wait on His timing for the results He has planned specifically for you.

But if I do it all wrong, and even if I neglect to trust Him, I just take refuge in God, access His strength, and pray for help and forgiveness during my trouble times.

151

Week Seventeen — Wednesday
Our Knowledge of God
Psalm 46:10

[10]Be still and know that I am God.

Psalm 46:10

There are certain scriptures which bring me to tears. This is one such scripture. It really speaks to me and my spirit and describes well what I need because of who I am.

"Be still" is one command that I am having trouble with. I am disobedient and can't be still. Sometimes not only do I fail to wait on God, I sometimes forget to consult with God about my issues. A baby taught me the best learned lesson about being still. My niece had a premature baby boy. My mother, grandmother, sister and nephew left for Virginia the Monday before Thanksgiving. She and her husband were in Virginia alone; he was with the U.S. Navy.

The problem (only for me) was that I was pregnant and grounded. I had already had enough scares of my own so I couldn't fly. BE STILL and know THAT I AM GOD! That's what He said to me. I could only focus on what I wanted and what I thought. Then He showed me: BE STILL & KNOW THAT I AM GOD!!!

"I fulfill all my plans and do whatever I want," says God. I just wanted to see my great-nephew. I only got pictures. I sent blankets and a special musical plush toy. Then Kendall left us. They were on their way with the baby for the services. BE STILL & KNOW THAT I AM GOD!!

Nehemiah was born the morning of Kendall's services! I still never met Kendall. I never really figured out why God wouldn't let our eyes meet, but I learned some very valuable lessons from someone who lived 5 weeks and 4 days. Kelsi (my niece) didn't meet Nehemiah until December; he was born in January.

BE STILL & KNOW THAT I AM GOD!!!

We have to be still to experience His fullness. We have to be still enough for enough time so that we can hear Him. We have to hear Him so we can be obedient. We have to hear Him so we gain knowledge about Him. We are still so we can become more intimate with Him. Practice. You will need Him and you will need to be still to experience.

STOP MOVING and KNOW THAT HE IS IN control no matter what we do.

152

Week Seventeen — Thursday
God Forgives Us
Psalm 103:3

[3]who forgives all your sins and heals all your diseases.

Psalm 103:3

God's ability to freely forgive overwhelms me. He forgives <u>all</u> my sins. All my sins – the big ones and the little ones. <u>ALL</u>. He didn't just choose the sins that I mistakenly committed and forgave those. He also chose the sins I forgot. He chose the sins I ignore. He chose the sins that were terrible and gross and indescribable. He chose to forgive them <u>ALL</u>. He picked them <u>ALL</u>. He didn't pick through a few of my sins.

I don't deserve any of His forgiveness – not any. He exhibits His unconditional love through His forgiveness of each of us. He forgives us because He promised to forgive, and He gave us an intercessor.

He further exhibits His love because He heals all your diseases. Broaden your definition of diseases. In this reading, diabetes, insomnia and addictions are also diseases. He heals those diseases which are public or private, known and unknown. Sometimes He doesn't heal the disease, but He may take the person. Then He heals your broken heart. God is faithful and His faithfulness requires our trust and faith in Him.

For another few moments, let's revisit forgiveness. Is there anyone you need to forgive, including yourself? This is the critical path to forgiveness from God. We have to forgive others. God empowers with the strength to forgive those who have truly hurt us. The opportunity to grow through experiences which force us to forgive others is <u>our</u> opportunity rather than others! God uses these opportunities to insure that we grow in Him. As we grow, He exposes us to more opportunities to grow. He continues this process with us so that we can reach the fullest understanding we can about God.

His forgiveness is important for our soul. We cannot be healed if we harbor unforgiveness in our heart. Forgive. Be forgiven. You will be healed.

Week Seventeen — Friday
Could You Do It?
Psalm 103:10-12

[10]He does not treat us as our sins deserve or repay us according to our iniquities. [11]For as high as the heavens are above the earth, so great is His love for those who fear Him; [12]as far as the east is from the west, so far has He removed our transgressions from us.

Psalm 103:10-12

Powerful scriptures require powerful questions. Could you do it? Your humanness says no. Your Christian spirit says of course.

Could you do it? Forgiveness says that you have let go the hurt, bitterness, pain, hate, shame, loss, and grief and other emotions associated with an event. Forgiveness signifies maturity as a Christian and a oneness with God. Forgiveness is not easy but expected. It is not fair but it is equal. Forgiveness is not common but unique. Forgiveness is not fun but loving. Forgiveness is not about others, not even yourself but about God.

Could you do it? When you ponder your answer, think about your exception list. The exception list is the people who won't forgive because what they did was so hurtful or similar emotion. When you consider that list, who could move off the list right now?

Let's pray: God, please move on my heart and my mind so that I am free to forgive those who hurt me. Please give me the character traits which allow me to forgive others when I might not want to. Lord, thank you for forgiving me for not forgiving others. Amen.

God forgives us and is quite patient about our stubborn nature. God is sensitive to what our hearts have experienced. God molds our character over time to develop us into the Christians He called us to be. Forgiveness requires practice. Once you start to forgive, it gets easier. Once you have forgiven, you learn to release more, hold onto less and honor God at the highest possible point.

Ask God for the power to forgive. Forgiveness possesses power.

Week Seventeen — Saturday
For Great Is His Love
Psalm 117:2

[2]For great is his love towards us, and the faithfulness of the Lord endures forever.

Psalm 117:2

Lack of forgiveness interrupts our love with God. His love is great. Monumental. Awesome. Unparalleled. Exciting. Wonderful. Special. Creative. Patient. Kind. Intense. Mysterious. Mind-blowing. Pure. True. Productive. Planned.

I'm sure you have some adjectives you would use to describe God's love. These are just a few I chose for now. His love is great and indescribable. This is because He does the unthinkable, impossible, amazing and the wonderful for each of us daily. He is the definition of loving His creation in spite of what we do and don't do. He loves us because He knows we need His love. We need His love and there are many times we reject it. He still makes Himself available. He's there for us when we are at our complete worse. Further, He's there when we don't feel we deserve to access Him.

Because His love is so great, we have unlimited access to Him, His love, His forgiveness, His faith and His comfort.

He does His best to extend His love toward us. In our experience, we need to do the best we can to be lovable by being obedient, honest, forgiving, focused, and loving.

God loves us. He created us. He has plans for us. He can bring those plans to life.

What is the greatest thing God ever did for you? Whether it was getting married, becoming pregnant, finishing college, overcoming a serious illness or whatever blessing, God did something great for you. Have you ever told anyone? This is your testimony. Testimonies are to be shared.

After God did that memorable great thing, did you say thank you? Did you recognize the awesomeness of God?

WEEK EIGHTEEN
LOVING YOUR SPOUSE

Ephesians is one of the most awesome books of the Bible. Paul outlines life lessons we will need forever. He examines several topics but the one we will focus on is loving your spouse.

Loving your spouse may not be easy. There are many reasons why. On the other hand, your spouse is there for you to love. Paul outlines some critical aspects of that love. He clearly explains God's expectations of that relationship and your love. Loving your spouse makes it easier to love your child. God designed your spouse for you to love. Your spouse should know you love him or her. Your spouse should feel and see your love. Mostly, your spouse will experience your love. Loving your spouse is a full-time, vacation-free, selfless, timeless and eternal commitment.

Further, marriage is a no-assumption zone. Neither of you can afford to make any assumptions. In relation to your marriage, assumptions create havoc. In your relation to your children and your marriage, making assumptions create triple the havoc.

Your child will challenge you and press you at difficult moments but do not neglect the house rules. If we haven't covered house rules, there are some.

We moved off the subject somewhat but it is critical that we understand how to love our spouse.

The enemy attempts attacks on us through those we love the most. It is wise to understand that and prepare for that. Now the start of that love is described as openly, honestly, fully, completely, sacrificially and eternally.

Does your spouse experience your love? If you are not sure, then we need to make some adjustments. Don't worry, pilots make in-flight adjustments all the time and they arrive at their destination and most often on time.

Sunday	Who loves like that?
	Ephesians 5:25-26
Monday	How does this work exactly?
	Ephesians 5:27-28
Tuesday	Where are the scissors?
	Ephesians 5:31
Wednesday	The Misconception of the Dirty Word
	Ephesians 5:22
Thursday	God holds him responsible
	Ephesians 5:23
Friday	"In Everything"
	Ephesians 5:24b
Saturday	Till Death Do Us Part – Love

Week Eighteen — Sunday
Who Loves Like That?
Ephesians 5:25-26

[25]Husbands, love your wives, just as Christ loved the Church and gave himself up for her [26]to make her holy, cleansing her by the washing with water through the word.

Ephesians 5:25-26

Whoever your wife is perceived to be, however she is thought of and whatever she achieves or doesn't is a DIRECT result of your efforts and a reflection of you. How so, you may ask. Does she have your support, your full, complete, and honest support? Does she know it? What do you directly and indirectly contribute to her success? You are responsible.

Further, whatever concerns, irritates, bothers or angers you about your wife and her behavior, etc., you are <u>directed</u> to fast, pray, study, teach, and whatever else is required to enhance her to God's image. You have to lead by example in order for this to be received as God intended. Jesus loves like this. This is the love that He shows. This love requires work and never tiring in our efforts.

Sacrifice required!!! She was made for you as a gift and you were designed to sacrifice for her. All couples work on this. The definition of sacrifice changes during each season of your life and your marriage. Ultimately, though, if the sacrifice piece is out of balance, then resentment develops. Keep in mind, this is usually a one-way sacrifice, meaning that the woman almost always sacrifices more but will usually resent her husband if his sacrifice is not equal or greater. Ultimately, he should appreciate her sacrifices.

What does sacrifice mean? Each relationship will dictate the definition. I will provide you with some explanation. As a husband, you increase your income streams so that your wife can work from home or stop working completely to be available for the children. Another sacrifice is hiring a maid to help your wife with the housekeeping and cooking, particularly if she is working.

Sacrificial love requires time and attention to detail. It requires listening to the answers to well asked questions. Finally, it means observation of your wife, getting to know her preferences, desires, moods and needs.

157

Week Eighteen — Monday
How Does This Work Exactly?
Ephesians 6:27-28

[27]and to present her to himself as a radiant church, without stain or wrinkle or any other blemish, but holy and blameless. [28]In this same way, husbands ought to love their wives as their own bodies. He who loves his wife loves himself.

Ephesians 6:27-28

Rule #1:   Don't expose the shortcomings of your wife.
Rule #2:   Don't expose the shortcomings of your husband.
Rule #3:   Pray, study and work for the best spouse God has in mind.
Rule #4:   Love your spouse.
Rule #5:   Study God's word so that you are confident in what it is saying to you.
Rule #6:   You love your spouse in the proportion you love yourself.
Rule #7:   Defend your spouse with others. Work out the details later between yourself.
Rule #8:   Love without strings, "if . . . then" statements, or conditions.
Rule #9:   Keep your assignment in perspective. God has plans for you and your spouse and your family.
Rule #10:   Define "experience my love" for yourself so you can express it to your spouse.

When your spouse experiences your love, your marriage elevates to a whole new level. While it progresses to the next level, it also deepens and strengthens. This is what most couples only dream of seeing in their relationship.

When you reflect on why you ever wanted to be married, you may recall that a deep, emotional bond with another wonderful human being may have been one reason.

When you reflect on why you married your spouse, then you will reflect on what you liked most about your spouse. Keep those thoughts at the forefront of your heart and mind. You will need that information.

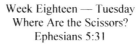

Week Eighteen — Tuesday
Where Are the Scissors?
Ephesians 5:31

[31]"For this reason a man will leave his father and mother and be united to his wife, and the two will become one flesh."

Ephesians 5:31

The old expression of "cut the apron strings" refers to breaking ties with your parents in particular areas of your life.

Frequent and unwelcomed in-law involvement inflicts stress on your marriage if handled improperly. This stress shows up in the form of disagreements, discontent, disconnect, and distrust. Each marriage is different so it is your responsibility to act accordingly starting with complete honesty. Tell him how you feel. Listen to her compassionately. I was dating someone once who shared a secret of mine with his mother. I found out about his breach because his sister asked me about the information which had previously been a secret. I told him that since he could not keep my secrets to himself then I could keep them to myself. And no, we did not marry; as a matter of fact, we didn't continue our engagement long after that.

Trust is huge here. This is often where the trust breaks down. You and your spouse have to trust each other.

Keep your business to yourselves. Sometimes you will need the wisdom of others. Sometimes that won't be your parents or even your relatives. Instead it may be a counselor, a pastor, a coach or a wise neighbor.

Your parents want the best for you – individually and as one: You will realize that throughout your marriage. They still are attached when something goes wrong even if it is your spouse.

Finally, your marriage deserves respect. Respect your vows and your mate enough to respect the boundaries of your marriage. Yes, your marriage has boundaries – its own personal space where no one – not even your mother – is allowed to occupy. This zone is a no-exception, relationship critical, low forgiveness space.

Just in case you are wondering, here's a list:

Women	Men
– Don't put him down or complain under any circumstances, if you are willing to forgive him (barring violence)	– Don't put her down.
	– Her spending habits
	– If she is making half or less than your income.
– Don't be out with your mother all the time.	

Cut the strings!

159

Week Eighteen — Wednesday
The Misconception of the Dirty Word
Ephesians 5:22

[22]Wives, submit to your husbands as to the Lord.

Ephesians 5:22

Men, husbands, in order for submission to go as directed, three elements have to be in place:

(1)   You have to submit completely to God. Lead by example. If you are not submitted and submitting to God, she won't properly submit to you;

(2)   She has to have something worthy to submit to. Your plans and ideas need to be well thought out, well designed, well prepared and well executed; and,

(3)   You still have to be the humble man called you to be. Don't be prideful about her submission to you. Don't take advantage of your role as head.

Housewives, regardless of what he does or does not do, be the wife you were called to be.

Tips for submission:

(1)   Obedience to God is key to showing Him your love.

(2)   Pray for a full submission attitude.

(3)   Respect yourself. Enhance your self-esteem.

(4)   Remember his image is reflective of you.

(5)   Seek the mentorship of a wise woman.

(6)   Adopt some rules for yourself about submission.

(7)   Pray for your husband's leadership and his submissiveness to God.

(8)   Pray for wisdom to be the wife God called you to be.

(9)   Once God grants you wisdom and experience, be a mentor to another wife.

(10) Let God provide for you in your marriage. God is responsible for the emotional gaps we sometimes experience in our marriage.

Submission to a liberal, independent, ninety's woman can sound like a revocation of our "rights." A God-centered marriage and the century's independent woman often attracts conflict. Even though God created us strong and capable of tremendous achievements, God designed marriage in a different structure. Successful marriages involve the success and communication of each spouse. A bit of advice: leave the power associated with each career in the car.

When we remember to whom we are submitting, then we are better equipped to submit correctly.

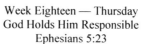

Week Eighteen — Thursday
God Holds Him Responsible
Ephesians 5:23

[23]For the husband is the head of the wife as Christ is the head of the church, his body, of which he is the Savior.

Ephesians 5:23

It is one thing to be held responsible for my own actions, but it is altogether different when you are held accountable for the well-being, Christian values and provision of the family God gifts you with.

God gave man the responsibility of what happens in our families. He knows what our needs are and He provides for those needs.

Husband, God directly addresses you about your duties and your role. You are responsible for her, her well-being, her spiritual health and her provision. And the same and more for your children. Big job. With God's guidance and leadership, maintainable, workable, doable. Now, how do I become the head of a woman who has done _____, _____, and _____ before we met? I am glad you asked. You are not alone. She was programmed to achieve all she could, not to ever depend on a man and keep a separate bank account. It may not have been those exact words but the independence was definitely primary. From birth to present, she has taken a survey of all the women in her life and from that complex collection, she determined what she would do, what she will tolerate, accept and reject. Because of what she saw, heard, experienced and read, you need God to help bring those walls down and get past her past. Whatever her stipulations are, trust me that God can move her beyond them in His time using you.

When I met my husband, I told him that he was not on my agenda for 2001. I wasn't ready to be married or focused on him. But most importantly, I didn't want to be hurt. My life had shown me divorce, death, infidelity and disappointment. I was in no hurry for any of that. I had measured my future on the evidence of my past. What if I had kept that mental stance versus trusting God? She's trusting God with His promises in your care.

God holds you responsible for upholding your role in your relationship with God and your wife. Yes, it is a heavy role but God also provides for you.

Week Eighteen — Friday
"In Everything"
Ephesians 5:24b

[24b]Now as the church submits to Christ, so also wives should submit to their husbands <u>in everything</u>.

Ephesians 5:24b

"In everything" extends some of us. The twenty-first century has provided excellent opportunities for women. There is still more work to do. There are still salary differences and benefit differences. We still have problems in certain industries. I worked for a financial services firm and was discriminated against as a mom. Tough pill to swallow.

What I want you to understand and consider are two points:

(1) Consider what your wife endures when her income is required for your family. She deserves the queen treatment. Just a note: she is not going to reveal everything she endures at the work place.

(2) "The Pursuit of Everything driven by the society in the 21st century" challenges her to be able to submit to you as her husband. In everything she will need some practice and some practical communication. She submits because God says so. And you need to provide a life where submission is honored, shared and appreciated.

Keep in mind, your marriage has to survive the culture, each of your idiosyncrasies, your pasts, and factors we don't think of as important. Marriage is work without rest and vacation. You have to work on it each day.

I was attending a women's conference workshop when I heard a woman say that she had asked her husband about buying a dress. I blurted out why was she asking him could she buy a dress. My thoughts were why does she and why should she have to ask him to buy a dress. She should have an allowance of money which allows her to buy a dress. How must she feel to have to ask but how must she feel if he says no?

These are the uncomfortable issues married couples face. How you handle these issues makes the difference in your relationship.

Wives, in everything means keeping him informed and involved. Husbands, in everything means be present when she shares and receptive when she speaks. You regulate the "in everything."

Week Eighteen — Saturday
Till Death Do Us Part – Love

Your spouse needs to experience your love. She needs to experience your love in her love language. He needs to feel your love.

If you have not mastered your spouse's love language, needs and "buttons," then it is wise to start your mastering process. This love language encompasses your personal investment in your spouse's life. You are your spouse's cheerleader and confidant, sounding board and shoulder, support and shield – all with God's leadership. Now, what does this experience look like? I'm glad you asked.

My husband's 35th birthday was special. I planned a week full of surprises and he enjoyed every minute. First, I planned a basketball tournament for him and his friends. Next, we had a family dinner after church. Lastly, his gift was some sports gear. This was a great birthday for him. He talks about this birthday like none other. Because I planned all of his favorite events, he experienced my love.

For my 30th birthday, he planned a surprise dinner of my family and friends at my favorite restaurant where we met in one of their private dining rooms. I experienced his love.

What does your spouse want to experience from you? Do you know their favorite places to eat, travel, shop, spend time, or do? If you don't know or you have checked in a while, ask and do a checkup. The real experience of your love starts with the interest, so asking the questions and starting the conversation will start that interest and the experience.

The full experience of your spouse's love is what makes your marriage strong and healthy and exciting. The experience of your spouse's love also keeps the communication open between you and your spouse. The experience keeps you wanting to be married. The love is for sharing with your spouse. This love insures that you are married until death.

Ask your spouse sincerely what they need and want. Listen actively to the responses. Invest time and resources to making it happen.

WEEK NINETEEN
LOVING YOUR SPOUSE

Experience requires time. Nothing is perfected overnight but over time. Set aside or schedule quality time with your spouse. You are not courting anymore so you no longer drop everything because she wants ice cream from the parlor across town. Or miss your favorite show because she wants to talk.

So how do you love your spouse with child(ren), or one(s) on the way, financial boundaries, family obligations, church, work, and on the list goes?

In the next several pages, we will address how to love your spouse, how to ask the tough questions, how to move from behind your pride to forgive so that you are equipped to love. We will give specifics along with an appendix of resources for more suggestions.

Keeping up with this fast, microwave lifestyle can be challenging. You need to remember we are here to please and glorify God. Everything we do should align itself with the word of God. Some of those "things" that stop us from spending time with our spouses should be completely eliminated from our lifestyles.

My husband's distraction is sports on television. After you ask your mate, then ask yourself what is distracting you from loving your spouse. Secondly, ask yourself what can you do to love your spouse more actively and effectively.

I mentioned overtime earlier in reference to a length of time but also overtime referencing more time than you may consider as enough to continue your relationship. Sometimes overtime is required.

My mother-in-law advised my husband to do all the things that he did to attract me in order to keep me. That advice would serve well to both spouses. Be honest and be prepared to make some changes. Wisdom dictates that you and your spouse reserve some renewal time for your relationship. Date nights need to be weekly, not longer than bi-weekly. Weekend travel needs to happen quarterly. Marriage retreats need to occur when they are offered, no fewer than semi-annually. These times will require your creativity. You will have children to find care for and you will need 3 plans for each occasion.

Make time to love your spouse.

Sunday	How to Love Your Spouse
Monday	How to Be Lovable for Your Spouse
Tuesday	Asking the Tough Questions Matthew 18:15-17; Luke 17:3-4
Wednesday	Forgiveness Equips Us to Love Ephesians 4:32; Matthew 6:14-15; 1 Corinthians 13:5
Thursday	Define Your Love
Friday	Define the Capacities You will Serve God
Saturday	Define Your Roles . . . Again

Week Nineteen — Sunday
How to Love Your Spouse

Loving your spouse can be difficult but doesn't have to be. I will make several points that may need to be tailored specifically to your spouse, but the main point is taking the time to do something positive to make positive results in your marriage.

1. Listen to your spouse.
2. Make an effort to understand your spouse.
3. Ask questions until you get all the details.
4. Remember. Remember the important details of his or her life.
5. Talk to your spouse.
6. Laugh. Laugh out loud. Laugh loudly. Laugh at the jokes he or she tells.
7. Have fun. Lots of fun.
8. Play.
9. Bathe together. Shower together. Swim together.
10. Work out together.
11. Exploit your commonalities. Create some common ground so that at several points in your lives you will be striving for the same thing at the same time in your life together.
12. Renew your investment in your relationship.
13. Surprise your spouse with balloons, flowers, lunch or whatever else will make him or her smile.
14. Be willing to accommodate your spouse. Do the "and then some."
15. Believe in your spouse.
16. Support your spouse.
17. Dream with your spouse.
18. Tell your spouse everything . . . FIRST!
19. Be a friend to your spouse.
20. Read enriching books and materials. Leave the garbage alone.
21. Look at enriching television. Don't take in the garbage.
22. Pray with your spouse.
23. Nurture your spouse.

Week Nineteen — Monday
How to Be Lovable to Your Spouse

We discussed how to love your spouse. Now how do you receive that love? How do you entice those actions? How do you welcome those actions? The following list will, in many ways, complement the previous one.

1. Maintain an open posture. Keeping your arms open, rather than crossed.
2. Keep an open mind. Don't linger on the past. Change can happen daily.
3. Respond with some zeal when your spouse greets you. A warm reception may be just the key to a better relationship. Your warmth invites your spouse to keep talking, sharing and trusting.
4. Listen completely to your spouse. Ask questions related to what your spouse says.
5. Be kind. Remember you are married. Your uniforms are the same colors. Treat your spouse better than you treat others. You don't work with this person, don't treat them like you do.
6. Talk to your spouse. He or she needs to hear your voice and know your feelings and know your desires. Be your spouse's best friend. Too idealistic? No, certainly not. I talk to my husband because I want him to know and I try to never let him hear me talking to someone else and hear something new about me or my life.
7. This is your spouse! God gave you to each other. If there are any issues, get them out on the table and resolve them quickly. Be committed to your marriage's health.
8. Forgive your spouse and forgive yourself freely. Your heart will be lighter and more open for your spouse.
9. Pray for your spouse. Pray for all the needs and wants and dreams and work and family and health and plans for your spouse. Prayer softens your heart toward your spouse. You cannot pray to God with a hardened heart.
10. Don't withhold your anger. Ephesians 4:26-27 reads: [26]"In your anger do not sin. Do not let the sun go down while you are still angry, [27]and do not give the devil a foothold." Share your anger and concerns with love and concern. Receive your spouse's anger and concerns the same way.

166

Week Nineteen — Tuesday
Asking the Tough Questions

Nothing feeds tension between a couple like not being able to ask a tough question. Tough questions need to be answered . . . immediately. Resolving these issues insures that you keep your communication lines open. The tough questions need to be solved before they become tough questions through communication.

Completely open and honest communication enhances your relationship, increases the bond of your relationship, and intensifies your love for one another. Getting to this step requires maturity and a deep desire to understand your spouse.

Asking the tough questions eliminates your comfort zone which should not exist with your spouse. What I mean is that you treat your spouse like a more intimate friend and you still tell your friends the critical information. Not a great idea. Your marriage needs your communication.

The devourer preys on couples who don't communicate. When you have children, your children absorb the discretionary time you once had. Every marriage experiences the "I don't have enough time to talk to my spouse" phase. How you overcome this phase is the difference between a healthy marriage and just existing in a marriage.

Address issues when they are small – not when they are extra large. Your courage and honesty earns your spouse's respect, rather than contempt or animosity.

Create space where and when you and your spouse can speak freely. This space and time needs to be protected and cherished.

Answer the tough questions.

Week Nineteen — Wednesday
Forgiveness Equips us to Love
Ephesians 4:32; Matthew 6:14-15

[32]Be kind and compassionate to one another, forgiving each other, just as Christ Gad forgave you. [14]For if you forgive men when they sin against you, your heavenly Father will also forgive you. [15]But if you do not forgive men their sins, your Father will not forgive your sins.

Ephesians 4:32; Matthew 6:14-15

Are you harboring resentment? Are you harboring guilt? Are you harboring anger? Are you keeping secrets? Are you keeping score of the times your spouse angers you? Or does something you don't like? If you have answered yes to any of these questions, you have become a prisoner in your own body.

Forgiveness equips us to love. You cannot love if you are not completely free or happy with yourself.

When you forgive yourself and your spouse, you are more free to love and to communicate with your spouse.

Lack of forgiveness results in the actions mentioned above and vice versa. It's a cycle – one that needs to stop. The cycle stops with you. You stop by forgiving the little things that interrupt you. Then you take the pegs out of the scoreboard and discard the scoreboard. The scoreboard wouldn't be a problem if only you cleared it daily. The scoreboard typically houses issues from ages, waiting to use that dated information when your spouse least expects it. Is this fair? NO! Is it the right thing to do? NO! Would you want to be the recipient of that? NO! Even if you experience that, you don't have to mirror that behavior. Be different. Do the right thing.

In our fourth year of marriage, my husband stopped talking to me. I asked why, and I continued asking until he addressed my needs. Why? I kept asking because it was important to me that he understand the impact of his lack of communication on our relationship. He didn't start talking the way I expected and still doesn't (we were married in 2001).

Now instead of asking him, I talk to God. In this context faith without works is dead means that I pray and ask God for help. While I wait on God to do His will, I still provide an audience for my husband to communicate.

Forgive and He will forgive you. Not before.

168

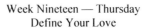

Week Nineteen — Thursday
Define Your Love

How long will your love last? How will you express love? How will you resolve conflict? What is your love based on? How do you define your love?

Do you have any house rules? For example, do you go to bed angry or not?

Your marriage and its health and success impacts more lives than you can currently count. Decisions you make today cause a ripple effect which outlasts your existence. Your children, their friends, and their families will be impacted by your marriage. It is your turn to start new traditions, new patterns, and to break any generational curses your family has experienced.

As you consider your past and family's history, this is your opportunity to do what God says to do. This is a huge undertaking but the opportunity of a lifetime. Take time to focus on what you experienced and do your best to be the agent of change.

In my life, my mother has had two husbands, one she divorced and one died. Of course I will fight against but first I will prepare myself and marriage to sustain through the tough times.

My relationship with my mother wasn't great and still leaves a lot of room for improvement. I work on my relationship with my children daily so I can be the agent of change for my life.

Defining your love is an ongoing project and will continuously evolve. It is the ultimate key to the strength of your marriage.

Most couples will never do this essential step. As a matter of fact, most couples don't know that it is a critical step, then still others don't know how to define, and lastly how to stay focused on the love you defined.

Defining your love is the changing element in your marriage. It's the extra bonus. Your marriage will be at the next level – the level most only experience after multiple decades of marriage.

Week Nineteen — Friday
Define the Capacities In Which You will Serve God

We discussed a family and couple's mission statement. If you still haven't done it, it's time.

MEN, you are the priest of the home. I repeat, <u>you</u> are the priest of your home. It is your job to pray for your wife, children, home and direction God wants you to proceed. Big job? Absolutely. But it's your job to make spiritual provisions for your family.

MEN, you are responsible for the spiritual nourishment of your family. This means you and your family attend regular worship and participate in ministry where you serve God by serving others.

So what shall it be? Where can you serve God that will meet the needs of your entire family? We have to worship and serve where there is a viable and active marriage and youth ministries. Without these two ministries, the needs of our families cannot possibly be met. When that happens then you add scheduling conflicts by trying to fulfill those needs elsewhere.

Lastly, MEN, it is your job to discuss with your wife what God says for you to do.

Now, WOMEN, you are still responsible for praying for your husband and what God tells him. You are to respect what he says provided what he says is biblical. You two are to be on one accord about your spiritual nourishment. We have an opinion but we have to follow what God says to him for us to do.

WOMEN, this is the hardest duty for him to do. Why? He is accountable to God for this area – completely and totally.

What if he doesn't do what God says? What if he doesn't feel adequate to be responsible for that area of your lives? Yes, you can help him but ultimately he has to hear from God about what to do.

Last word, WOMEN, in the meantime, no complaining, no nagging, no "I told you so," no undermining his role, no asking for something different when God has spoken, and no challenges.

Pray for his clarity of mind, spirit and heart when God speaks to him. Pray you keep your peace when you really want to challenge what you see without knowing what God has planned.

Week Nineteen — Saturday
Define Your Roles . . . Again

What do you want your marriage to look like?

What does it take to make that work?

Your ideal marriage and the reality will be different but by how much is the difference. The measure of this difference will be the measure of your success.

Start with the end in mind and build your marriage based on the picture you have in mind. I mentioned that we want to be focused on the ideal marriage without decades passing by without any progress. Great marriages require work daily.

Children change the dynamics of your marriage. When they go to college, your marriage changes again. How you start and develop will determine the legacy you live and leave for your children and grandchildren.

I always dreamed that my husband and I would be a power couple with stable financial backgrounds, successful careers and a fabulous lifestyle. Our marriage is not quite what I dreamed which is great. When I dreamed about being a power couple, I had no idea what other issues can arise from that dream. When you define your roles and likes in your marriage, you have to consider all the possible issues which arise between couples.

Questions/Topics you need to pray about when you define your roles and your marriage:

1. Who pays the bills? Separate accounting? How will daycare factor in to our budget?
2. Will a parent stay home? Will you start a home-business so that one of you has flexibility for the child and maybe even keep the baby at home for a certain time frame?
3. Are we hiring a housekeeper?
4. Who researches the best options for baby?
5. Who is in charge of date night? When is date night?
6. Who finds the sitters for special occasions?
7. Who plans the birthday parties?
8. How do we manage change in our life? Family? Relationship?

Define and redefine the roles until they work. Get past your pride and employ some help.

WEEK TWENTY
LOVE YOURSELF

Congratulations! You are about to be the proud parents of a wonderful baby. Hats off to you for accepting God's gift of parenting! He doesn't choose everyone to parent. By the way, your job description just changed . . . dramatically, to say the least.

First things first: take care of yourself. Renew, revive, and rejuvenate yourself as often as possible. Babies change your ability to care for yourself.

On the other side of that, babies require love! No, you won't run out but do you love yourself enough to unselfishly love this baby whose very existence depends on your love-ability.

FACT: babies grow faster and healthier when they are held. They thrive when they are hugged and held. Premature babies when held early and often gain their body weight, strength and health. Further, when twins are both struggling to hold on to life, in order to help their survival chances they put them in the incubator together.

LOVE is required! We are in week 20. You have 18 weeks to build your love tank, self-esteem and love-ability. Find out what makes your love ability grow. Find out what makes you thrive. Invest in yourself. Believe in yourself! Love yourself! You are designed to love! Your love list: God, your spouse, your children, your family, other Christians, other people who need Jesus and YOURSELF!!!

Start working on loving yourself more. Read, go to workshops, counseling and any other mechanisms. ASK God and read His word.

Similar to sharing your body with your child, you will need to share how to love with your child. I am not leaving love lessons for my child in the hands of the world. Loving yourself is not easy but can be attained and maintained with God's help. Loving yourself is quite rewarding beyond measure.

Sunday	Love Yourself Defined: What loving yourself means; What God says. Psalm 139:14; Genesis 1:27; Deuteronomy 6:5
Monday	Love Yourself Defined: What it does not mean 1 Corinthians 13:4-7
Tuesday	Why Loving Yourself is so important Ephesians 5:29
Wednesday	What Steps Can I take to Love Myself Galatians 5:22-23
Thursday	Love Yourself Unconditionally: Forgiveness Matthew 18:21-22; 6:12
Friday	Love Yourself Purposely: Mission/Vision Jeremiah 29:11
Saturday	Love Yourself Properly: Your Health at its Best 3 John 2

172

Week Twenty — Sunday
Love Yourself Defined: What God says about Loving Yourself
Psalm 139:14; Genesis 1:27; Deuteronomy 6:5

[14]"You are fearfully and wonderfully made."
[27]"So God created human beings in His own image. In the image of God He created them; male and female He created them."
[5]"And you must love the Lord your God with all your heart, all your soul and all your strength."

Psalm 139:14; Genesis 1:27; Deuteronomy 6:5

I love math, specifically geometry. The deductive reasoning and logic upon which geometry is based fascinates me. By deductive reasoning, we are supposed to love ourselves. This has previously been a mystery at various times of our lives because when we see it we stop loving ourselves. We treat ourselves worse than we treat others. We meet others' needs before we meet our own. We stop loving ourselves when we feel like stopping – any old reason will do.

Not vanity run amuck. Not pompous. Just pure love. Sensitive love. Forgiving love. A God kind of love. When you love God, you love yourself. When you love yourself, you love God. There are some times when you do not like your actions, attitudes or behavior. These are not the times when you stop loving yourself. God says He hates the sin, not the sinner. We must learn that philosophy.

When you love God and yourself, it is easy to love your spouse, children and others.

Love is contagious. Love draws others near you. Love is a command God gives us. Love translates into peace. Consider the wealth of this world if we loved ourselves as Christ prescribed and we all loved Him as He commands.

With all said, why don't you love yourself? Why did she stop loving herself.? Why don't you feel you deserve your own love?

These are critical questions you need to answer as we move forward.

You deserve to love. And you deserve yourself.

173

Week Twenty — Monday
Love Yourself Defined: What It Does Not Mean
1 Corinthians 13:4-7

[4]Love is patient, love is kind, and is not jealous; love does not brag and is not arrogant, [5]does not act unbecomingly; it does not seek its own, is not provoked, does not take into account a wrong suffered, [6]does not rejoice in unrighteousness, but rejoices with the truth; [7]bears all things, believes all things, hopes all things, endures all things.

1 Corinthians 13:4-7

This is a difficult set of scriptures. The word challenges our daily behavior. How do we harness this anti-love behavior? Who helps us to overcome these challenges? God and only God, of course.

Jealousy exists even in the most minute form. I was jealous that my husband was working and enjoyed adult conversation when I was home with the baby. Whatever your jealous "button," confess it. I shared with my husband how I felt. He tried to become very sensitive to my need for conversation.

Have you ever kept count of how often your wife didn't put the mail in your favorite place? This is not love. When we are not loving, we create divisiveness. This division leads to conflict and so on.

Paul speaks of wanting to do good but not being able to do the good. In some situations, I can be provoked. We all can. In love, we learn to exercise self-control and self-restraint. Simply stated, we need to arise above submitting to provocation. We are provoked only by our own consent.

We have to consent to being provoked. STOP consenting to provocation! Decide not to be provoked. Change your perspective on what you allow to upset you.

Now lastly, skip the "I told you so's" and the "na na na na na" kid-like responses when you are correct or when your spouse is wrong. I cannot love if I have these obstacles in my path. Lack of love burdens me. Often when we respond in this manner it is because of missing love.

Love can only exist when these other behaviors are in the person.

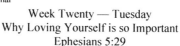

Week Twenty — Tuesday
Why Loving Yourself is so Important
Ephesians 5:29

[29]For no one ever hated his own flesh, but nourishes and cherishes it, just as Christ also does the church.

Ephesians 5:29

While Biblically speaking it seems impossible to hate your own flesh, many people despise their own flesh. Difficult times, unfulfilled dreams, broken promises and any other unfavorable circumstance offers the opportunity to hate your own flesh. Not to mention not having the perfect physical attributes also contribute to hating your own flesh.

Loving yourself is critical because we are fashioned in His image.

To hate yourself means to hate Christ. Extreme? No. Caring for yourself is caring for Christ. Realistically, you don't look into the mirror and say or think, "I hate myself." But address what you really do – you neglect yourself! Be honest! Be true! Stop putting you last all of the time!

When you neglect yourself, you are neglecting the temple in which Christ dwells.

Renewing your mind, body and soul is caring for yourself, thus loving yourself and providing a great dwelling for Christ. It is okay to love yourself. We are not defined by our material possessions, address, social status.

We are defined by Christ's death for our sins. We are defined by the Holy Spirit's dwelling within us. We are ultimately defined by God's creation of us in His image.

When you love yourself, you can freely serve God. Praising, serving and glorifying God is your reason for living.

My daughter asked about death. I responded that we die after we have done God's work.

Love yourself so that you can freely serve God. Loving yourself is a part of that work.

Will you serve Him without any of the "things" that you want? Will you serve Him without the "stuff" which causes you to lose focus of God? Will you serve Him through loving others, even those who don't love you at all?

Week Twenty — Wednesday
Love Yourself: The Essential Steps
Galatians 5:22-23

[22]But the fruit of the Spirit is love, joy, peace, patience, kindness, goodness, faithfulness, [23]gentleness, self-control; against such things there is no law.

Galatians 5:22-23

Memorize this verse. I took a class where this is a memory verse and I have known the content and concept of this scripture but didn't have it memorized.

Christians are expected to possess the 9 parts of the fruit. While some parts may be stronger than other parts, they all need to be developed in a fashion which pleases God.

It is easier to love a being which possesses the fruit, even yourself. Love, as defined by God in John 3:16 where He sacrifices for us, where we would sacrifice for someone else, is the love the fruit of the spirit demands. You will share with your spouse all the love types. With your child(ren) you will only experience two of the types. What you will find is that your sacrificial love for you child may be greater than for your spouse. Simply because you birthed the child. You have shared your body with this being in ways your spouse will never know.

As you consider the fruit, discover which element you possess. Rejoice. Stop. Consider the elements you lack, confess. Pray. Ask for filling with these. Don't be dismayed if you ask for more of all. Be encouraged.

The fruit of the Spirit evolves in one's life. Consider the glow you have because of your pregnancy. Now add the fruit, the internal glow which outlasts pregnancy. Double Good News!!

Just as fruit trees need fertilizer, your fruit needs the word of God and the Holy Spirit.

Pray in your daily quiet time for the fruit of the spirit to become evident in your life. Diligently work on the areas which cause you unrest.

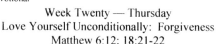

Week Twenty — Thursday
Love Yourself Unconditionally: Forgiveness
Matthew 6:12; 18:21-22

[12]And forgive us our debts, as we also have forgiven our debtors. [21]Then Peter came and said to Him, "Lord, how often shall my brother sin against me and I forgive him? Up to seven times?" [22]Jesus said to him, "I do not say to you, up to seven times, but up to seventy times seven."

Matthew 6:12; 18:21-22

Forgiveness is hard, especially when you come to a greater understanding of Christ. Why do I say that when it should be easier? First, you haven't forgiven yourself for anything – because you don't know to forgive you, then you must learn how to come out of your own judgment.

The first scripture is so powerful. Geometry was the first of my favorite math courses. In geometry, we learn that results hinge on a process: If . . . then. So in this scripture, Lord forgive me as I forgive others. If you don't forgive anyone, why would God forgive you? If you forgive, then God forgives you. I had known that scripture for years, but one day it slapped me in the face.

Coupled with the first verse, the second verse really explains God's view of forgiveness. He forgives me all day daily but I have a limit. One time today I will forgive one person. Who will it be? Isn't that how we act?

Math time again: $70 \times 7 = 490$ times per person! Is the scripture literal? No. Jesus is referring to a forgiveness where your forgiveness is infinite and limitless like His.

If He only forgave me 490 times a week I would've been cut off by Tuesday.

Start with yourself and then it will be easier to forgive others. Master the concept of getting out of the way of your own blessings by forgiving yourself as well as others.

Seek to forgive. Do it because your life depends on it. Do it because your life deepens on it.

177

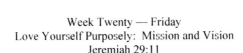

Week Twenty — Friday
Love Yourself Purposely: Mission and Vision
Jeremiah 29:11

[11]"For I know the plans that I have for you," declares the Lord, plans for welfare and not for calamity to give you a future and a hope.

Jeremiah 29:11

Love yourself with purpose – the same way God does. Franklin Covey publishes a guide for writing a mission and vision statement. Once you author those two documents personally and your family, then you can proceed to live by these two documents. Now these two documents do have to live up with God's will. However, it is not our job to know God's specific will for our lives until He reveals it to us. It is our job to live according to His word as He reveals His will for our lives.

Now the plans He has for us are better than the ones we have for ourselves. Yes, God's imagination is bigger than yours. He knows your thoughts, dreams, desires, fears and all our details. Isaiah 55:9 says that "As the heavens are higher than the earth, so are my ways higher than your ways and my thoughts than your thoughts."

God is a completer and finisher. You will see the plans God has for you. Despite yourself, you will accomplish the plans God has for you.

You have to live purposely so you are prepared for God's actions. He does not put us in positions or give us material possessions we cannot handle. Just as He doesn't give us more trouble than we can bear, we will not get more power, possessions or positions than we will handle with humility and meekness.

He wants to prosper us and He wants us to succeed. He has great plans for us. We are special to God.

When I first discovered this scripture and realized that I cannot stop the great things God plans for me, I learned to prepare to be blessed.

When you met and married your spouse, that meeting was God's plan, not yours.

When you conceived this baby, the conception is God's plan. With all of that, I couldn't help but love myself thus loving others.

178

Week Twenty — Saturday
Love Yourself Properly: Your Health at its Best
3 John 2

[2]Beloved, I pray that in all respects you may prosper and be in good health, just as your soul prospers.

3 John 2

In logic, this would be classified as an if . . . then statement. Your soul prospers in pace with your financial and health and relationships.

So what does this mean? Your soul needs to prosper. How do we accomplish that? Read your Bible. Fellowship with other believers. Pray. Meditate. Investing in your own soul and self.

What you consume is what you produce and output.

Your inner health is most important: your physical health and your emotional health.

Your diet is critical! WATER! 64 ounces per day! Half a gallon – no exception! VEGETABLES! Real ones: fresh, or frozen; canned as last resort! FISH! NO JUNK FOOD!!! Stop the sodas! DOCTOR once a year for a full checkup! And anytime you have a pain that doesn't subside with over-the-counter medication in 12-16 hours. Don't get this confused with medical advice. Use common sense and call the doctor's office.

Now, you are a parent. You are someone's livelihood. You are responsible for the shelter, food, clothing, education, health and well-being of these little people.

You have to be healthy enough to parent, both physically and emotionally. You have to be healthy long enough to be available for counsel, wise counsel, to your children. Keep your health a priority.

Stop the generational curses that exist in this area. Start a great health attitude in your children. Believe me you will learn how to go to the doctor once you take the baby for all of her check-ups.

This is your one body. You don't get another one. Medical interventions are not guaranteed.

Remember the Holy Spirit resides there, too. He deserves a healthy space to live.

WEEK TWENTY-ONE
LOVE YOURSELF

Love yourself with the fruit of the Spirit. If we haven't said so already, loving yourself is crucial to loving your child.

The fruit allows you to do the unimaginable, like love others, walk away from temptation and exercise good will with yourself and others. The nine characteristics of the fruit are treated separately but operate as a unit. They all need to work together within us to be the product of the Spirit. As we walk through each element of the fruit, we will examine life instances where this characteristic comes into practice.

Having spiritual fruit grants us access to the Father, Jesus and the Holy Spirit. With this access, we gain power of influence in our interactions and relationships. We are only granted this power because we will not misuse its value. As with any power, there is also accountability. We are now completely knowledgeable about our accountability to the Holy Spirit because we are equipped to handle the situations with which we are presented.

Now, the fruit is love, joy, peace, patience, kindness, goodness, faithfulness, gentleness and self-control. The elements are co-dependent and co-existent. We may not have them to the same degree but they are proportional. For example if we measured the amount with 10 being the max, I would not be a 10 in love and a 1 in gentleness. How will people view you as love or loving if you are harsh or rude? You will have them in proportion and in order. As one or several strengthen, they will all strengthen. If one area is weak, they are all considered weak.

Pick a starting point for your fruit work and move the fruit toward the spirit.

Now, each element of the fruit needs attention so we will discuss them individually. The fruit which you bear announces itself as it grows. Fruit also has a self-replenishment factor so that you will not run out. As a matter of fact, the more of the fruit you share, the more fruit you will be able to share.

Sunday	Love: Membership Leadership Has its Privileges Galatians 5:22; John 3:16
Monday	Joy: A Measure of Wealth Galatians 5:22; James 1:2
Tuesday	Peace: Not a Choice, a Provision Galatians 5:22; Philippians 4:7; 1 Corinthians 7:15; Colossians 3:15
Wednesday	Patience: Can you do the same Galatians 5:22; 1 Thessalonians 5:14
Thursday	Kindness Galatians 5:22; Ephesians 4:32
Friday	Goodness Galatians 5:22; Timothy 6:18
Saturday	Faithfulness Galatians 5:22; Hebrews 11:6

Week Twenty-One — Sunday
Love: From Privileged Beginnings
Galatians 5:22-23; John 3:16

²²But the fruit of the Spirit is love. ¹⁶For God so loved the world that He gave His one and only Son, that whoever believes in Him shall not perish but have eternal life.

Galatians 5:22; John 3:16

Love is mentioned in over 300 scriptures, sometimes more than once in the same scripture. Love is important to God and the Holy Spirit and especially Jesus. What concerns God needs to concern us. Love needs to be at the top of our priority list.

Privileged defines our position because He shows exactly how much He loves us by His actions. In His image, yet so unlike Him. He loves those who despise Him. I don't. Privileged to have His presence and not engaged enough in His presence. The most profound act of His love is when He loves me when I don't deserve it. He knows I don't deserve it and He still loves me. Although we have privilege, power and purpose, we do not follow His leadership. We offer our love selectively. We consider you to be privileged to receive our love. We have it wrong – it is our privilege and gift to love; not the recipient's to receive.

Not to mention God witnessed the birth, burial and resurrection of His son and never changed His course. He could've changed His mind, but He didn't. As a parent can you do it? Could you sacrifice your child for people who don't know him, don't love him and some really hate him? I couldn't which is why I'm not Mary.

Now the question is can we take Jesus' love, learn to love like He does, then teach by example your child, family, spouse the Jesus love we have experienced?

We are privileged to love. We are called to love. We are commanded to love. John 13:34-35 states that "A new command I give you: Love one another As I have loved you, so you must love one another. By this all men will know that you are my disciples, if you love one another."

Look and listen to the as . . . so statement. When you read that aloud, clearly Jesus states that your love should look like My love, feel like My love and your love should lead others to seek Me. I am overwhelmed by those words because I fall short daily of the love He expects me to share.

The first component of the fruit is love. Interestingly enough they all work together and shape each other. Love is the thermometer of the group. Without love, none of the other elements exist, and likewise the other elements can grow where love lives.

181

Week Twenty-One — Monday
Joy: A Measure of Wealth
Galatians 5:22; James 1:2

[22]But the fruit of the Spirit is love, joy, [2]Consider it pure joy, my brothers, whenever you face trials of many kinds.

Galatians 5:22; James 1:2

Joy is defined by Webster as a very glad feeling, happiness, great pleasure, and delight.

Gage's definition of joy is great, insurmountable, awesome and sometimes indescribable state of mind expressing contentment and excitement that is shown outwardly in expression and deed.

Using these definitions, joy is a measure of spiritual wealth. Joy speaks volumes about your relationship with Christ. Also speaks to your spirit and your relations with others.

Joy is not easily accessible, yet a wonderful experience. Joy is the completer to the fruit.

James tells us we should seek the joy in all situations no matter the circumstance, especially when trials arise. Why would there be joy in our trials? Does finding joy in your trials require wisdom? Absolutely.

Wisdom to understand that trouble will not last always. That revelation should spark joy. Joy develops when you become excited about the result of the trial.

Jesus expects you to be joyful. However most of us have never acknowledged the concept of joy; we reflect a down-trodden spirit when we face any adverse circumstances.

Joy, as a measure of wealth, should be passed on to your spouse, children and others.

God's blessings flow more easily when you are joyous. When you are joyous, you are focused on God. When we give our full attention to Christ, we are able to hear from God, wait patiently for Him to complete His plans and have joy in the process. Having joy enables you to fully experience the fruit of the Spirit. With joy, you are poised for blessings as well as warfare. A wealthy spirit and life requires joy.

Week Twenty-One — Tuesday
Peace: A Provision, Not a Choice
Galatians 5:22; Philippians 4:7; 1 Corinthians 7:15b; Colossians 3:15

[22]But the fruit of the Spirit is love, joy, peace.

[15b]God has called us to live in peace.

[7]And the peace of God, which transcends all understanding, will guard your hearts and your minds in Christ Jesus.

[15]Let the peace of Christ rule in your hearts, since as members of one body you were called to peace. And be thankful.

Galatians 5:22; Philippians 4:7; 1 Corinthians 7:15b; Colossians 3:15

God provides peace. God calls us to be peaceful, to live in peace and let your hearts be ruled by peace.

Peace provides power and protection. Peace provides.

Peace is a provision. Peace is not a choice. Peace should be sought. Our testimony should be leading up to a point of peace. The high point of our lives happen when we begin to experience His peace. Not only experience His peace, but anticipate the experience of His peace, then learned to recognize His peace – that's our goal.

Can you share your life where you've experienced His peace?

Can you decide to be peaceful? Will you decide to be peaceful? DECIDE.

Peace will guard heart and minds. Anxious, worry and peace will not co-exist in the same space. Prayer and decisiveness is required to extinguish anxiousness and worry so that peace can rule your heart and mind.

Stop being quarrelsome. Stop picking fights. Stop gossiping. Stop worrying. Stop arguing. Stop being the source of disruption. Start seeking His peace. Start being kind. Start with some actions and attitudes about your behavior.

Peace is so important for at least 2 reasons, which we will discuss. I am a debater and am typically correct. I do my homework on the subjects' facts. I read the fine print. When I present the argument, I can stand on my information. Because I was correct, I felt justified in my argument. Now that would be okay except my presentation was boisterous, demanding and degrading of the person whom I was addressing. Since that time I have become respectful of the person to whom I am speaking, slow to anger, lower my voice and carefully explain my point in a slow and deliberate manner. I am still correct but I represent Christ better while leaving the associate with her dignity.

When I do need to debate my point or stand my ground, I am mindful that my children are watching my behavior. They act like I act. They say what I say. My job as parent is trainer. So when I "train up a child in the way they should go," I eliminate loud, boisterous, disrespectful and ungodly behavior. As my children started speaking and repeating conversations, I warned strongly those around me to be careful of their word choices. As soon as her aunt said some words that were on the "don't say" list, my daughter told her not to say that. My daughter then went on to tell my mother that her aunt said a word on the "don't say" list. So we let that pass. The next event occurred at school when she repeated a statement an adult made. This statement was disrespectful and I was quite concerned that a school employee would say that statement in earshot of children at a Christian school. Being peaceful is a life lesson for all of you. Just as a reminder, your peace guides your child(ren) to peace.

183

Try to live peacefully. Try to be the peacemaker. Be ready for questions about your peace. Be ready for new levels in your life because of the peace. Be sure to give God the glory for his provision of peace. Be sure to thank Him for His thoughtfulness.

Week Twenty-One — Wednesday
Patience: Can I expect the same from you?
Galatians 5:22-23; 1 Thessalonians 5:14

²²But the fruit of the Spirit is love, joy, peace, patience
¹⁴And we urge you, brothers, warn those who are idle, encourage the timid, help the weak, be patient with everyone.

Galatians 5:22; 1 Thessalonians 5:14

Job was rich and wealthy one day. Then one day it was gone. During this period, Job remained faithful to God. Job was encouraged to curse God. Job was challenged about his belief in God. Job remained faithful to God. God kept His word to Job that He would never leave or forsake Job. Further He restored Job's family and doubled Job's wealth. Job was patient and faithful to God. Can He expect the same from you? I ask myself that question: What would I do if that had been me? What would I do now?

God wants us to be patient with others, as well as ourselves. Many times, we get upset because we didn't achieve what we had in mind or we didn't get that promotion when we thought. Be patient with yourself. Finally we need to be patient with God about what we want Him to do. Patience is a virtue. I know that love and patience are a couple. One will not exist without the other. God is patient with us so we need to be patient with others. When I am patient, I ask myself if my patience saved her life? Our days don't always go as planned and sometimes we have had all that we can handle. We are sometimes at the brink of breakdown. Then there is someone who shows up and who is patient with us and helps us. Then we feel like we can move forward then.

Be patient with yourself. God's will for your life will happen. Not even you can stop that from happening. Stop putting yourself down. Stop berating yourself. Sometimes when things don't happen as you planned may be God's way of insuring that no harm comes your way or that you don't miss what God really has for you.

Be patient with God. His timing is impeccable. He always does His work on time. We receive His blessings when we are ready with the desired maturity and attitude. Not before. I often have to remind myself of that because He said that He would give me the desires of my heart. He didn't say by age 25 nor did He say that it would happen all at the same time.

Patience instills appreciation for all events and blessings in life.

Week Twenty-One — Thursday
Kindness: The Golden Rule Updated
Galatians 5:22-23; Ephesians 4:32

[22]But the fruit of the Spirit is love, joy, peace, patience, kindness
[32]Be kind and compassionate to one another, forgiving each other, just as in Christ God forgave you.

Galatians 5:22; Ephesians 4:32

The old Golden Rule is do unto others as you would have them do unto you. The Golden Rule has been revised: Do unto others better than you would have them do unto you. In other words, treat others better than you are treated and better than they expect to be treated.

Wise persons share with you that when you are having trouble with someone, you should "Kill them with Kindness." This statement suggests that you respond in a kind manner no matter what they do to you.

Overwhelm other people with your kindness. Genuine kindness that overwhelms their spirit and countenance. Several years ago, Oprah promoted "Random Acts of Kindness." This new neighborly attitude sparked people to change their thinking and encourage others to do the same.

Paul teaches us to be kind and compassionate to one another. But we are not. We suffer from road rage, cut-throat behavior at work and at church and socially, lack of trust, and poor relationships. How can we each govern ourselves, then we show our children, then our families, then strangers?

Reality is that we find it hard to be kind because people are not kind to us but Jesus wants to change our behavior and that choice may spark a change in others. Besides, when I consider why I should be kind at all times, I cringe.

God is kind to me daily and I don't say thank you for each occurrence. God is kind to me when I don't deserve His kindness. Who am I to offer selective Kindness to others when He is bountifully Kind to me – always.

Kindness to others is a thank you to God for His kindness to us.

Lastly, when we are not kind, we decide that the opportunity God presented for us to represent Him was not important.

Show your children how to be Kind by being Kind.

186

Week Twenty-One — Friday
Goodness
Galatians 5:22-23; Timothy 6:18

[22]But the fruit of the Spirit is love, joy, peace, patience, kindness, goodness
[18]Command them to do good, to be rich in good deeds, and to be generous and willing to share.

Galatians 5:22; Timothy 6:18

Goodness is hard to come by. I want to be good and I want to share goodness but will it be received well and with pure motive?

Let's define goodness. First of all, goodness is an attitude. Goodness requires a decision. The decision to be good is mostly learned rather than natural because of our sinful nature. Most people will do good as long as the good doesn't inconvenience them or cost anything. But the real challenge is will you do good when it costs, inconvenient, trouble or it's a sacrifice. That's the measure of Christianity.

Because of today's climate, it is hard to decide to do good. Will you stop on the freeway to help someone? I call help for them. Others want to stop to help. In 2006, a man was killed after he stopped to help someone. After that will people stop to help others? Very difficult to do.

Let's move closer to your daily life. Do you help your co-workers, family or friends? Do you do good to others on the road, in the grocery store? Do you offer good deeds to elderly people you see or disabled people you pass? Do you share your possessions? Why or why not? Goodness is who God is and what God does. God expects us to do what He would do. God expects us to be good to those He sends in our paths. Offering goodness is our reasonable service.

God sends people to us to see if we will do His will by being good to others. We often fail.

Goodness means helping the homeless, less fortunate, people who seem in need, those who are seeking help and children. Will we do it? List of possible "goodness" deeds:

(1) Clean your closets out and donate them to a shelter
(2) Clean out your kitchen cabinets and donate them
(3) Volunteer to feed the homeless
(4) Volunteer to teach classes at a shelter
(5) Give money when you are asked and/or to a shelter or other worthy organization
(6) Be sensitive to the needs of others
(7) Be compassionate to others
(8) Love others unconditionally
(9) Treat others better than you are treated.
(10) Considering the heart of Christ.

Goodness is crucial for the love of Christ to continue to be shared.

Week Twenty-One — Saturday
Faithfulness
Galatians 5:22-23; Hebrews 11:6

[22]But the fruit of the Spirit is love, joy, peace, patience, kindness, goodness, faithfulness
And [6]Without faith it is impossible to please God because anyone who comes to him must believe that he exists and that rewards those who earnestly seek him.

Galatians 5:22; Hebrews 11:6

I would rather have a few people in my corner with a great attitude than a bunch with lukewarm enthusiasm. I know that God feels the same way. [15]"I know your deeds, that you are neither cold nor hot. I wish you were either one or the other!" "So, because you are lukewarm – neither hot nor cold – I am about to spit you out of my mouth." Revelations 3:15-16.

God measures faithfulness by your perseverance to seek Him at all times, through the good and the bad. Likewise, He focuses on your consistency in prayer, study and Christian fellowship. Be reminded that in your time of need is not only time you seek Him but in your great times even more.

When you look back over your life, when have you been the most faithful? During what circumstances are you least faithful? Why are there differences?

As we consider faith, Gage's definition is believe in Him – not what He blesses us with nor what He does in our lives – just Him, not even His promises; just what He has already done. The Bible says that "now faith is being sure of what we hope for and certain of what we do not see." Hebrews 11:1.

How did my faith grow? How do I live a life of faith that my children understand how to live by faith? How can I share my faith?

The greatest exercise of my faith has been being married and having children. God intimately intertwined my life with three other preselected people whose lives I impact and guide and influence daily. My question is why did God choose to trust me with His gifts? To carry out His will and commands is faith in action. All of my dreams haven't come true but things I never dreamed of have happened in spectacular proportion. An exhibit of His plan and my faith.

Children exercise in faith daily until we show them how not to be faithful.

WEEK TWENTY-TWO
LOVE YOURSELF: THE FRUIT CONTINUED

We spent last week on the fruit of the Spirit and how they relate. We will continue our study on the last two elements, then we will move on to the Fruit Lifestyle.

These last two elements are by far a challenge for me. They call me to a life of excellence. I have to master them so that I can be an example for my children and their children. Also as I grow closer to Christ, He helps the fruits better active in me. The Spirit desires for the fruits to be active in each of us. In order for that to happen we are required to focus on the Lord daily. Luke 9:23 says that "If any man would come after me, he must take up his cross daily and follow me."

Daily time with God is required. Growing closer to God assures that you grow closer to your loved ones. Daily time is hard to come by sometimes but prioritize His time. His time develops the fruit. These last two fruit elements are gentleness and self-control. Certainly, they are not the most difficult yet they are critical to our whole package.

Keep a growth journal for notes on how you've grown as you study.

As a leader of my children and as an example for other children, gentleness extends to each life and strengthens relationships. Gentleness builds the self-esteem of others and any exhibit of gentleness is the epitome of what Jesus would do. Also your gentleness encourages others' gentleness. Gentleness is necessary for the growth of the Christian world. Self-control cannot be more important now than ever before. With road rage, crime, and threats of national security, self-control is a commodity and crucial to raising responsible children as citizens. Self-control includes language, overall behavior, how you handle the sales associates to how to handle disagreements with your spouse.

Self-control and discipline are synonymous. Self-control includes eating, driving, education and maintenance and spending.

The fruit of gentleness and self-control truly minister through the whole person to the whole community, which starts at your address.

Sunday	Gentleness Evidence Galatians 5:22-23; Philippians 4:5
Monday	Self-Control Galatians 5:22-23; Titus 1:8
Tuesday	His Provision and Power/The Power of His Provision 2 Peter 1:3-4
Wednesday	My Homework, Part 1 2 Peter 1:5-6
Thursday	My Homework, Part 2 2 Peter 1:7
Friday	Promises Fulfilled 2 Peter 1:8-9
Saturday	Promises Fulfilled and Complete 2 Peter 1:10-11

Week Twenty-Two — Sunday
Gentleness
Galatians 5:22-23; Philippians 4:5

[22]But the fruit of the Spirit is love, you, peace, patience, kindness, goodness, faithfulness, [23]gentleness
[5]Let your gentleness be evident to all. The Lord is near.

Galatians 5:22-23; Philippians 4:5

By gentle, I do not mean pushover. Jesus' example of gentleness is our model. Your ability to be gentle becomes tested when you must discipline. This applies to your children and others who cross your path.

If people fall when your mouth opens and your tongue starts to move, then we have a trouble with gentleness. I pray over my gentleness with others. My compassion in general is overwhelming but my gentleness requires prayer. I have the ability to hold others to my standards and level of accountability without mercy. God, Jesus, the Holy Spirit and the Bible expect us to act in excellence. They do not excuse simply because of our economic status or health conditions. Their expectations of us are the same. However, Jesus forgives us without debate when we are wrong. That is where our paths diverge. I demand excellent service. I remember the sequence of your words, tone and body language. I enforce your own rules on you. Sound harsh? Sometimes it is but what makes it hard is that I can be unrelenting. I have started being gentle but maintaining the same standards. Different results: no, I usually get what I seek, however the sales associate or manager leave with dignity yet learned about the situation.

Why is this significant? I debate. I am armed with facts and figures and other valuable instruments which prove my point or case or gives me privilege.

I have to be mindful that in my delivery I may not always be gentle, neither do I want my daughter to adopt my stern ways.

I practice being gentle when I shop by smiling, speaking slowly and listening to the other person when I am dealing with people. Also, I have learned that when I do those things, the other person is compelled to respond the same way and I achieve the desired results.

A much better Christian behavior.

Week Twenty-Two — Monday
Self-Control
Galatians 5:22-23; Titus 1:8

[22]But the fruit of the Spirit is love, joy, peace, patience, kindness, goodness, faithfulness, [23]gentleness, and self-control. Against such things there is no law.
[8]Rather he must be hospitable, one who loves what is good, who is self-controlled, upright, holy and disciplined.

Galatians 5:22-23; Titus 1:8

Self-control challenges most of us. Consider the fact when you cannot control yourself then you've submitted to that as master. If you cannot control yourself then you have given control to someone or something else.

What is our challenge? Is it shopping, drinking, television, eating, or/and sex? Some may be past challenges or they may be current challenges.

Whatever your challenge, prayer reinforces self-control. Prayer produces self-control.

When I face my issues where my self-control is challenged, I talk to God – I am specific with my request and ask for an escape. I also ask that the thought and desire be removed immediately.

When we exercise self-control, we honor Christ, we are able to witness, we strengthen our testimony and we make Christ proud.

Self-control allows God to work in your life.

I remember when I was single and would be tempted. That period of time was the first time I addressed self-control in a direct approach. I recall the conversations I would have with God. I would literally yell help so that I could overcome the temptation and establish an escape.

Several scriptures address self-control. The one that I use the most is 1 Corinthians 10:13 which reads "No temptation has seized you except what is common to man. And God is faithful; He will not let you be tempted beyond what you can bear. But when you are tempted, He will also provide a way out so that you can stand up under it."

God trusts those of us who exhibit self-control. Although 1 Corinthians 10:13 doesn't address self-control, the scripture offers us direction when tempted. When we choose to take the way out He provides, that choice is a choice of self-control. Self-control is honorable and Christ-like, not worldly and not sinful.

Week Twenty-Two — Tuesday
The Power of His Provision
2 Peter 1:3-4

[3]His divine power has given us everything we need for life and godliness through our knowledge of Him who called us by His own glory and goodness. [4]Through these He has given us His very great and precious promises, so that through them you may participate in the divine nature and escape the corruption in the world caused by evil desires.

2 Peter 1:3-4

Awesome! I cannot remember completely consistently what I need when I leave home daily, so how can I know what I need before I really need it? I don't. That knowledge is God's job.

There is power in His provision, His thoroughness of thought and His complete view of my well-being. These scriptures overwhelm me. In other words, we have everything we need for a godly life because of our knowledge of Him. Further, He called us to provide us with our needs for life and godliness because of his own glory and goodness. Just based on His desires and plans, He provides for me. He does all of this in spite of myself, my deeds, my failures and my misunderstandings and my mistakes. He is forever providing for me and planning for me. He did all of this "so that through them you may participate in the divine nature." He planned us for His glory. He says so in several scriptures but none has ever touched me in this manner.

My job now is to avoid embarrassing God through my sins. Further, as a parent, I shall teach my children the power of His provision.

After nine days of discussion of the Fruit of the Spirit, these two scriptures elegantly summarize why we should strive to get closer to Him and stretch to gain the fruit of the Spirit. I work diligently daily to not disappoint Him but I do anyway. I eagerly seek His face and still have trouble with sin.

He has promised me an escape from the corruption of this world and if that is all He ever does, that escape is a great provision.

I look forward to what else He will do for our lives.

Week Twenty-Two — Wednesday
My Homework, Part 1
The Prescription for Righteousness Living
2 Peter 1:5-6

[5]For this very reason, make every effort to add to your faith goodness; and to goodness, knowledge; [6]and to knowledge, self-control; and to self-control, perseverance; and to perseverance, godliness;

2 Peter 1:5-6

Similar to the fruit of the Spirit, these two scriptures and the verse 7 gives us homework.

Peter shares the assumption that we already have faith. Not always a great assumption. Nonetheless, trying to be good and extend goodness, requires work and diligence. And a decision. Then add knowledge. Read. Study. Pray. Use the wisdom you have as you request more. Use godly sense, rather than common sense. Sometimes common sense encourages you to act in a common manner rather than in the excellence of God.

Self-control requires knowledge and love of God. Exercising self-control is a testimony of God's presence in your life. Just a note, exhibiting self-control now stops future embarrassments. Your children's behavior is molded by your life on display before them. Self-control communicates your love and concern for God's opinion of you, your actions, attitude and behavior. Perseverance is the fulfillment of the promise – one where God says He will be with us always. Perseverance teaches us pure joy. James says consider it pure joy my brothers when you encounter trials of any kind. Perseverance builds character. Perseverance cultivates the wisdom and provides the area where drive is produced. Lastly, perseverance yields appreciation. You appreciate that for which you earn.

Lastly, godliness defines your attitude, your attire, behavior, gestures, consumption and language. Examine your life for areas where you need godliness. Consider one area at a time for methods to self-correct for godliness. I have considered that my body is a temple and the temple needs maintenance: more exercise, more water, more fruits and vegetables, fewer breads and sweets.

Let's start doing our homework.

193

Week Twenty-Two — Thursday
My Homework, Part 2
2 Peter 1:7

[7]and to godliness, brotherly kindness; and to brotherly kindness, love.

2 Peter 1:7

For the last several weeks, there have been many events in my life that have caused me to question my faith. I have been thinking that no one cares for me. That I am always the server and not the served. I have accounted for times in my life when I have had my biggest challenges and no one seemed to be there.

I am always the one to love and help and aid and serve. I am always the one who is kind and wonderful and thoughtful and innovative and loving. I give myself away all the time.

I had to stop expecting any measure of those qualities and traits back. I was wrong to expect anything in return from them. God enables us to give to others when they are in need. Can you imagine someone more in need emotionally than you? There is someone who needs you; someone who needs you more than you need another person.

One day I even threatened to stop. Yes, I did. I threatened to stop offering to help, hug, love, support, go above and beyond, go out of my way, go beyond my comfort zone, be kind when others are awful, to be wonderful when others are horrible and be loving when others don't recognize love in their presence.

I felt so unloved and empty because of constantly giving and not really receiving that I promised I would stop. One day the Holy Spirit spoke to me and said that I was not being godly.

God commands us to love as He would, which means we are to love unconditionally. We are to love without any strings attached and without any return expectations.

I told the Holy Spirit but I feel so empty. "What about me, God?"

God responded, "Well since I replenish you, because I and only I can replenish you. I have always replenished you and always will."

Since He commanded us to love, God replenishes our love.

"I supply all your needs," says God.

Week Twenty-Two — Friday
Promises Fulfilled
2 Peter 1:8-9

[8]For if you possess these qualities in increasing measure, they will keep you from being ineffective and unproductive in your knowledge of our Lord Jesus Christ. [9]But if anyone does not have them, he is nearsighted and blind, and has forgotten that he has been cleansed from his past sins.

2 Peter 1:8-9

We have spent the last few days discussing the fruits of the Spirit and living righteously for Christ. We need to do a few more things to please Christ.

First, we need to increase them in measure. We need to become progressively more of all of the fruits and qualities which please God.

Secondly, we need to continuously be conscious of Jesus' death and resurrection for our sins.

Is our living with the fruits of the Spirit our repayment to Christ for all He does? Arguably so.

Similarly, when we judge others who have survived great tragedies, we determine that they need to do great things. We decide because they were the lone survivor of the greatest car crash, train wreck or worst hurricane or flooding that they owe their lives to a higher cause. We know that there is a great purpose for their lives and we don't mind sharing our feelings. And we judge them when they don't.

Why is that person's life not just simply a gift? It is a gift, just as ours was saved in a great tragedy and an even greater miraculous resurrection. We owe our lives to His purpose. He has a plan for our lives and while it is not easy to know what He wants us to do exactly, whatever we do needs to please Him.

By most standards, this is a tall order, but because of God, Jesus and the Holy Spirit it is as simple as asking what His will is. In His time, He reveals His will to each of us.

The question is will we do what He wants us to do?

Week Twenty-Two — Saturday
Promises Fulfilled and Complete
2 Peter 1:10-11

[10]therefore, my brothers, be all the more eager to make your calling and election sure. For if you do these things, you will never fall, [11]and you will receive a rich welcome into the eternal kingdom of our Lord and Savior Jesus Christ.

2 Peter 1:10-11

The "calling and election" refers to our commitment to Christ and the work He requires.

In poker (which I have only viewed on television when the celebrities play for charity) there is a strategic move that a player makes when they bet all they have. The statement they make is "I am all in."

Are you all in? Are you all in all the time? Does God have your attention? Undivided attention? Does God have your all? Are your talents dedicated to Him? Do you seek His will in all you do? Love is in the action. Do your actions state that you truly love God? Does He know how you feel by your behavior rather than your words? Does He know by your feelings and attitudes that you will serve selflessly?

What are you willing to do?

He's prepared to give it all. He's prepared to fill each promise, provide for each need, purpose each life, and preconceive each need. God has planned and prepared for your life. What are you going to do with what He promises and what He has given you?

The word encourages us to get excited and tell everyone who we serve and why. His word urges us to have a clear decision made in a timely fashion. As usual, He has gifts when we do such declarations but is that important? In the grand scheme of life, that gift is the least important of the possible outcomes.

Have you rushed to make your calling and election sure?

Does He know?

WEEK TWENTY-THREE
TAKING CARE OF YOURSELF: AN ACT OF LOVE

When I was pregnant with Hillary, our first child, I learned the hard way that taking care of myself is my top and only priority. I know that by now you have realized that you have to eat properly, drink lots of water and take your vitamins. This week we will go further. What are you doing for your emotional and spiritual health and well-being? Are you able to relax and stress free? This should be a pleasant time with some work but not the work which is stressful and not liked.

The best thing my husband did for me was throw me a surprise party, a Valentine's Dance and a pre-natal body massage. What do you do to relax? Do you read? Write? Walk? Shop? Spa visits? What do you do that allows you to regroup from your workday?

The ideal show of love is taking care of yourself. Resting, drinking plenty of water, relaxing, monitoring your weight, vitamins, regular exercise, and the spa are all key to your health.

Taking care of yourself is not optional – it is required. Your total person affects the growth and well-being of the baby, and ultimately, your entire family.

I remember several nights when I arrived home, ate dinner and laid down for some rest at seven in the evening and slept until seven the next morning. These twelve hours indicated that I need more rest.

Pay attention to your body. Don't ignore any signs or pains or discomfort or twinges. Your baby and body will help you understand what you need.

I remember my first pregnancy so well that with my second pregnancy, I did a better job taking care of myself. I owed my care to my baby and to my family and to myself. Your body is a temple for Christ to dwell. It is my job to care for myself.

Your health and the health of the baby are not replaceable. Your health is a precious gift you should cherish. Taking care of yourself is the best thank you note you can write to God.

Sunday	Sleep? Who needs it anyway?
Monday	Water – THE necessity
Tuesday	Relaxation. Stop cleaning and sit.
Wednesday	Weight management
Thursday	Vitamins and the Health Diet
Friday	Exercise for the Expectant Couple
Saturday	The Spa: Our Destination

197

Week Twenty-Three — Sunday
Sleep? Who Needs It Anyway?

You need 9-12 hours of rest each day. Your body replenishes itself during rest and you have more to replenish. You need to sleep now because remember when your bundle of joy arrives you are then on her schedule – not your own.

Invest in some nice sheets. Increase your thread count. The thread count is how many stitches are in one inch of the sheet, which defines how smooth your sheets are.

Invest in some better pillows. Be sure to solicit advice from experts in this area. Be sure that you are able to tell the sales person how you sleep. Of course, how you sleep now may differ from previous or later.

Research how your sleep patterns influence your child's sleep attitudes. Did you know that your position affects your baby's heart rate? I discovered this fact during my second pregnancy while in delivery.

Resting keeps you happy and calm and pleasant. Lack of rest and sleep causes irritability and causes some health concerns.

Create a wonderful sleep environment for you and your spouse. There are countless statistics about sleep and what environments create the best sleep. They have information on colors, temperature, cleanliness and countless other details.

Protect your sleep time and your rest routine with all that you have. Sleep and rest are just that important.

When the baby arrives, the sleep routine changes slightly. My husband's rule was to sleep whenever the baby sleeps. I couldn't do that. When my sleep is continuously interrupted, I don't feel well. I worked through my new sleep routine by helping my baby sleep longer.

Overall, the fact is that you cannot be a great parent or spouse or friend or person without the proper amount of sleep.

Last word, lead by example. This is not a do what I say, not as I do. You have to sleep so that your child will also know the value of sleep, too.

198

Week Twenty-Three — Monday
Water – THE NECESSITY

64 ounces per day is the minimum. Your body needs hydration. Water is the best form. WATER. Not juice, milk, punch, sports drinks or electrolyte drinks or diet supplements.

Figure out how you best like it: with lemon or lime or orange or cucumber, in a bottle, in a glass, in your favorite mug or thermos, or whatever brand, not flavored, you like. Pick one – decide now. Water is critical to your nutrition and the health of your baby. During my first pregnancy, I was slightly dehydrated and didn't realize it. I spoke to the doctor and at the end of the visit, he urged me to drink water or he threatened to "park" me in the hospital. We never had that conversation again. I learned the value of water.

Develop a system so that you drink the appropriate amount daily. I drink out of a bottle so I number the bottles I need to drink today. When I am done and I still have meals left to consume, I still drink water but I also add 6 to 8 ounces of something else. I am careful of the sugar content.

There are facts about how long you can survive without water. Seven days sounds familiar or three days. You may be asking yourself why didn't the author research that before writing that. I didn't research it because how many days you can survive is unimportant. You are carrying a child now who needs water the most. And even though it's a "nice to know," we are also not interested how long the baby can survive without water.

Drink water. Start now so that for the rest of your life you can adequately hydrate your body. 60% of your body is water. That percentage needs to be maintained for the proper body functioning.

Water – required. As you increase your water intake, you will witness your health improve. As you replace your sodas, juices and other fluids with water, you will also experience an energy boost and some weight loss. If all else get a partner or reward system so that it's easier for you to start and be consistent.

Week Twenty-Three — Tuesday
Relaxation – Stop Cleaning and Sit

So relax. Just sit down. Put your feet up for twenty minutes each day. This increases your circulation which prevents future issues.

Put aside some money for someone to help you with the house. You need to avoid the cleaning fumes and the heavy workload. There are superstitions which exist about what a pregnant woman can and cannot do. For example, she should not lift her arms above her head. Now how are you supposed to get your blouse on? At any rate, whether it's real or not, you need to take care of yourself at whatever cost.

Also, learn the new limitations of your body. You are with child. You are sharing a body with a little someone. You need more rest and more sleep. You can walk for the same number of miles in the same amount of time. Be careful to consider your actions so that the child doesn't suffer the results.

Treat yourself to a pedicure to keep these feet in tip-top shape. Be careful of the nail treatments which produce fumes. I changed my nail routine by going as early as possible to avoid the extra fumes. Also I went less frequently.

Most importantly, a prenatal body massage. I remember my first one. I was so relaxed. The massage was great. I will never forget the experience. They have become more widely offered in salons and spas. The therapist treats you well and the massage relaxes and appeals to your senses. Needless to say, I had subsequent visits.

The key is to find your favorite mode of relaxation and do that more often than regular. Your relaxation insures the child's health and well-being. When you are stressed, the baby feels that and your stress affects the baby's growth.

Relax!

Week Twenty-Three — Wednesday
Weight Management

Begin with the end in mind. Most of us have heard that statement before now, so we will use that to direct us in our weight management.

Manage the weight now so you will have a head start on it after the birth. Eat with that in mind. Visit a nutritionist for the best plan for your food intake.

Vitamins are critical for the growth and health of your child. I prefer chewable vitamins. They were great.

Ask your obstetrician about an appropriate exercise regimen. No you cannot continue to use that same program you are using.

Weight management requires work for some of us. I strongly encourage you to include God in your weight management. I took a class which was Christian centered weight loss. This class met for 13 weeks with tapes to listen to and a workbook to complete each week. This class helped me lose weight and come into a better understanding how to manage my food consumption. Further, how God instructs me to consume food and beverages is covered in this study. I feel strongly, and I am sure that some studies support my feelings, that self-esteem are inversely related. Higher weight means lower self-esteem; lower weight means higher self-esteem. This may just mean me.

Weight loss tips:

(1) Do not give in to all cravings.
(2) Do everything you can breast feed for at least the first 90 days.
(3) Exercise regularly. Start slow with walking. Consider a DVD at your local sportstore or multi-purpose retail venue; and
(4) Drink water. Water cleanses your system and does not have any calories. Calorie reduction is a great plan to manage weight.

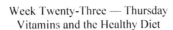

Week Twenty-Three — Thursday
Vitamins and the Healthy Diet

If you recall your first pre-natal visit, you were prescribed vitamins immediately. Vitamins are an important part of your baby's health and your health. I didn't use vitamins prior to my pregnancies, so taking daily medication was somewhat challenging. Chewable vitamins made life easier. I highly recommend them.

The Healthy Diet is equally important. More water, more green vegetables, more protein, fewer carbohydrates, fewer complex sugars, etc. JARGON?! Yes, for those of us who were not focused in high school health class. Get a nutrition education. What foods are high in protein and which ones are low in sugars are the most critical. Read a book, visit nutrition websites or visit a doctor/nutritionist.

Read labels for sodium content. Monitor the amounts which exceed 200 mg.

Be conscious of what you consume, your baby now consumes. A healthy diet and vitamins and water are critical. Maintaining a healthy diet inclusive of calorie management insures weight management. Healthy habits provide a platform for later which lowers the chance for obesity in our children.

I am viewed as the strict parent because I don't carry or chew or buy gum. I rarely eat chips, ice cream or other higher calorie snacks. I read labels and try to serve nutritious foods and snacks at all times. My children drink lots of water, because I do. This is a choice I make. I am not the most popular parent at mealtime but I am not embarrassed or upset when I visit the doctor.

Moderation is key. Effort is important. Decisiveness matters most.

Your health is not to be compromised.

Week Twenty-Three — Friday
Exercise for the Expectant Couple

Exercise with your spouse is a rewarding time spent together. Walking, yoga and bicycling (not while pregnant – check with your doctor) offer the perfect exercises for bringing you and your spouse together, closer at heart. Make it a fun and romantic time. Most couples won't admit that many obstacles come into their lives which discourage closeness. I want you to know that you need to have many "touch-points" in your marriage. Gage's definition of "touch-points" is points in your marriage where your hearts and bodies touch, physically, emotionally and spiritually.

Yoga provides some touching as you lean and stretch together. Yoga is a stress-reliever and relaxing for us.

Birth practice can also be wonderful for this experience.

I suggest recreating this contact time as you read, watch television or have the family meeting in this position. Create time for you to touch your spouse.

Walking provides time to talk and exert energy simultaneously. Three miles guarantees to cover all pertinent family issues. Walking provides enough cardiovascular activity to keep additional pounds away. Make time to walk with your spouse. Miles walked could enhance your marriage by incredible measure. Long-lasting marriages have some similar testimonies, some of which are walking with your spouse, others are simply routines the couple have established. No matter what you decide to do, the important point is that you decide, establish and execute a routine and an exercise plan.

Week Twenty-Three — Saturday
The Spa: Our Destination

Gentlemen, this will be a definite treat. Earlier, I mentioned the pre-natal massage. In addition, regular massages are great therapy for you. Massages keep stress low and lower the opportunity for other health issues stress induces. Have a massage with your spouse in the same room. It is a wonderful experience.

Part of growing as one is trying new things together. Gentlemen, as a hint locate the nearest spa and call the manager. Spend time talking to the manager about your needs and plans and your budget. While the spa manager is describing her recommendations, you need to have some dates for her to check for availability.

Expect to be enlightened. The massage may not be new. The two of you may not be new. However, the newness is the experience together. Learn to enjoy the moments you have together. Learn to create moments when you share, reminisce and re-create those moments. You will need these moments later in your marriage. You will need these moments when you haven't slept in hours and are yearning for a nap.

I use these memories to help me through the nights when the children are awake all night. Children change your lives. You will need to seek refuge. The spa is that refuge.

Check your budget so you can have that experience together on a regular basis. Schedule your spa occasion. Make it special. Keep your appointment. Remember to enjoy.

WEEK TWENTY-FOUR
PARENT AS TEACHER

"More is caught than taught" is a phrase that I have heard more lately as a new parent than ever. Being in the new parent club introduces you to personal growth through reflection. You are your child's first teacher and you will be her teacher all of your life. She does what she sees you do and repeats that action or words. He is a reflection of you.

Your child learns everything from you until she starts school and visits others. Be careful, this could be a compliment or a complaint.

Construct your lesson plans carefully. Decide on your parenting rules carefully. Remember once you establish your standards, take a stand for your rules and beliefs. Someone will challenge your rules.

Our rules:

(1)   No secular music in front of the children.
(2)   Certain words/phrases are not permitted (shut up).
(3)   Can chew sugar-free gum.
(4)   Proper grammar.
(5)   No violent television/movies in front of children.

Remember that we live by these rules before them so we don't create a double standard. Otherwise when you tell your child to do or not to do something, you may hear the words, "But you do it." You won't be able to prevent all instances but those things you feel strong about, you discipline yourself accordingly. My daughter watches us so closely that I am so conscious of my behavior, the good and the not so good. They do what you do. They say what you say. Would you like to see your reflection when it is less than positive?

You are the teacher. You are the model. You are the example. You are the standard. Prepare for the best. Prepare to be outstanding. What is your lesson plan? What is your strategy? Who will assist you? When my children do something that I don't necessarily care for, I call my mother and apologize for doing that to her.

As a parent, I study and pray a lot. Also, I have personally taken some of the limits off of my life. I have enrolled in a master's program for business and will earn two other degrees, one of which is a doctorate. I will do it and expect my children to do the same.

Sunday	Salvation Romans 10:9-10; Ephesians 2:8-9
Monday	Spiritual Gifts Matthew 25:14-30
Tuesday	Love John 14:15
Wednesday	Faith Hebrews 11:6
Thursday	Tithing and Money Malachi 3:10 (8-9)

Friday   Worship and Praise
                          John 4:24; Psalm 139:14

Saturday   Peace
                          Philippians 4:7

Week Twenty-Four — Sunday
Salvation
Romans 1:9-10; Ephesians 2:8-9

[9]That if you confess with your mouth, "Jesus is Lord," and believe in your heart that God raised him from the dead, you will be saved. [10]For it is with your heart that you believe and are justified, and it is with your mouth that you confess and are saved.
[8]For it is by grace you have been saved, through faith – and this not from yourselves, it is the gift of God – [9]not by works, so that no one can boast.

Romans 1:9-10; Ephesians 2:8-9

Are you saved? Do you remember your transformation experience? Do you remember your baptismal experience? Will you share your experience with your children? How will they know how to come into relationship with Christ? You are their first teacher on salvation. Teaching salvation is refreshing. Coupled with sharing Jesus with your child your passion for Christ should be evident. The passion for God is what you are teaching, developing and sharing. Your passion for God is truly on display when you are sharing God and Christ with your child.

Your child's thirst for knowledge should spark a spiritual renewal for you.

Often seasoned Christians become complacent and removed from the best experiences with God. I believe God uses our children to ignite the best of our spiritual lives.

He will also use our children to hold us accountable to Him. He did that to my mom. She became more active because He used me to propel her into action. God has used my children to remind me that He is right here for me, at times when I began to doubt.

Teaching salvation predominantly depends on your lifestyle. It is mostly what they see, hear and feel, rather than what you say directly to them.

Knowing scriptures will assist you in explaining how we enter that relationship. Romans 3:23 & 6:23 are the additional scriptures needed to support the salvation.

Caution: it is extremely difficult to explain that mommy and daddy sin and are wrong sometimes. Proceed with care.

Week Twenty- Four — Monday
Spiritual Gifts
Matthew 25:14-30

[18]But the man who had received the one talent went off, dug a hole in the ground and hid his master's money.

Matthew 25:18

What are your gifts? Are you using them as prescribed by Christ? If not, why not? If so, you have chosen to pass on the life God endowed you with. Part of our responsibility as parents is to pass on a legacy of Christ, which includes teaching how to realize our gifts and using those gifts to increase God's Kingdom.

Will they use their gifts at school and work? Certainly.

Teaching them to use their gifts for the benefit of Christ is what counts. I love teaching lessons on spiritual gifts. I love the transformation in those I teach. Most people simply don't realize. Once they do know, I witness a transformation in their lives. They start to work in the church, they do a better job sharing Christ, and they focus on what Christ needs of them. Further, they are better accountable Christians. They are more involved in church and fellowship with other believers. They have the tendency to be more knowledgeable about Christ because the involvement has increased.

The first way to teach use of gifts is by example. Do you use your gifts? Have you explained your gifts to your children? Have they seen your gifts in action? Have you invited them to participate as you use your gifts?

The second way to teach the use of gifts is giving them opportunities to develop their gifts. When you consider what they do at home use that same activities for them to share with elderly persons or other children, at church, or at the hospital or shelters.

When we teach spiritual gifts and teach giving of themselves earlier, we raise responsible children at an earlier time.

Start a legacy of giving back to God what He has given to us to use for His kingdom.

Week Twenty- Four — Tuesday
Love
John 14:15

[15]If you love me, you will obey what I command.

John 14:15

Gage theory: "If I love them, they will obey me." I suggest this because obedience with any other source is temporary. Fear and intimidation only last until they leave home. Love lasts and teaches more, builds confidence and self-esteem.

Teaching love is based on what they see, feel, know, hear and experience. Why are we teaching love? "Won't they just get it?" you may be thinking. Well no. Love is taught at home.

I learned how to love and how not to love at home. I consider my home life and sometimes, I made up love. As an adult, I still love differently than most people. I love too easily. I love completely or not at all. I still think that everyone should love me, regardless. Does it happen – no. We also need to teach the source of Love: God. God and Jesus are the true and only examples of love.

Love and trust will become synonymous, even though they shouldn't. I have to teach how not to be so trusting with people – even her "friends" at school. She defines them as friends, while I don't. We then engage in quite careful conversation about love, friendships and trust.

Love is the foundation of who we are. Love is like air and oxygen. Without love, similar to oxygen, the brain and body doesn't function properly, creating issues later in life.

Love is nurtured. Love is an action. Love is really a verb. Dr. Gary Chapman authors a series of books entitled The Five Love Languages, one of which addresses the love language of children. He addresses strategies to love your child in her language.

Love is critical. Teach through loving. Live love.

Week Twenty- Four — Wednesday
Faith
Hebrews 11:6

[6]And without faith it is impossible to please God, because anyone who comes to Him must believe that He exists and that He rewards those who earnestly seek Him.

Hebrews 11:6

How do we teach faith? This may not be fair but hold up a mirror and check your faith. Do you have faith or do you worry? Do you fret? Do you need consistent reassurance? Are you overly anxious? When you pray, do you really give <u>all</u> of your burdens to God? And leave them with Him permanently? While we may not be able to answer no to all the questions all the time, answer according to your usual behavior.

Your child is watching your behavior, listening to your words, listening to the tone of your voice and feeling your emotional vibes.

Teaching faith is modeling faith. Do you believe in His Power? Do you believe in His will? Do you "earnestly" seek Him? Do you trust Him and His word? That is your exhibit of faith.

Faith is the evidence of what is hoped for but yet unseen.

Modeling faith is work. Waiting on the Lord requires work, real work. Faith is not thinking that God will deliver a job to your door. Faith is applying for each position where you are interested and knowing that God will supply a job based on your efforts. Faith is not thinking that God will make you debt-free when you acquire more credit cards and keep them at the limit. Faith requires us to stop spending, diligently pay down the debt and cut up the cards. Faith is praying and fasting in belief that God keeps His word. Faith is our refuge in the Lord. He is our strength. Faith is our thank you. Faith is us believing that He is who He says He is. Faith is knowing that what God has for you is for you.

Faith is professing the positive over your life. Faith is believing God and doing what He said.

Faith is modeled behavior.

Week Twenty- Four — Thursday
Tithing and Money
Malachi 3:8-10

[8]"Will a man rob God? Yet you rob me." "But you ask, 'How do we rob you?'" "In tithes and offerings. [9]You are under a curse – the whole nation of you – because you are robbing me. [10]Bring the whole tithe into the storehouse, that there may be food in my house. Test me in this," says the Lord Almighty, "and see if I will not throw open the floodgates of heaven and pour out so much blessing that you will not have room enough for it.
Malachi 3:8-10

There are unlimited testimonies about what God does when we are obedient. Tithing is hard for some people; there have been times when it has been hard for me. I know it is something I must do.

There are unlimited testimonies about people who don't believe in tithing. They also have a long list of other Biblical principles they don't believe in. It calls into question whether they are truly Christians.

Tithing is an act of trust and obedience. Sometimes it's hard and sometimes easy.

Teaching it requires transparency. Place three jars or boxes in your child's room. Label the first as "tithes." Label the second as "savings." Label the third as "the rest." Do this when they start receiving an allowance. They also need a dream notebook. In this dream notebook, they gather up ideas for "the rest." Use this exercise to teach dreaming as well.

The jars will hold them accountable. When it's time to go to church, they empty the jar and give it to church. They will be proud and they will be disciplined. They will need to be reminded.

Tithing is one of God's requirements.

Week Twenty- Four — Friday
Worship and Praise
John 4:24; Psalm 139:14

[24]"God is spirit, and his worshippers must worship in spirit and in truth."
[14]I praise you because I am fearfully and wonderfully made, your works are wonderful, I know that full well.

John 4:24; Psalm 139:14

Worship is personal, yet your children should know that you WORSHIP the Lord. Hillary, our older child, loves worship. She taught her brother about worship. Worship is your reverence to God. Your quiet time, prayer time and meditation time constitutes worship.

Praise is more fun and more expressive. I taught Hillary how to PRAISE. She sees me clap, hears me sing and asks me if I am crying when I praise the Lord. She taught Nehemiah. He watched her clap and sing and dance before the Lord. Nehemiah claps, sings and dances before the Lord now, too. Hillary has corrected his dancing, as well. Correcting his praise aside, Hillary knows how to praise God and does so daily. My greatest accomplishment is that my children praise the Lord because they love the Lord. They learned it from me.

I have a rule that we don't listen to random secular music. There are certain songs, mostly ones from movies that they can listen to as well as instrumental jazz. Music becomes a part of your soul. You must monitor their, as well as your own, musical intake. They learned to praise because they see me praise the Lord in my truck on the way to our destinations <u>daily</u>.

Worship is the meat on the plate. Praise is the everything else, including the beverage. This is the description of a balanced diet. We cannot leave one of them alone. For properly living, we need both.

The Lord knows that we love Him through obedience, worship and praise. We were created to praise and worship Him. Don't let the rocks cry out in your place.

Week Twenty- Four — Saturday
Peace
Philippians 4:7

[7]And the peace of God, which transcends all understanding, will guard your hearts and minds in Chris Jesus.

Philippians 4:7

God's peace transcends all understanding. Teaching peace requires seeking His peace. Keep in mind, understanding His peace is not required, since it's nearly impossible. Do you seek God's peace Do you expect God's peace? Do you need God's peace? Do you want God's peace? Do you ask God for His peace?

Teaching peace requires peaceful behavior. Peacefulness requires submission.

Now let's talk about what His peace will do: His peace guards your heart and mind in Christ Jesus. The definition of guard is to cover; prevent from hurt, harm and danger; to protect from all issues and persons.

God protects your heart and mind. God protects your heart and your mind with His peace. God's peace protects our heart and your mind. With all that we encounter and face and manage and seek and cope, HE protects our hearts with His amazing peace. For all that we see, hear, ignore, persevere and feel, HE protects our minds with His magnificent peace.

When I start to meditate on those very words and consider the events that were an attempt on my sanity and designed to hinder my ability to love, reason, function and think, I have to THANK Him for His peace.

When I consider the unkind words, thoughts, and intentions of others to me, I consider His peace, which I do not understand, bestowed on me unexpectedly, and His peace overwhelms and consumes me.

Be overwhelmed, consumed and functioning with His peace. That is how a parent teaches peace.

WEEK TWENTY-FIVE
LIFESTYLE CHANGES

A baby changes your routine. A baby changes everything about your life. Forever. Once that baby arrives, your life will never be the same.

Most men think that it is impossible for that to happen but it is true. Anticipate, expect, and plan for change.

In the areas of home dynamics, career, priorities, goals, money, house rules and decisions and answers, you can expect change. Immediate and definitive.

My priorities definitely changed. My goals changed. When I consider what I wanted out of life for myself, once I had children, now I want more because I want my life to positively influence them.

My husband went back to college. He wanted his degree. I went back to earn my master's degree. These are all concepts to consider when you consider your life and the life you create for your children and yourself.

Dust off that dream and goal sheet. Chart your progress. Re-ignite that spirit. Remember that your life is defined by more now. A little person with her own personality changes your perspective. He moves your boundaries. He causes you to step up to the plate and do your best in all areas of your life. During our first pregnancy, we were at dinner. A couple approached our table, congratulated us and suggested that we enjoy all of the hot meals, naps and quiet time that we could. He continued by saying that when the baby arrived, most of that would cease. We said thank you graciously and had to carefully consider the timing and delivery of that information. I was initially in doubt or denial about the validity of their information but I consider the source – they had five children. As the parent of five children, I had to admit that they were a credible enough source to share and not be challenged.

There is wisdom in that information and regardless of whether they earned that knowledge or someone else shared it with them, I am passing it on to you with the same intentions they had when they shared.

Sunday	The Family Goals Jeremiah 29:11
Monday	The Home Dynamics Proverbs 31:11, 15, 26, 28; 1 Timothy 3:12
Tuesday	The Family Priorities Joshua 24:15; Matthew 21:13
Wednesday	Your Careers Proverbs 31:16-17, 22a, 24, 27; Ecclesiastes 5:10
Thursday	Money & Its Differences 1 Peter 5:2-3
Friday	House Rules: Decisions: How are they made? Ephesians 5:17, 23
Saturday	House Rules: Answers: Who has them? Ephesians 4:26-27; 5:21

214

Week Twenty-Five — Sunday
The Family Goals
Jeremiah 29:11

[11]"For I know the plans I have for you," declares the Lord, "plans to prosper you and not to harm you, plans to give you hope and a future."

Jeremiah 29:11

God has plans and goals for your family, collectively and individually. Your family needs written, measurable goals with dates for when they are to be achieved. A goal without a date is a dream. I use a goal folder with a goal on each page. I outline the steps, process and plans for each with dates. As you develop your goals and plans, remember that a vision and mission statements should start your process. Your family needs a family scripture – very important. Our family has a few. Jeremiah 29:11 is one of our scriptures because God clearly outlines that He has a plan for my life, offering His best.

The family needs to be on one accord when your goals are developed and established. DO THE BEST FOR YOU FAMILY! Remember as you work <u>together</u> on these goals, you were chosen to marry each other, so you should remember to work together. Not against one another. Your goals should propel your family forward and should move you closer to God. The goals should reflect God's views and His commandments.

Goals examples: The wife returns to school for her MBA. During the development of this goal, the attendance dates, what institution, cost and how paid should be considered. Other important factors are what will degree help to achieve and why does she want this degree.

As you create the goals, remember the dreams need to be included as well. If you have always wanted to travel to Paris, France, when will you go, how will you pay, what will you see and how long will you stay.

Put all of the goals and dreams on paper. This is a working document. The goal notebook reminds you of what you are praying for. The goal notebook reminds you that you and your spouse are working together to achieve these goals.

Week Twenty-Five — Monday
The Home Dynamics
Proverbs 31:11, 15, 26 & 28; 1 Timothy 3:12

[11]Her husband has full confidence in her and lacks nothing of value.
[28]Her children arise and called her blessed; her husband also, and he praises her.
[12]A deacon must be the husband of but one wife and must manage his children and his household well.

Proverbs 31:11 & 28; 1 Timothy 3:12

The book of Ephesians clearly outlines the role of husbands and wives. The three scriptures further outline the parental and spousal roles.

Your children do what they see done. Respect your husband. Wives bridle your tongue. Tell your husband your "complaints" in private. Watch your tone when you ask him to complete his chores. Speak to him kindly. Uplift him publicly. Thank him and compliment him. Do more for him than he expects.

Husbands please don't treat her as the maid. If you do, your children will, too. Men remember to be excited to see her when you return to each other's presence. Be kind to her. Treat her with love and respect and dignity. Don't ask her what she did all day. Do ask what can you do for her. Be a servant leader. PRAISE her publicly and PRIVATELY. Treat her better than you want to be treated. PROTECT her from others who intentionally or unintentionally hurt, offend or disturb her.

Her motivation and inspiration and actions are based on YOUR behavior. You are the head of the household. You are the manager of that home. She facilitates your leadership. If you are not providing that leadership, you should not expect anything.

Your children know when the home is comfortable or insecure. They know when you have issues or are uncomfortable or when you are happy. They need all of you when you get home. They need you to supply them with comfort and security. You are the protector of your family, HUSBAND.

Family dynamics depend on you. It changes when one of you changes. What your children see they do. What you want them to do, you will let them see.

Week Twenty-Five — Tuesday
The Family Priorities
Joshua 24:15b; Matthew 21:13a

[15b]But as for me and my household, we will serve the Lord.
[13a]"It is written," he said to them, "My house will be called a house of prayer."

Joshua 24:15b; Matthew 21:13a

What are your priorities? Does your talk match your walk? Difficult at best to balance when you first have a baby, but you and your spouse must make time to pray, study and serve the Lord.

Prayer is a form of worship. Your children need to know that prayer and worship and praise is what you do for God because of who He is; not for what He's done or what we want Him to do.

Now when I say prayer, I do not want you confused with the good blessing. They need to see you on your knees or prostrate before the Lord. They need to hear their names in your prayer. You are the example of a successful relationship with God. You are the Bible study leader and teacher and minister, and everything that they build their initial relationship with is based on what you do and say and practice.

Do not depend on "church" to teach your child. As a minister, Sunday school teacher, Vacation Bible School Leader and new member orientation teacher, I have seen other leaders give bad information or come unprepared to teach effectively. In both cases, those persons posing as teachers have been excused.

Your child's relationship with God is the most important relationship your child will ever have. Why trust its development to strangers? This relationship is too hard to correct when it is not being built well. Why take chances when you can be sure by doing most of the work yourself. Once you've done your job, then others can add to the relationship. When your child is presented with wrong information, she will know how to address that person and most importantly that the information is wrong.

What are the family priorities? When will we pray? Who leads that prayer? When will the child lead the prayer? Where is the prayer board of requests or petitions, answered prayer and persons who we need our prayers? When does the family fast?

Decide on your priorities prayerfully and hold each other accountable for those priorities. The strength of your family depends on it.

217

Week Twenty-Five — Wednesday
Your Careers
Proverbs 31:16-17, 22a, 24, 27; Ecclesiastes 5:10

[16]She considers a field and buys it; out of her earnings she plants a vineyard. [17]She sets about her work vigorously; her arms are strong for her tasks. [22a]She makes coverings for her bed; [24]she makes linen garments and sells them, and supplies the merchant with sashes. [27]She watches over the affairs of her household and does not eat the bread of idleness.
[10]Whoever loves money never had money enough; whoever loves wealth is never satisfied with his income. This too is meaningless.

Proverbs 31:16-17, 22a, 24, 27; Ecclesiastes 5:10

Your career is not first. Husband, your job is to provide – completely. Wife, you are an entrepreneur. She is not lazy but quite resourceful. I like this description of the wife's role because she lives a balanced life and is not consumed with one area over another. Further, she is a genuine woman.

Husband, if your family is living on two incomes, now is the time to fix that budget. Use your resources to eliminate debt. Look at your expenses and cut those unnecessary ones. Practice paying cash. Stop using credit. Pay them off. Develop a strategy where one person's income was to eliminate debt, including your home. Put a time limit on it. For example, two years from today you will have a mortgage burning celebration because you make four principle only payments. These aggressive financial goals influence your decisions. When your wife knows that your family is not depending on her income, then she can be the woman God called her to be.

I didn't say that she had to stay at home. I said that her income or lack thereof will not bring the house into financial ruin or cause upheaval.

You need to plan for her not to work financially; if she does that money is retirement savings, college funds, and other wise monetary decisions.

Husband, your work life needs balance. She and your children still need your time and energy when you get home. Just because you work does not exclude you from reading to the children or playing Scrabble with your wife.

Your career is protected by God when His order is respected in your life and home.

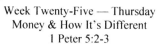

Week Twenty-Five — Thursday
Money & How It's Different
1 Peter 5:2-3

[2]Be shepherds of God's flock that is under your care, serving as overseers – not because you must, but because you are willing, as God wants you to be; not greedy for money, but eager to serve; [3]not lording it over those entrusted to you, but being examples to the flock.

1 Peter 5:2-3

Money cannot successfully be our focus as Christians. We have to settle that "greed" for money early in our Christian walk so that we do not lose sight of what is the ultimate priority.

Money is important but for the advancement of the family and God's family but it is not why we live. We were created to serve God. God did not create us to be greedy. God has abundance and is the owner of everything. God does not need our money. God judges our monetary maturity based on our obedience to His word about money.

What do you do with your money? How did you learn to manage money? Did that process go well? How will you teach your child about money? Are you following the advice of a financial advisor? Are you prepared to answer questions about money? Are you prepared to share information about the household bills with your children? How can you use your money to serve God? How can you teach your child to be a great steward of their finances and resources?

For some of us, we have promised to provide a better life for our children than we did. How are we really measuring "better"? I define "better" as my children graduating with all desired education debt-free. In addition, I want to gift them with the down payment for their home. I will match dollar for dollar the car down payment. This is "better" by my standards, rather than all the clothes the store produces or the toys or the games.

Money should be used discreetly, not flaunted. Keep a discreet lifestyle rather than brag about possessions. Your life will be simpler if you don't train your child to keep up with the Smith's (the Jones' moved). My daughter once asked if we could have a television in our truck. I asked her why we needed that. She responded that another family had one. I asked her why would we do what someone else did without a great reason or needing that item. At 5 years old, it is hard to explain that we do not covet the belongings of others but this is necessary for your sanity and personal accountability.

Week Twenty-Five — Friday
House Rules: Decisions: How are they made?
Ephesians 5:17, 23

[17]Therefore do not be foolish, but understand what the Lord's will is.
[23]For the husband is the head of the wife as Christ is the head of the church, his body, of which he is the Savior.

Ephesians 5:17, 23

Husbands are responsible for the decisions and the outcome of those decisions. Wow! That's the reality of being the husband.

Prayer is required when making great decisions. Seeking God's voice to reveal the unseen factors of your decisions. Give yourself some time to make decisions so "hasty decision mistakes" are not made. As you develop your family plan and goals, you should include when you buy new vehicles, specifically the month and year, rather than generic every ten years. How is that decision made? If your goal is one car note at all times then ten years sounds feasible if you have 60 month financing, however, all life events were not considered here. Is your current vehicle able to accommodate the car seat, a stroller and both parents? Is you current vehicle able to accommodate two car seats, a double stroller, and luggage to take a family vacation? If not, then you need to plan for that or plan to replace that vehicle in three years.

Seek God for wisdom when making household decisions. Wisdom may come from anywhere. Husband, you are the head of the wife and home, however, you need the eyes and hands and other parts to be whole.

Seeking advice from your clergy, financial professionals, wise persons and your family is wise. These individuals have some experience in your area of need. They experienced some things so they can pass it on to you, so that you don't repeat those errors.

House rules set boundaries and establish guidelines. House rules are the road map. Most children adopt these same house rules as they grow older. Some of us promised, as children, that we would do things so differently when it was our turn. A word of wisdom before you dismiss your childhood "house rules," consider what God has shielded from you with these rules. If available, check with your parents about why those rules were instituted. Be wise.

Husband, listen to your family. Use that information according to God's will. Make sound decisions. Simple enough?

Week Twenty-Five — Saturday
House Rules: Answers: who has them?
Ephesians 4:26-27; 5:21

[26]"In your anger do not sin." Do not let the sun go down while you are still angry, [27]and do not give the devil a foothold.
[21]Submit to one another out of reverence for Christ.

Ephesians 4:26-27; 5:21

House Rules for answers:

(1)   Do not argue with your spouse in front of your children.
(2)   Do not discipline your child when you are angry.
(3)   Do confer with your spouse about gray areas of your "rules."
(4)   Do offer honesty to yourself, spouse and children.
(5)   Do be consistent in your rules and answers.
(6)   Do not be divided in the answers or the parenting.
(7)   Do pray when you need answer guidance.
(8)   Do remember that you are not perfect.
(9)   Do remember that we make mistakes so when we do APOLOGIZE!
(10) Rules are not made to be broken.
(11) House rules are up for discussion. Just because we discuss them doesn't mean they changed.
(12) Do allow for "group rule development." Let them decide on the house rules. When they are involved, they are more accountable.
(13) Agree as a couple. Honor the agreement.
(14) Honor your word.
(15) Do not relax the rules when the other parent is not around. Do not use the statements "Don't tell your mom/dad" or "this is just between us" where discipline is concerned or anything that is not related to gift or surprise party.

Keep in mind that your children rely on you for guidance for knowing what discipline is and how important it is in their lives. The Bible says spare the rod and spoil the child (Proverbs 13:24). I would rather discipline now rather than have to discipline later and I would rather discipline than have the authorities discipline my children.

Last note, be sure that you remember that you and your spouse need to be on the same page to be effective parents.

WEEK TWENTY-SIX
PARENTHOOD HAS ITS REWARDS

When you were a child, you and your friends who pretended to be the mom. Your sister could play mommy for hours and you wondered why and how. When pretending to be a parent, she does not count all of the costs or pains or joys. When she pretends to be a great mother, it is a one-sided relationship. The pretend baby doesn't smile unexpectedly or cry for 15 non-stop minutes or have bumps or accidents. Parenting has its rewards and its privileges. Parenthood is a relationship. It is the first relationship that your child experiences. This is your first reward. This baby responds to you and only you until you expose them to others. This relationship with you is the second most important relationship, second only to God. You influence heavily both of those important relationships. How these relationships develop determine how they develop the rest of their relationships, marriage and friendships. Parenting has many rewards, ones you will not experience elsewhere. We will cover God's promises, the gift and responsibility of parenting, and accountability.

One of the rewards that I like the most is the accountability children provide. I dream big. Goals have a date. When I consider what I want for my children, I know that children challenge who you are when you demand their best. I have always wanted my MBA and JD. I want my children to earn a Ph.D. or doctorate of some description. So I am pursuing my MBA, deciding about the JD but will be pursuing a doctorate personally. I want the best for them, so I have to be my best self. Another reward – discovering the best of yourself. A chance to pursue your own dreams to inspire your children to do the same. Parenting is rewarding because it is a clear sign that God trusts you.

Finally, while considering the rewards of parenting, parenting enhances your responsibility. Become more responsible for yourself, your environment and your community and your finances. It is hard to recognize where to enhance your responsibility but examine closely your life because your "microscope" is going to be delivered soon. Your child will be able to see things in your life that you have dismissed. Be responsible.

Sunday	God Keeps His Promises Luke 1:13-18
Monday	Just Enough For You to Handle Matthew 11:28; 1 Peter 5:7
Tuesday	The Gift of Child Bearing Luke 1:26-38
Wednesday	Responsibility of Parenting James 1:5
Thursday	Design Your Future (Within God's Will, of course) Proverbs 3:5-6; 16:3-4
Friday	Set A Standard Proverbs 20:11; 22:6
Saturday	Raise The Bar Psalm 139:14; Galatians 5:22-23

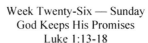

Week Twenty-Six — Sunday
God Keeps His Promises
Luke 1:13-18

[13]But the angel said to him: "Do not be afraid, Zechariah; your prayer has been heard. Your wife Elizabeth will bear a son, and you are to give him the name John. [18]Zechariah asked the angel, "How can I be sure of this? I am an old man and my wife is well along in years."

Luke 1:13, 18

God keeps His promises. When I consider what God has done, I am mostly amazed of what He has promised and what He has fulfilled.

God promised that Elizabeth would give birth to a child. God fulfilled that promise through John the Baptist. As a part of God's promise Mary gave birth to Jesus. God orchestrates His plan in His way and in His time to fill His will and purpose. He planned those two births to fulfill His purposes. I was amazed that God picked two women who knew each other so that Mary could leave Elizabeth to seek wisdom and consult.

God will keep His promises to you as well. What has God promised you? God has created the plans for your life and He will orchestrate His plan until it's fulfilled. You can't even stop the plans He has for you. Not even you can stand in the way of God's plans for your life. One day God revealed that to me and I was overwhelmed to tears.

When we reflect over our lives, we should consider those areas where God has been faithful to us and true to His words and fulfilled His promises and fulfilled His purposes in us. God has done the unbelievable in all of us. We may not keep our part of the deal but God keeps His promises all of the time. Elizabeth, Mary, Sarah, Abraham, David, and so many others have experienced God keep promises.

God has done so much for each of us that we cannot do for ourselves. We have to consider the blessings of even the promises before we evaluate the fulfillment. The fact that He promised. I don't often promise. I don't want to be accountable to anyone for the promises that I make. Perhaps I forget what I have said or change my mind or simply can't fulfill the promise because of lack of resources. I may accidentally promise something that is impossible.

But not God. His promises are not prompted by us. His promises are already in place from the beginning. He has a plan to the end to fulfill each of them. He doesn't need to be reminded. He doesn't have to be coaxed or bribed. He doesn't need any help.

He is God and God keeps his promises.

Week Twenty-Six — Monday
Just Enough for You to Handle
Matthew 11:28; 1 Peter 5:7

[28]"Come to Me, all you who are weary and burdened, and I will give you rest. [7]Cast all your anxiety on him because he cares for you.

Matthew 11:28; 1 Peter 5:7

ALL means all. He invites us all to come to Him with our burdens. Bring our weariness to Him. "Come to Me" is His invitation but we don't RSVP to Him. Instead we go to our friends and family and strangers and therapists. They have the same questions we have, as many as we have and NO ANSWERS. I give great advice when it's Biblically based and God-ordained. But God gives the best advice and support when I am in trouble or in need or anxious.

What I need to do better is recognized God's limitations for me. There is a song that says that "He'll never put more on me than I can bear." We often take that for granted. We forget that during our tough times God carries us. Our trials are designed to build strength and character. Our trials become our testimony for what God does and who He is.

So what can you handle? We don't know until it happens but what I do know I will live. I made a decision. I decided to move past the issues presented to me with knowledge, understanding, and diligence.

What I am capable of and my burdens belong to God. When I consider the burdens we live with each day: bills, children, spouses, and family. These things can overwhelm you if you are not careful.

God is there for you in all of your circumstances. God only gives you what He can trust you with, meaning that He knows what you can handle. Secondly, when He presents you with what you think is more than you can handle, He is testing you and stretching you. During this time, He is growing you.

Lastly, during each of these trials, He is creating your testimony. He will never leave you, nor forsake you. As a promise to you, He fulfills this regardless of the situation.

Everything that you need, God has.

Week Twenty-Six — Tuesday
The Gift of Child Bearing
Luke 1:26-38

[30]But the angel said to her, "Do not be afraid, Mary, you have found favor with God. [31]You will be with child and give birth to a son, and you are to give him the name Jesus. [34]"How will this be," Mary asked the angel, "Since I am a virgin?" [38]"I am the Lord's servant," Mary answered. "May it be to me as you have said," Then the angel left her.

Luke 1:30, 31, 34, 38

Mary's pregnancy is often referred to as the Immaculate Conception because God appointed Jesus in her womb rather than the traditional manner of conception. As a women, you don't know if you can conceive or not until it happens or you are tested. When a women cannot become pregnant, emotions run high. One of the questions is why can't I get pregnant.

Based on what we know, child bearing is a gift. God chose you to give birth to this baby at this time for His purposes. This is His child.

What do you do with this gift? First, thank God for the gift. Second, dedicate His baby to Him.

Remember that God chose you. Listen to Him. He will direct your path. You had faith that God would choose you. You had to have faith that you would carry that baby. You had to have faith that you would be a great mom.

So why did God choose you? He trusts you. He wants to bring you closer to Him. He loves you. He has granted you the desires of your heart. He has invested in you what you cannot do for yourself. He changed your life. He made promises for your life because of the plans He had for you. He fulfilled those promises with this pregnancy, this life, this new love. He has increased your faith and hope. He has increased the standards. He has raised the bar. He has showed out on your behalf. He has added to your testimony. He has enhanced your life. He has met your needs. He has lived through you. He is God and God alone. He has gifted you. He expects great results from His gift.

Week Twenty-Six — Wednesday
Responsibility of Parenthood
James 1:5

[5]If any of you lacks wisdom, he should ask God, who gives generously to all without finding fault, and it will be given to him.

James 1:5

Parenthood is a responsibility. A huge responsibility. You are responsible for their health, nourishment, education, shelter, love, cleanliness and everything. You are responsible for all that they are and all that they need.

The responsibility of parenthood requires wisdom. Hillary is now five and a half years old. I made a decision to have her repeat kindergarten. I was torn all summer about this decision. I made this decision for two reasons: she didn't seem confident in her reading and she would've been seventeen when she graduated from high school. She would've then been in college at seventeen for almost the entire first year. I was mortified at that thought. However, wisdom had to overrule my personal desires of her not repeating kindergarten. This will be better for her in the long run. My responsibility is to make wise decisions which benefit her and her well-being. The decision made about her college entrance age could only be effected now – not at any other later time.

Again wisdom is required. I have to think ahead, read about situation, recall my own experiences and those of my husband's, and seek wisdom from God as I make decisions for our children.

My biggest fears as a parent are making a mistake which impacts us longer than twenty minutes, not paying attention to my children and leaving them somewhere. Your first responsibility is to keep them safe. We lose sight of that responsibility when we take our eyes off the "ball." Keep your mind on what you are doing. For some of us that means clearing your mind of your issues. For most of us, it means that we need to slow down so that we can keep focus on them. Whatever needs to happen, the bottom-line is that the children are the most important persons when they are present.

226

Week Twenty-Six — Thursday
Design Your Future (within God's will, of course)
Proverbs 16:3-4; 3:5-6

³Commit to the Lord whatever you do, and your plans will succeed.
⁴The Lord works out everything for his own ends – even the wicked for a day of disaster. ⁵Trust in the Lord with all your heart and lean not on your own understanding; ⁶in all your ways acknowledge him, and he will make your paths straight.

Proverbs 16:3-4; 3:5-6

When I consider my future, I have been mostly amazed how my children have opened my eyes. My personal life was always good but they force me to be better than my personal BEST. As a mother who desires to leave a very powerful legacy, I decided to do some BIG things. I pursued my MBA (Master's of Business Administration). I am planning for three additional degrees: law degree, master's of divinity and a Ph.D., undecided on the topic. I will publish at least ten more books and the accompanying pieces.

In addition to the education and publishing, I also decided that dreaming wasn't enough. We will travel to Disney, Paris and other places that have interested me.

Of all that I can teach, I want to live a life that teaches how to LIVE completely, with wholeness and without regret.

Step one: Give your "little" plans to God and commit them to Him.

Step two: He is flattered by your assistance but the end is His to have.

Step three: Remember that the Lord knows it all and the Lord knows what is best.

Step four: When you notice that you are following your own path, acknowledge God and He will re-direct you to the right path.

Remember that your future is planned by God to glorify God to advance His purposes. God has great things in store for us. It is up to us to do His will.

Develop the life you always wanted. Everyday you have the opportunity to do something great and to be someone great. Do you take advantage of that opportunity? If so, great! If not, why not? Normally, we don't give ourselves admission to be great because we have been programmed to be mediocre. Take a stand for your life and your future.

DECIDE. TAKE ACTION. TODAY.

Week Twenty-Six — Friday
Set A Standard
Proverbs 20:11; 22:6

[6]Train a child in the way he should go and when he is old he will not turn from it. [11]Even a child is known by his actions, by whether his conduct is pure and right.

Proverbs 20:11; 22:6

Gage's definition of standard is when the expectation is set through behavior, consistently. The standard of etiquette and manners is the use of please, excuse me, thank you and I apologize. I use them and expect my family to do the same. When that doesn't happen, I ask why or I correct the request or statement. I am mannerable and desire mannerable children.

This principle applies to all facets of life: church, faith, education, love, grooming, eating, just to name a few. I mentioned earlier about my education. I will earn my Ph.D. When my child considers her life, she is able to feel free to pursue that same level of education. She knows that more is available and expected. Children respond to what we have evidence for, meaning that when I say you need to earn your master's degree, she will not be able to say, why. She already knows I have one so end of conversation. Similarly, the Ph.D. is becoming more common but no one in my family has one. I will be the first. This lays the foundation for my children to do the same. My achievement empowers them to achieve more than the average young person as well as being free to achieve.

"Being free to achieve" means that there is not family/peer pressure to remain average. "Being free" also encourages them to pursue goals beyond what others around them have done.

I am the first in my family to earn a master's degree. I will be the first to earn a Ph.D. My children will be free to achieve all that they can imagine.

Setting a standard also includes showing great behavior as a parent. My biggest goal is to teach my children better study habits so that they can get a great start. Establishing a standard for education lays the foundation for educational success. My involvement in their education sets the tone for their success, engagement and interest.

Set the standard also requires honesty. I will have to tell each of them the mistakes I made so that they don't repeat them unknowingly. Because I am honest, I can expect more.

Set a standard.

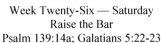

Week Twenty-Six — Saturday
Raise the Bar
Psalm 139:14a; Galatians 5:22-23

[14]I praise you because I am fearfully and wonderfully made; [22]But the fruit of the Spirit is love, joy, peace, patience, kindness, goodness, faithfulness, [20]gentleness, and self-control. Against such things there is no law.

Psalm 139:14a; Galatians 5:22-23

Give your child permission to exceed your achievements. Encourage them to build a "bigger" box. We have defined ourselves and others by the box where we figuratively live. Share with them what you dream about, what your goals are, what else do you plan to achieve as a person. Be honest about your own life. Your honesty will inspire them to reach their dreams.

"I am fearfully and wonderfully made" is a fact. Self-esteem is at risk in each of our children if we don't make a move. As parents we need to assess our own self-esteem. Next, we need to work to enhance our own self-esteem. Stop letting the negative in your spirit. Guard your own ears and mouth against evil, just like you do for your child. Pour positive into your life as well as your child. Change your mind to do great things and being a great person. Your child accesses her self-esteem with the keys you give her. Only issue keys that unlock greatness and love and the other fruits of the spirit.

Step up to the bar and change those things that jeopardize your self-esteem. I needed to lose 63 pounds. I decided on a program that required me to drink only liquid for twelve weeks. During that time I lost 40 pounds. I feel better. I have more fun. I will lose 23 more pounds. My children, even though they are young, know that change is occurring in mommy. When I do something that is great, then they have the power to do great as well.

My attitude and my fruit of the spirit will furnish a platform and foundation for a healthy spirit, if and only if I have a healthy spirit.

When I first heard verse 14, I cried because that verse moved my self-esteem from the garbage to the top. God is not concerned with what you wear or how you look or what you have. God is concerned with your heart.

Raise the bar in your life and your child will raise her life's bar as well.

WEEK TWENTY-SEVEN
FAITH IS REQUIRED FOR PARENTS

In the childbirth preparation class, we did an exercise where we closed our eyes and picked from some cards. On these cards were printed on either side: vaginal/cesarean, no complications/NICU, long labor/short labor, etc. In all of the scenarios, the facilitator explained what to anticipate. Some of the possibilities were horrible but not impossible.

The outcome requires faith.

Our daughter was born at 5 pounds and 7 ounces. The team tried to explain all of the negative possibilities, including feeding her with a tube, and bottle, putting her in NICU, and they were the picture of doom and gloom. I had no problems with the pregnancy, or the birth. She was simply "underweight." I placed that in quotes because while she may have been in an area on the weight chart where they were uncomfortable, God is in control. They threatened me with all kinds of consequences if she didn't gain weight. She needed two ounces. My husband and I prayed over her with our hands on her. God responds to our faith, or lack thereof. Hillary never lost an ounce, gained the two ounces, came home on time and never visited the NICU, tube or bottle feeding.

What do you trust God with?

What are you believing God for?

Our son was born cesarean style. Not what we wanted or expected but truly necessary. The event means nothing once God has shown up. No need for panic or alarm. God's will be done. Submit and surrender. Consider it all joy. Yes, it is easy for me to say.

My niece faced a tragedy after a birth but God is still profoundly awesome. God continued to bless her and she gave birth again triumphantly. God blesses those who believe.

Trust Him with all – it all belongs to Him anyway. Give it all to Him – He knows it all anyway.

Believe that He will handle it all – He is in charge because it is His plans and design.

Sunday	The Faith Quiz: Can you Pass? Hebrews 11:1, 3
Monday	Faith: A Commitment to God Hebrews 11:6
Tuesday	Faith: Walk the Walk, Stop Talking Matthew 14:28-31; Luke 8:43-48
Wednesday	Faith: Sometimes Alone Genesis 12-Genesis 22
Thursday	Faith: Pass It On 2 Timothy 1:5-6; Romans 1:12
Friday	Faith: An Action, Not Discussion James 2:26; Matthew 17:20
Saturday	Faith: The Final Word Hebrews 12:2; Matthew 25 :21

Week Twenty-Seven — Sunday
The Faith Quiz: Can You Pass?
Hebrews 11:1, 3

[1]Now faith is being sure of what we hope for and certain of what we do not see. [3]By faith we understand that the universe was formed at God's command, so that what is seen was not made out of what was visible.

Hebrews 11:1, 3

Are you faithful?
Do you worry?
Do you submit to faith?
Do you speak with as if greatness is possible?
Do you share the great things that happen?
Do you believe God will do what you ask?
Do you ask believing that will answer and provide?
Do you pray? Regularly?
Do you fast? Regularly?
Do you have a prayer partner?
Do others know that you are faithful?
Do you speak with belief?
Do you think faith is important?
Do you know that God expects you to have faith?
How do you measure faith?
How does your measurement compare to God's?
Do your children know that you have faith?
Do you encourage others to have faith?
Do you know any scriptures about faith?
Do you move with faith?

When you consider your answers to these questions, would you pass if this were a test? More importantly, how does God grade your faith? Are you an example of faith?

In this week's introduction, I asked you two questions: (1) What do you trust God with?, and, (2) What are you believing God for? I want you to ponder these questions because you need to know and share the answers. I trust God with my "stuff" and my children. I share my dreams and my feelings and disappointments. I'm believing Him for the goals and dreams He lets me have. I'm believing that He will keep His promises even when I don't keep mine. When you want to know when you really believe you will tell others too. When we are afraid that God will make a fool out of us, we keep our "stuff" to ourselves.

I pray a powerful faith for you.

Week Twenty-Seven — Monday
Faith: A Commitment to God
Hebrews 11:6

[6]And without faith it is impossible to please God because anyone who comes to Him must believe that He exists and that He rewards those who earnestly seek Him.

Hebrews 11:6

Read that scripture aloud. When I heard it in a sermon, after I heard it, there was silence in my own mind. It was as if God quieted everything around me so that I hear HIM say that – just to me.

Faith is a commitment to God. Faith commits us to God. Faith communicates to God that we believe, that we trust, that we hope, that we dream, that we have plans.

Faith is our plan to make God happy. My faith pleases God. It may be the only thing I have done correctly. The fact that I consider how to increase my faith pleases God. My faith validates His unrelenting commitment to me. My faith is a love relationship, where my faith shows I love Him and I am responding to His love. My faith communicates in a responsive manner that I hear Him and am ready for more of what He has for me.

My faith communicates that I test well and can receive larger blessings. I want God to know that I know that my faith, my belief, my trust, and my perseverance moves Him in amazing ways. My faith is tested just like everyone but the difference is that from my test, He has already foreseen the outcome. Sometimes I disappoint Him by faltering during a test but there's even a lesson in that. When I fail, He doesn't fail me. He tests me to stretch me and to grow me. Because growth requires change, I must be tested. The test is designed to increase my faith for bigger tests and so on.

He doesn't fail me, rather He continues to love me and keep me in His care.

My testimony includes my faith, expands my faith, increases my blessings and increases my opportunity to share.

Without faith, it is impossible to please God.

Faith is required. Faith is enough. Faith is an exhibit of hope. Faith is your expression of love. When I act and live faithfully, I demonstrate my love for God.

232

Week Twenty-Seven — Tuesday
Faith: Walk the walk, stop talking
Matthew 14:28-31; Luke 8:43-48

[31]Immediately Jesus reached out his hand and caught him. "You of little faith," he said, "why did you doubt?"
[47]Then the woman, seeing that she could not go unnoticed, came trembling and fell at his feet. In the presence of all the people, she told why she had touched him and how she had been instantly healed. [48]Then he said to her, "Daughter, your faith has healed you. Go in peace."

Matthew 14:31; Luke 8:47-48

Get up and take action! Faith requires action. The story of the woman in Luke is the woman who had the issue of blood. She is very inspiring. She decides to make a move about her situation: she leaves home. She decides that nothing will stop her: she gets past the crowd. She determines her method of help: she grabs Jesus' robe. She accomplished her goal: she was healed. Great story, huh? It doesn't end there, though. Jesus NOTICED her. He felt her touch his robe because she had accessed His power. She didn't go unnoticed. He stopped what He was doing and asked, "who touched me?" Initially, no one answered, then she finally confessed. Here is the blessing. Jesus speaks to her and encourages her to remain faithful and He offers her His peace.

When God grants you what you are believing Him to do, He is encouraging you to be faithful. Remember that God will be glorified when He delivers the promises He has made to you. When I am given the desires of my heart, I am immediately encouraged to remain about the items I am yet believing Him to deliver.

"Why did you doubt?" Such a powerful question, one we don't have a great answer for. We doubt because we forget and we fear. The implied statement that Jesus could've added, "Have I ever failed you? Why would I let you down, now? I am able to do all things." Jesus could've said anything proving that He was capable IF we believe. Jesus doesn't need to continuously remind us of what He is capable. However, we think He does because we keep demonstrating that we need reinforcement.

Faith requires action. Stop talking! Do what you need to do so that God can bless your work. God cannot bless anything that you haven't put any work toward.

Get up and take action!

233

Week Twenty-Seven — Wednesday
Faith: Sometimes Alone
Genesis 12 - Genesis 22

[1]The Lord had said to Abraham, "Leave your country, your people and your father's household and go to the land I will show you.

Genesis 12:1

God told Abraham to leave his country, his family and GO! ALONE! Abraham was disobedient and took a cousin, Lot. At some point in the journey, they had to separate. Abraham had been distracted by the extra people he invited along. After all that was corrected, God could complete His work. Where is or has God leading you alone? Consider carefully your life and times in your life where God seemed to have you alone?

When we are alone, we can hear Him best. So when He has our attention, He is able to get us to work. Work is defined as prayer, fasting, forgiving, praising, and loving – all to Him.

God will fulfill His promises when you are faith-filled. I hear this among believers and "church-folk," but what does that mean for your life, your family and your children?

From the mother of two, take my word for it: You will never be ALONE again. ALONE starts with a re-prioritization of your own values, goals and time. ALONE leads to faith-filled. Faith-filled develops from spending time ALONE with God. As a mom, we spend our waking moments answering to the call, "MOMMY!" But God is screaming "Onedia," can I hear Him? Not all the time. When God wants to talk to you, can you hear Him?

From one mommy to another, ALONE happens when they, including your spouse, are asleep. Now Dads you may be wondering why am I addressing only mom and you should: the success of your family depends on her faith because of her time with God. Your prayer time and your study time needs to be established and announced and regular and respected.

During this time, God will meet you in your prayer time and in your study time so He can renew and revive you and refresh you. Yes, I know you go to worship and Bible study and other church events and you are not alone. Your prayer life and study time is more critical now than ever. Fight for it. Prepare for it. Plan for it. With just as much detail as you have spent on preparing for the baby's arrival, create some private space for you and God.

Husband, you need prayer time and study time, too. Paint her space whatever color she requests.

234

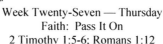

Week Twenty-Seven — Thursday
Faith: Pass It On
2 Timothy 1:5-6; Romans 1:12

[5]I have been reminded of your sincere faith, which first lived in your grandmother Loris and your mother Eunice and, I am persuaded, now live in you also. [6]For this reason I remind you to fan into flame the gift of God, which is in you through laying on of my hands. [12]That is, that you and I may be mutually encouraged by each other's faith.

2 Timothy 1:5-6; Romans 1:12

You cannot share without experience. You cannot give what you don't have. You cannot pass on what you do not possess. I have discussed my education philosophy legacy throughout these pages but the most important is to leave my children a legacy of faith. I intend for Paul to be able to use me as an example. I want my children to experience faith because they see my faith in action.

Paul encourages Timothy "to fan into flame the Gift of God, which is in you." While faith is not in our DNA, this scripture begs the question: "Is faith hereditary?" Do we pass our faith on to our children? Did we get our faith from our parents? Certainly I can not prove that faith is hereditary or not, but what I do know is that faith is experienced and observed, rather than heard, taught, or discussed.

Faith is lived and experienced. Our children need to see us access the faith we possess in order to understand faith. My mother acted in faith but lived in silence. She never shared her concerns with me and rarely the outcomes of these concerns. I had to discern and decipher based on clues and conversations and silence. I really wanted to be there for her but couldn't because she didn't share.

Faith covers a multitude of areas of our lives – ALL. Not one of our issues is exempt from faith. God expects us to exercise our faith and act faithfully and respond in faith on all occasion. At all times. In all circumstances. In front of all persons – especially our children.

Faith is not foreign when felt on familiar fronts. Share your faith with your children.

Week Twenty-Seven — Friday
Faith: An Action, Not Discussion
James 2:26; Matthew 17:20

[26]As the body without the spirit is dead, so faith without deeds is dead.
[20]He replied, "Because you have so little faith. I tell you the truth, if you have faith as small as a mustard seed, you can say to this mountain, 'Move from here to there' and it will move. Nothing will be impossible for you."

James 2:26; Matthew 17:20

Do you have enough faith? What is the size of your faith? A mustard seed is described as small. Jesus says that nothing will be impossible for us if our faith is at least this size – meaning that we don't need a lot of faith. At first glance, one may think that faith is sized or is measurable. However, when considering the possible metaphorical references, I am considering the fact that Jesus may have been explaining that faith doesn't have an actual size but rather an either you have it or not characteristic.

I also find that some people think they have faith but they really don't. They don't have it for many reasons: (1) they don't know what faith is, (2) they think about faith but there is no matching effort, and (3) they expect God to do all the work. The popular example is employment. The cliché is you don't expect God to knock on your door with a job if you never send a resume or send an application or make a call or even tell anyone you are looking for work.

A more applicable example is parenting. By faith, you have been given parental custody. However, you are on assignment. God has specific assignments for you as a parent. While I trust that she will grow to know God, it's my "work" to share God with her. It is my job to teach him to pray. It is my "work" to buy her a Bible, read it to them and provide a great spiritual environment for them. By faith, God will lead them to Him, keep them close and His will with them individually. God chose me to parent them by His will. When we realize that our daily work we do so that God can develop the results. While this may not seem as tangible as the defined job example, the parenting is more impacting and important. One doesn't simply change parents. Jobs change. Parents don't. Just a thought to consider: while you didn't pick one another as parent-child, you certainly don't want to be without one another.

This is most evident in adopted and foster children. They almost always want to know their real parents even though they have never had a relationship. The child just wants to know who was originally assigned to him. Profound, huh? It doesn't matter who got the reassignment, they spend an unaccountable amount of time on the original parent.

Finally, why would God bless something you don't spend any time on? Faith requires work. Thinking, wishing and hoping don't count as work.

236

Week Twenty-Seven — Saturday
Faith: The Final Word
Hebrews 12:2; Matthew 25:21

[2]Let us fix our eyes on Jesus, the author and perfector of our faith, who for the joy set before him endured the cross, scorning its shame, and sat down at the right hand of the throne of God. [21]"His master replied 'Well done, good and faithful servant! You have been faithful with a few things. Come and share your master's happiness!'"

Hebrews 12:2; Matthew 25:21

Jesus is always our example for what we should do. Jesus is obedient and action-oriented and determined and energetic and discerning and forward-thinking. Jesus prays and is compassionate and caring and thoughtful and considerate and Jesus.

The goal for all Christians is for God to say, "well done, good and <u>faithful</u> servant! You have been faithful with a few things. Come and share your master's happiness!"

"Well done" are words the general human would love to hear from anyone, however God is the ultimate at this compliment. To hear His voice utter those words is the ultimate gift. "Good" means that I have been on good behavior. At least redeemable. "Faithful" is not a generally used term. The use of the words indicates a strong commitment through some unusual events and circumstances. Life constitutes that level of "faithful." "Servant" in the secular world is the lowest being. The Highest being in the spiritual world. When God uses servant and Onedia in the same sentence, He honors me for my service and obedience. In my service, I always have to remember that my service is to God rather than the person. He continues to admonish me to serve despite my personal feelings. To God, servanthood <u>and</u> the desire to serve defines leadership.

"You have been faithful" denotes long term faithfulness, not short-term, for-show "faith," a proven faith that exists when no one is looking, just what God sees.

"With a few things" indicates only what God defines as ultimately important. On His list are children, spouse, parents, and others He has called you to serve. God is not expecting us to do everything well (don't think this releases you from general accountability), but the ultimately important assignments is what the "few" defines. Does it mean your job? No. It does refer to the person or person(s) to whom you are assigned at work.

"Come" is an invitation with a promise of reward.

"and Share" is the completion of the reward for faithfulness.

"Your Master's happiness" is something at the top of the desire list and what we spend our time searching for and His happiness is the ultimate gift.

His gift of happiness is a certain reward for a mustard seed size faith over a few things.

WEEK TWENTY-EIGHT
THE LESSONS AHEAD

Your child also has the job of teaching you lessons. There are many lessons you have ahead. For those of you who may miss the lessons on the first round, there is great news. The lessons are presented until we get it. I promise. These lessons are for both of you. The lessons also expose your character traits and sharpens them. When this happens consider that education that is for you now, will later be used for them as well. God wastes nothing. God does not waste any opportunities for His glory to shine as well as for us to learn more ways to praise and glorify Him these lessons.

Lessons are multi-dimensional. These are the lessons we learn to move us forward. These are lessons we learn so we become closer to God. Then, these are lessons we learn so that we can reprioritize our lives. In all of these, the lessons are not new, but function as a reminder of how God really designed life.

Children do not possess fear. We teach fear based on our actions. Or lack of action. When we learn from their fearlessness, we learn to move forward and release our fears. Further, we learn to stop preventing them from moving forward. We also learn to stop teaching fear and start teaching abundant thinking and living. Finally, we are reunited with God's teaching of casting our fears on Him.

Next, there are the lessons which bring us closer to God and reestablishes accountability. As they grow older, they hold you accountable for your activities. We have a list of words that are off-limits. When my daughter hears us say one of them, she immediately says that she will tell our mothers, and that we know better. When the five year old in your life challenges your obedience to your rules, she reminds you that you are the parent and she is expecting your best. Her accountability also reminds you that you are accountable to God. Your parental relationship brings you closer to God.

Another lesson is remembering to dream, set big goals, and work hard.

Lastly, God wants us to leave our fears with Him. You must teach that to your child. In order to do that, you have to live that command.

You can only teach what you live.

Sunday	Show her your prayer life early 2 Chronicles 7:14; Luke 6:28; 1 Thessalonians 5:17; Matthew 5:44, 6:5
Monday	Document his many firsts Ecclesiastes 3:1-8
Tuesday	Hug her as often as possible Matthew 3:17
Wednesday	Make every moment count – each one is important Ecclesiastes 3:11-14
Thursday	Your marriage still requires the same attention Ephesians 5; 1 Peter 3:1-7
Friday	I rarely remember the disadvantages or hard times

1 Corinthians 13:5; Matthew 18:21-22

Saturday   Your career and family sometimes conflict
                            Genesis 1:26; 2:18; Proverbs 31:10-31

Week Twenty-Eight — Sunday
Show her your prayer life early
2 Chronicles 7:14; Matthew 5:44, 6:5-13; Luke 6:28; 1 Thessalonians 5:17

[14]if my people, who are called by my name, will humble themselves and pray and seek my face and turn from their wicked ways, then will I hear from heaven and will forgive their sin and will heal their land.

[44]But I tell you: Love your enemies and pray for those who persecute you.

[28]bless those who curse you, pray for those who mistreat you

[17]pray continually

2 Chronicles 7:14; Matthew 5:44; Luke 6:28; 1 Thessalonians 5:17

Intuition doesn't come to an unprepared mind or heart or spirit. When she needs access to power and strength, she needs PRAYER, not mom or dad. Teaching her the power of prayer early gives her access. My daughter knows the power of access. She will pray anytime, for any reason because she has witnessed the power of prayer. When she says, "Let's pray." She stops and starts to pray. Children who learn to pray, never forget that access and power. They also know that they have unlimited access to God. This is when knowledge is the most powerful. They can pray without your knowledge, consent and interference.

The earlier you show her your prayer life, the longer you have to coach and check her knowledge. If you teach later, it will take longer for her to develop a prayer life and keep it consistent. As they grow up, they become influenced by outsiders and you need to set the foundation before the house is sitting there and you are trying to place the foundation under a built house. She needs to see prayer and hear prayer and pray before she has to rely on her own prayers or believe she is anyway.

As you show her that you pray, share with her the principles of prayer. Pray with humility. Pray sincerely. Pray consistently. Pray for those aspects for which you are thankful. Pray adoration to God. Pray your confession to God. Pray your commitment to God. Pray for your friends. Pray for your family. Pray for your enemies. Pray for those who persecute you. Pray for your concerns. Pray for the desires of your heart.

Remind her that prayer pleases God. Show her how to pray out loud. Encourage her to pray with the family, her friends, and on programs at church.

Pray at night with her. Pray for her in her presence. Listen when she prays for you.

Week Twenty-Eight — Monday
Document his many firsts. Record all you can as many ways you can
Ecclesiastes 3:2

[2]A time to be born and a time to die.

Ecclesiastes 3:2

So when he's born, we do all the stuff for the birth and photos and baby book! We are excited parents! Then reality sets in and life gets back to hectic and then out of the "blue," someone asks you to see some pictures. The last picture is when he was six months old, now he is three years old. Then you are embarrassed because the picture is so outdated.

We take pictures on a quarterly schedule as a family: February, May, August and November. In February, my daughter takes the pictures for her birthday. In May, we take our generational photograph – my grandmother, my mother, my husband's mother, my daughter and myself. We also take a family photo. In August, sometimes optional, but fun pictures are taken. Finally, in October or November, we take holiday photos as well as my son's birthday pictures.

Pictures and memories are all we have to recall the many firsts and any stories that they generate. Also you'll want pictures to show them later and into their adulthood. I grew up taking pictures all of the time. My mother has volumes of my life on Kodak paper. I want the same for my children.

Firsts are non-repeatable and non-transferable. Do the most you can for all of your children equally. It does get harder when there's more than one but I encourage you to be diligent. I am always thinking about the future and I never want their lack of memories to be my fault. I also don't want there to be more memories of one child than there is of another.

To adult children, memories translate into love because of time spent as a family.

Consider your own situation. Recall your childhood – can you share it with your children? I can and my children will be able to as well.

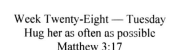

Week Twenty-Eight — Tuesday
Hug her as often as possible
Matthew 3:17

[17]And a voice from heaven said, "This is my Son, whom I love; with him I am well pleased."

Matthew 3:17

My daughter's favorite spot is in my lap. When I am sitting, she wants to be in my lap. Of course, this is great except I don't get to sit that often. Lesson to master: sit more often. That is easy to say if you don't have another child or a spouse or anything else. However, the reality is that we are all busy, but she should be third only to God and your spouse or self. We make two mistakes: (1) we put other "stuff" before our kids; and, (2) we put everything before ourselves.

First of all the airline's instructions are clear, yet ignored. Help yourself then help the child. Putting the air mask on her first could kill you, but placing yours on first will save you both. Secondly, when she <u>needs</u> you, you have to have enough fuel or emotional energy to help her. I have to hug her and comfort her and that requires energy that I have to save for her.

Next, we give our families the leftovers. I worked in customer service for years. When I get home, my children run from wherever they are and hug and kiss and yell my name. They are happy to see me and that I am home. They then expect to sit with me immediately – and sometimes I don't. They deserve my best. They thrive from my touch. I arrive home exhausted because I actually gave my best leftovers away at work. I only have mediocre leftovers to give them because I don't take time to care for myself.

I developed my new routine, which I'll share because I needed to a great ME to be an awesome MOM! I take more baths with real bath bubbles and lotions and scrubs and oils. I take more time in the bathroom when I need to. I enforce my bathroom time boundaries with everyone. My hair, nails and feet have regular, standing appointments so that I look my best so I can feel my sharpest. I developed a wish list and mark off the things I receive, whether I purchase it myself or my husband gives it me.

After all that, I sit down and <u>invite</u> her to sit in my lap. I invite her because it lets her know that Mommy loves her. It tells her that Mommy loves you and wants you to know it.

I need to hug her as often as I can because there will be a time when I can't. NOW is all that I have.

242

Week Twenty-Eight — Wednesday
Make every moment count – each one is important
Ecclesiastes 3:11-14

[12]I know that there is nothing better for men than to be happy and do good while they live.

Ecclesiastes 3:12

Time is precious. Time is unrecouperable. Time moves when you wished it would stop. Time is not rewindable. Yesterday is a distant memory. Tomorrow is not promised to you. The time you have is the moment you are in.

You have the same 24 hours as I do. What are you going to do with those hours?

I have some timing rules that you may find helpful:

(1)   Washing machines, dryers, and dishwashers don't need supervision – turn them on at night or early morning.
(2)   Saturday is not the cleaning day.
(3)   Find a maid. If you don't think you can afford one, check you budget, eliminate something else and get a maid. The work 3-4 people do in 2-3 hours saves you time and you reserve your energy for those who need and love you the most – your children.
(4)   Learn to go where they like for fun. It saves time for later.
(5)   Establish time boundaries for bed. Their health depends on proper rest.
(6)   Make a list before you leave home so that you don't waste time trying to remember where to go or what to buy.
(7)   Schedule and respect your fun time. Fun and family don't just happen. It requires effort and energy and priority.
(8)   Treat your time with care. Make your time special.
(9)   Cook in bulk. Warm as necessary. Eat together. Cut off the television.
(10)   Cut off the television. Yes, it was so important, it needed another mention.
(11)   Read to your children as often as you get a chance.
(12)   Spend your time wisely. Only spend your time on things that have a great return on your investment.

Capture your moments. You can't count them but you want and need every one of them.

In the movie, "Hitch," Alex says, "Life is not the number of breaths you take but the moments that take your breath away."

What takes your breath away?

Week Twenty-Eight — Thursday
Your marriage still requires the same attention
1 Peter 3:1-7; Ephesians 5

[7]Husbands, in the same way be considerate as you live with your wives, and treat them with respect as the weaker partner and as heirs with you of the gracious gift of life, so that nothing will hinder your prayers.

1 Peter 3:7

Your marriage requires the same attention. Now more than ever you need to dedicate yourself to your marriage. Recall your courtship. Recreate those moments. Start interviewing babysitters so that you can keep your dates. Yes, you still need to date. You need time with your spouse – uninterrupted.

You need this time to remember what your spouse likes and finds fun. Find time to converse about each other's thoughts and fears and needs and dreams. Remember how he likes his coffee. Remember her nail appointment. The little things mean the most.

Pray for each other and <u>with</u> each other. Keep your word – your promises. Women remember the promises men make and women fully expect those promises to be kept, without being reminded.

Men, don't forget what the scriptures say about your sacrificial love for you wife. SHE IS FIRST, after God. Husbands, your love equals her respect. When she respects you, she can love you. Without that love, you have no marriage – just a roommate and co-parent.

Ideally, you will "date" bi-monthly. These dates will be romantic and full of wonderful conversation, followed by wonderful lovemaking. If that's not your fantasy, that's great, however, whatever you desire for your date, make it happen. Your dates are an important quality time in your relationship. Take it seriously. Time goes quickly and if you have not committed any time to each other, you will be co-habitating with a stranger.

He still <u>needs</u> sex. She still <u>needs</u> conversation. Get creative. Be cooperative. Be flexible. Be committed. No whining. No excuses. Your marriage deserves time, attention and care.

Your marriage is precious. Take care of it accordingly.

Make every conversation count. Ten minutes of uninterrupted daily face-to-face time with your spouse will kindle your relationship. Keeping all examples equal, treat your marriage like your vehicle. Rotate the tires every 5000 miles. Change the oil every 3000 miles. Wash it every weekend.

This is consistent and required maintenance, which you do so that the car is reliable and that the engine does not lock up. Each marriage is different but the basic principles are the same. Your marriage requires the same amount of attention.

Week Twenty-Eight — Friday
Your Grudge is Your Anchor
(I rarely remember the disadvantages or hard times)
Matthew 18:21-22; 1 Corinthians 13:5

[21]Then Peter came to Jesus and asked, "Lord, how many times shall I forgive my brother when he sins against me? Up to seven times? [22]Jesus answered, "I tell you, not seven times, but seventy-seven times.
[5]. . .(It) love keeps no record of wrongs."

Matthew 18:21-22; 1 Corinthians 13:5

Love keeps no record of wrongs. Tall order. Sometimes taller than others. But tall all the same. Yes, wives, it means put the scorecard in the trash. Yes, it is hard to do.

My friend said to me one day when you are having a hard time in your marriage: "Give your husband over to the Lord. It is not your job to fix him. He belongs to God. Give him back." Her statement took my breath away. I could barely breath. Give it up! Stop keeping a record of things gone wrong. You are still human. We all make mistakes. Forgive each other for EVERYTHING!! When you don't forgive, you stop the Lord from forgiving you. You also delay your own blessings.

In Ephesians 4:32, Paul also talks about love and forgiveness. It is hard to love freely, and openly, when you are holding a grudge. Holding a grudge is like a closed fist. When the fist is closed, you can't receive anything or give anything. Holding a grudge also stops your creativity.

Forgiveness is essential to growing as a person and in your marriage.

Love has to be able to flow freely in your marriage.

In the previous page, the scripture mentioned that certain actions would not "hinder your prayers," similar to this scripture, you forgive so that your prayers won't be hindered.

Keep forgiving! Yes, I know it is hard to do and it's hard to say. Keep forgiving! Forgiveness keeps the lines of communication open. Keep forgiving! Obedience to God means more than anything. God will honor your obedience. Keep forgiving! Your child benefits from this discipline. Keep forgiving! Forgiveness is key to a long and fulfilling relationship.

Just to clear the table of pre-existing issues, forgive yourself and spouse of all previous issues.

Week Twenty-Eight — Saturday
Your career and family sometimes conflict.
You may challenge your decision to return to work
Genesis 1:26, 2:18; Proverbs 31:10-31

[26]Then God said, "Let us make man in our image, in our likeness, and let them rule over the fish of the sea and the birds of the air, over the livestock, over all the earth, and over all the creatures that move along the ground." [18]The Lord God said, "It is not good for man to be alone. I will make a helper suitable for him."

Genesis 1:26, 2:18

God gave Adam a job. Husbands, you have a job. God provides for your family through you. In this century, half of last and the future centuries, women have become more independent and prominent in the workplace. God gave Eve a job, too. She was designed to help Adam. Wives are designed to help husbands. However, wives' jobs have changed since that time. Wives have evolved. Even though that is the case, husbands, your job hasn't changed. You need to have a plan for her to help you with. Yes, she can help you develop some of those plans, but the plans' foundation should be Biblical and established and shared with her.

I am that independent working woman who regretted not being able to stop working after my regular maternity leave. I was working when she took her first steps. I DECIDED that for the second child, that I would work from home. I did that for eighteen months before I went back to work. There was definitely internal conflict with my strong desire not to return to work and the need for the money. Your current household budget may not allow you to stop working but it is necessary everyone to commit to the decisions made.

Several issues need to be considered: (1) if you can't currently afford to stay at home, what would it take? What would need to be cut so that you can? (2) What can each of you sacrifice to make it happen? (3) What work can you do from home? What independent businesses which target moms can you do so that you can stay at home? (4) What sacrifices can you make in order to stay at home?

If the decision to stay at home is important, then the sacrifice is inevitable.

Do whatever it takes.

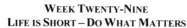

WEEK TWENTY-NINE
LIFE IS SHORT – DO WHAT MATTERS

Life is to short for worry, anxiety, anger, bitterness and grudges. I was pregnant on September 11, 2001. I was at home, going to work later but not really feeling great. I watched the tragedy happen. 2002 brought the one year anniversary of the day our national security was breached. I watched the special hosted by Diane Sawyer about the 65 children born of the September 11 tragedy. Each day 63 women are reminded of the day which changed their entire lives. Best scenario: They were all at peace. They were perfectly happy. Worst scenario: They were unhappy. They had just had a fight. The fact is they were never able to make it right. Don't fall victim to that – make it right always.

When you consider your marriage and any issues, contemplate whether they are serious enough to hold on to. Ask yourself will it matter in twenty minutes. When you consider life's overall impact on your life, then some of the issues that really bother you may not be that important.

Life is too short. Do what matters. Decide what's important. Family time is ultimately important. What time is allocated to family? Are your dinners family style where everyone is at the same table and there is no television? This is true family time. How do you spend your weekends? Are your weekends dedicated to growing closer as a family? Do you take time to listen to the children? Can you modify your hours at work so that the family can eat dinner together?

There were several thousand stories from the survivors of 9/11. There is one that touches my heart the most. The owner of a company who was on floor 104 one away from the top, was walking his child to school the morning of the tragedy. His child asked him to walk her to school that morning. He agreed reluctantly because he would be late to work. He agreed and walked the child. He arrived at the area after the explosions. If he had been on time, if he had not walked the child to school, he would not be alive. It doesn't matter who he was, what he owned, the gender of the child, however, it does matter that he did what was important. We have 18 short years before they are no longer children. We need to make the most of each of those days.

What are you going to do to make the moments count and matter?

Sunday   Prayer is Power
                          Romans 8:26

Monday   Love
                          John 3:16

Tuesday   Timing Is Everything (Quality Time)
                          Ecclesiastes 3:7-8a

Wednesday   Listening is a Skill
                          James 1:19

Thursday   Quiet Time
                          Psalm 1:2; 19:14; 145:5

Friday   Conflict Resolution is Essential
                          Ephesians 4:26-27; Proverbs 15:1, 18; 17:9, 14

Saturday   Family Philosophy
                          Joshua 22:5

247

Week Twenty-Nine — Sunday
Prayer is Power
Romans 8:26

[26]In the same way, the Spirit helps us in our weakness. We do not know what we ought to pray for, but the Spirit himself intercedes for us with groans that words cannot express.

Romans 8:26

Prayer is powerful. Beyond measure, prayer is extremely powerful. Prayer is our access to God. Unlimited access by praying to God in the name of Jesus is a provision made by Jesus' birth.

God is waiting on us to pray. He expects us to pray. He provides an avenue for us to pray. He has provided an intercessor, Jesus, who goes before us to pray. He also gives us the Holy Spirit to intercede when we don't know what to pray for. He is waiting for us to pray. He is concerned when we don't.

Prayer offers us several opportunities. We can adore God in our prayers. When we adore God, we simply love Him and the many ways that we love Him. Also when we pray, we confess our sins, reconciling our hearts to God. Sin separates us from Christ, so we need to be conscious of our sins and remember to confess them. God already knows what happened so go ahead and confess what will cleanse you of your sins and revive your relationship with God. Also, in prayer we offer thanksgiving; thanking Him for what He has done, but most importantly who He is. Then we pray with supplication. Align yourself with God, offering your best.

God is complimented by prayer and praise and scripture. When we pray, we tell God our needs, our wants and the desires of our hearts. The word says that if we delight in the Lord, then He will give us the desires of our hearts.

Prayer is powerful. Prayer is awesome. Prayer is required. Prayer does not have to be poetic, but sincere. Prayer is not perfunctory, but an honor we give back to God because of what He grants to us. Prayer is a form of praise. Prayer is also a time when God can talk to you. Prayer is when we can hear from God. We need to hear from Him.

Prayer is critical. Prayer is our lifeline to God.

Week Twenty-Nine — Monday
Love
John 3:16

¹⁶For God so loved the world that He gave His only begotten son that whosoever believes in Him should not perish but have everlasting life.

John 3:16

John speaks of the most profound love one will ever experience. Jesus died for my sins and I wasn't there when He was flesh. As humans, we don't consider dying for those we do not know. We have reservations for those we do know <u>and</u> love. But without knowing me or you like He knew the disciples, He died for me. That's real love.

Will you die for them? Will you donate your organs to them? Do you <u>love</u> them? If so, how much? What are you willing to sacrifice? Is your love Conditional? Provisional? Earned? Real? Dr. Gary Chapman authored several books on <u>The Five Love Languages</u>. In these books, he defines love languages and shows that there are 5 and how to keep your spouse and children's love tank full. He also defines love tank. Love tanks and languages are subjective. Jesus is love is objective and unconditional.

Life is too short not to love fully and completely. We have a finite number of years here with our loved ones – make each one count. Love is required to have family as God designed. I may be selfish but I want to know that I am loved. My love language is time and conversation. When a person doesn't spend time with me, then I am not feeling the love they say they have for me. If we are not talking, I'm not feeling the love. For me, this is like air. To others, it's not important at all.

Children require time and equate time to love. There is an email where a boy wanted to spend time with his father. The father replied that he was busy. The boy left the room for about 20 minutes and then returned. When he returned, he asked his dad how much money did he make an hour. His dad replied, $20. He said okay and left the room and came back to the room with $20. He presented the $20 bill to his dad and said can I have an hour of your time.

If I could add an addendum to 1 Corinthians 13 as verse 14: Love is not busy and is not put off easily.

When I want to say wait or mommy's busy, I am suddenly reminded of that email. I stop and address my children and give my love through my undivided attention.

249

Week Twenty-Nine — Tuesday
Timing is Everything
Ecclesiastes 3:7b-8a

[7b]a time to be silent and a time to speak, [8a]a time to love and a time to hate.

Ecclesiastes 3:7b-8a

One of the many lessons that you will teach as a parent is one of the hardest – timing. My mother's lesson is "think before you speak." Although she said it dozens of times each week, I never fully understood until I started working. Timing in speaking is critical. Teaching that lesson requires honesty and fortitude and diplomacy. As I start teaching that lesson, I find that I have used the rule personally myself. My children repeat what they hear me say. If I want a parental report card, I listen to my children – grammar, vocabulary, tone, slang and attitude.

As I start sharing with my daughter how to think before she speaks, I have to remember that she is still small, five to be exact. At five, she has learned honesty but doesn't understand that honesty doesn't have to be shared with all parties. Caution is needed here because I don't want to inadvertently teach her to lie. I use "when we are honest we also are careful to be kind." This statement communicates that honesty is important and preserving the relationship, respect, dignity and integrity of both parties is equally important. Thinking before you speak and deciding to be silent requires wisdom and maturity. Teaching that lesson to a child also requires fortitude. You will have to say that same phrase several times in differing variations in order to make your point.

Teaching this lesson requires personal diplomacy and the ability to teach tact and diplomacy. How you say what you say is more important than the actual message. Tone and body language communicate loudly what you are saying and sometimes drowns your message.

Finally, love has its place and time. Love has interesting parameters. Timing and love normally don't work in the same platform. Although you can't time when you love someone, you can certainly work on your time to love those who deserve and desire your love. There is also a time to spend on love. Spend time with the idea of love.

Timing is everything. When you do something is as important as how and what you do. Using time wisely is equally as important.

Week Twenty-Nine — Wednesday
Listening is a Skill
James 1:19

[19]My dear brothers, take note of this: Everyone should be quick to listen, slow to speak and slow to become angry,

James 1:19

Listening is a skill. Listening is a requirement in healthy relationships. Listening is required in all levels and stages and events in your life. Listening is the first step in love and conflict resolution. Listening is a very valuable skill.

Teaching my daughter requires that I speak slowly so that she can process what I am asking. Repeat what I need. Ask her if she understands what I need. Offer her the opportunity to ask questions. Sounds easy? It's a little more difficult than I explained.

The key to listening is connecting at some level of understanding. In order to effectively listen, I have to engage the speaker. When you are the parent, you have to engage the listener. I have to insure that she understands by using vocabulary she knows and using a tone she responds to well. Then I have to ask if she understood what I said. When she indicates that she did, then I know that we have communicated effectively.

The other component of listening is the follow-up and follow-through. The follow-up is me walking upstairs to be sure she is working on what was asked. The follow-through is her doing her share and knowing that I am holding her accountable for our conversations.

Now as the parent and even the spouse, you need to do some additional listening. I "listen" to my child's body language when she is talking to me. This body language communicates to me her happiness, fears, anxieties, joys, pains, excitement and her urgency.

As a parent, you also need to listen to their tone of voice. The tone will tell the second most important portion of the dialogue.

Lastly, I use my eyes and ears equally when I listen. I have trained myself to stop what I am doing to look at her when I listen to her. When I look at my children, I communicate that I am listening to them and I care about their concerns.

When I do these things, I am also teaching them those same skills.

251

Week Twenty-Nine — Thursday
Quiet Time
Psalm 1:2; 19:14; 145:5

[2]But his delight is in the law of the Lord, and on his law he meditates day and night. [14]May the words of my mouth and the meditation of my heart be pleasing in your sight, O Lord, my Rock and my Redeemer. [5]They will speak of the glorious splendor of the majesty, and I will meditate on your wonderful works.

Psalm 1:2; 19:14; 145:5

By Gage's definition, meditate means to seek God in a quiet place with a receptive spirit, soul, heart, and mind.

Further, meditation means taking time to reflect on what you have read, what you have seen, what you have heard and what God has for you.

Doing what matters should be priority. Quiet time needs to move to the top of the list. When do you sit down and let quiet cover you? When do you sit still without interruption? When do you seek the Lord and refuge in Him? When do you relax in the arms of the Lord?

When you become parents, your quiet time happens at a cost. You know that it is critical that you have to have quiet time. You will sacrifice other areas of your life so that you can have the quiet time you need. You <u>need</u> quiet time to refuel and reenergize yourself. You <u>need</u> that daily quiet time to reflect on the <u>great</u> things that God has done today. You <u>need</u> that <u>daily</u> quiet time so that you can resolve in your mind that today is passing and tomorrow is future. You <u>need</u> that <u>daily</u> quiet time to focus on God who redeems us from poor choices and bad consequences.

Don't feel guilty when you have your quiet time. You may self-inflict the guilt or maybe others will attempt to make you feel guilty. What is accomplished when you have your daily quiet time with God is worth far more than the guilt you will experience.

Quiet time with God is so valuable that it increases your effectiveness as a parent and a spouse. When you have had time to commune with God, you are able to maintain through life's ups and downs. You are closer to God because of this time. Remember the triangular relationship we discussed earlier, recall that we grow closer to Christ, we are growing for those we love. Further, your time with God becomes an example for those you love.

252

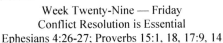

Week Twenty-Nine — Friday
Conflict Resolution is Essential
Ephesians 4:26-27; Proverbs 15:1, 18, 17:9, 14

[26]"In your anger, do not sin. Do not let the sun go down while you are still angry, [27]and do not give the devil a foothold."
[1]A gentle answer turns away wrath, but a harsh word stirs up anger. [18]A hot-tempered man stirs up dissension, but a patient man calms a quarrel.
[9]He who covers over an offense promotes love, but whoever repeats the matter separates close friends. [14]Starting a quarrel is like breaching a dam; so drop the matter before a dispute breaks out.

Ephesians 4:26-27; Proverbs 15:1, 18, 17:9, 14

As you parent, there will come an occasion when you ask yourself what impression did I just make on my child? I learned this the hard way when one day my own words slapped me in the face. My daughter said something that was inappropriate at which point I promptly chastised her and then asked, "When did you hear say that?" She responded, "You," quite innocently, I might add. I was appalled and embarrassed and completely enlightened. It was clear now that her memory was excellent. Her hearing was great too. And also that her sponge was absorbent. Our children are sponges, meaning that they catch everything in their presence. There is also an assumption they use daily: my parents are great examples and role models. As my parent, I should be able to repeat what they say and do. Is this a good assumption? Not always. As parents, we don't know it all, we make mistakes, and we are not perfect. Because of these facts, we need to be careful on how we approach these areas, such as anger, fear, and any other life pitfall.

Conflict resolution needs to be handled well at all times. Our children use we show them on how to handle conflict. My husband thought his parents never argued because he never saw or heard them. When his mother revealed that they actually did argue, he was surprised. The same example could be used for you. What can you show your child? What can you shield from her? How do they see you resolve issues on the phone? At a restaurant? At home? With them? With their siblings? At the store?

When I shop with my children and the customer service is poor, I prepare to leave my potential purchase in order to avoid the situation. I now select where I take them and where I have stopped shopping in order to avoid having to be angry or upset.

Be careful as these situations arise. Remember that what you say cannot be reversed nor erased from her mind.

Week Twenty-Nine — Saturday
Family Philosophy
Joshua 22:5

[22]"But be very careful to keep the commandment and the law that Moses the servant of the Lord gave you: to love the Lord your God, to walk in all his ways, to obey his commands, to hold fast to him and to serve him with all your heart and all your soul."

Joshua 22:5

What is your family philosophy? The family philosophy is based on your desired legacy, grounded by your beliefs and upheld by your daily activities. Your family philosophy has a long history as it has been passed on through all the generations in your family, then influenced by etiquette, social values, others, and Biblical principles.

How do you share your family philosophy? I share portions of it with my family as often as possible through conversation, discipline, behavior and faith.

I attended a wedding recently where I returned to my table from the buffet line. I noticed that the four seated people, one of which was my husband, were not eating. Immediately, my husband and I prayed so that we could start eating. Before we picked up our forks, I asked the lady also at our table, "Are we using all of our manners today?" When I asked smiling, I already knew the answer. She replied, "Yes. They are almost done with the line. We can eat as soon as they are seated." My family philosophy included that etiquette. I chose to ignore it for a moment but I know the truth. Family philosophy provides instructions and guidelines for life and relations. A sample of our family philosophy is: "You have not because you asked not"; Family sticks together; Family spends holidays together; Family are concerned about each other; do not wear hats in the house or sunglasses; do not run with sharp objects; and, no singing at the dining table.

Some of these may be familiar to you, and if not, feel free to borrow them.

The point is to equip your child and family with an anchor and foundation for life which creates common ground.

Lastly, be prepared for the challenge when you steer away from the philosophy.

WEEK THIRTY
IN TEN WEEKS

In ten short weeks, you will be a parent. Excitement and fear may have anchored themselves within you. You may be exhausted and also tired of people asking when you are due, what you are having, what you will name that person and rubbing your stomach.

In ten short weeks, you will experience sleepless nights, odd hours, cold meals, pure exhaustion, and a new person. This new person comes equipped with her own personality and temperament and love. This person, this baby, will steal your heart even before you hold him. Absolutely promise. In the next ten weeks, you have work to do, though. Dreaming has to be allocated. This time will pass quickly.

As you prepare for the arrival, a birthing preparation class assists you in knowing what to anticipate. During the class, after you exercise your breathing, they share valuable information about pain medication options and the side effects and any associated risks. Also, they share the other possible outcomes, particularly changes in the birth plan. When I had Hillary, I didn't have pain medication and gave birth naturally. When I had Nehemiah, I had to have a cesarean section and pain medication was required. The surgery wasn't optional.

Consider over the next several weeks how your lifestyle will change. Do you need a housekeeper? Who will help you after your husband returns to work? What is the family plan? Now is when those discussions are important. Eat as many hot meals as possible and enjoy the lack of interruption. Decorate the nursery. Prepare for the bundle with the energy you have.

Remember to relax and respond to your body's needs. You have a lifetime ahead. This is an exciting time and you want to remember this time as exciting.

Names are important. Carefully select his name. He has to use it his whole life. I don't like nicknames so I expect his name to be used without modifications or changes. Lastly, it needs to mean something and be respected. His name attaches him to his family.

Sunday	The Arrival
Monday	A Room of Her Own
Tuesday	Names Are a Legacy
Wednesday	Care for Your Child
Thursday	Your Revised Lifestyle
Friday	Your Thoughts are Important
Saturday	Your Feelings are Important, too

Week Thirty — Sunday
The Arrival

What is the plan? What is the backup plan? What is the third option? What happens when all plans fail?

We know a couple who went to the hospital for a checkup. Her doctor decided to induce her labor. The mom thought she had to go home and get her hospital bag and car seat. She gave birth within the hour. None of that was planned so the plan was that we took those items to them. The plan was altered and in fast forward.

Write a couple of plans. Then know that the possibility is that you will have to change some parts of that plan. Feel comfortable with that decision and tell everyone so that there's no misunderstanding.

What have you envisioned? What does it take to make that happen? Share your desires with your circle. What will the arrival home look like? What will the baby wear home? Have you purchased a car seat and other safety accessories? What will the weather be like? Will the house be ready? What will it take to get ready? Do you have your time off arranged? Does your spouse? Do you have a plan for videotaping and films? Do the people who will be present for the birth know that is what you want?

How can you insure that your birth experience and your baby's arrival are special? Be proactive. At six months, I had the hospital reserved. I was excited. My husband and I spent too much time on that and not enough in other places but it worked out. Develop a realistic mindset and move on your desires. Share in the plan.

At the end of the day, remember when you see, hear and feel your baby that the most important detail is happening. Be present in that moment – you will never get that time or experience past back.

Enjoy it. It doesn't last long.

Week Thirty — Monday
A Room of Her Own

What will the nursery look like? What theme? What kind of crib? Will you want a chair in the nursery? Details. Details. Details.

There are many options. You may even select something and then change your mind.

The room design should be warm, welcoming and friendly, and fun. The room design ideally should grow with the child. There are cribs that convert into full size beds with a converter kit. Please purchase them at the same time.

In our case we decorated a nursery in primary colors so that we could use it again. When my daughter climbed out of her crib, she moved into her room with a queen-sized bed. The nursery remained ready for my son. There are days that I wished that I had done the completely pink, plush, out-of-the-movies nursery. Do what is going to enhance your moments. The room is not the moment – the baby is.

Hang photos of the family in the room. Recognition starts early. Music is essential as well. Music can help soothe and will work wonders for relaxation for all of you. Make this the place to unwind. Make this a great place that will stay the same, essentially, for a few years. A library is critical as well.

Make it comfortable. Shop for a chair that is comfortable enough to sleep in. You may need to sleep in it many nights.

Be creative. Decorate with love. Invest in this room. It is the room where your baby will grow.

Week Thirty — Tuesday
Names are a Legacy

Is that a family name?
How did you get your name?
What is the origin of your name?
What does your name mean?
How do you spell that?
Can you repeat your name?
Do you know _____ (someone with same name)?
Are you related to _____?
Are you _____ little sister/brother/daughter/son?

Your name has a story. A legacy. Your name was carefully selected. It means something to have your name. It may be a family name. It may have been selected out of a baby book. It may have been the name of friend or a doll or an actor. Your name attached you to someone or an event or a group of people, known as your family.

Take this opportunity to create a naming tradition and legacy in your family. My grandmother started with mother by using her grandmother's first name as her middle name. My mother continued it with my sister and myself. And that legacy continues in my family. My daughter and my husband have the same first name but spelled differently. Hillary has my middle name. My mother and I have the same first name, spelled the same.

Needless to say, there is a tremendous amount of pride that exists when someone asks our names or discusses names with us. Remember the naming rules (I may have created these):

Will that child be able to spell that name?
Will they grow up to be proud of that name?
Will they feel attached to that family through the name?
Will that name be respected in writing?
Will children tease him at school?
Will the teachers respect her name?
Will your race be obvious by the name selected?
Will she be discriminated because of her name?
Will she feel strong when she says her name?
Will he want to change his name later?

Just a little suggestion on names from someone who loves her name and has to spell and correct it for others daily.

Week Thirty — Wednesday
Care for Your Child

Decisions for the rest of his life are being made as your eyes cross this page by you and many others who don't even know your child, such as governmental officials.

Your decisions are critical and essential and important. These decisions include:

1. College fund – where, what type
2. Life insurance
3. Early interaction – at home with mom or daycare
4. School – when, which one
5. School – when do we change
6. Lifestyle
7. Toys, television, internet usage
8. Music
9. Laws, government, elected officials
10. International affairs and relations

How will these affect you, your child and the best you can do for the child?

Keep your focus on your child. Care for this child is the most important factor of all factors. Nothing is more important than caring for this child, emotionally and fiscally. Children are gifts and their care should be deemed to be supreme on the priority list.

Keep in mind you were gifted with their care. Take your job seriously. Act wisely. Ask for help. Stay focused on the fact that your decisions impact your life but also that child's life. Caring for your child is important. Sharing with them is important as well.

Protect your child.

259

Week Thirty — Thursday
Your Revised Lifestyle

No, you can't just do what you feel like doing. No, your meals will be different. No, you don't go to the bathroom alone anymore. No, all of your money is no longer yours anymore.

No, your life is no longer your own. No, you can't just get up and go on a date. You have to have a babysitter so that you can go on a date.

Learn to plan if you don't already. Planning is critical with a baby. Your marriage needs that planning. Your spouse still needs the same amount of attention. Your friends still want to see you and spend time with you. Your baby needs your time. Your family needs your time. Your personal time is still important, too.

Your schedule needs some revision, though. You will need to allocate time to drop the baby off and still get to work on time.

There will be different demands on your time now. You may need to spend more time planning your days and weekends. I found that I shopped more online from non-essential places, such as the bookstore, electronics and anything that offers free shipping. I had never been an internet shopper but when my time allocation changed, I had to be flexible.

Your relationship with your spouse will be impacted. Yes, it will change. Your previous "free time" will now be spent with the baby. What does that leave for you and your spouse? Date nights are helpful. Arranged times at home and away from home, that is dedicated time to spend with your spouse, doing what you both like to do.

Your lifestyle will change. Consider how proactive you can be about it. Remember to be flexible. Remember the person you parent this child with – please do not neglect your spouse. The baby is important and everyone else is too.

Week Thirty — Friday
Your Thoughts are Important

Your thoughts are important to God, your spouse, your family, your friends and people who care about you. Your thoughts need to be shared and your impact into decisions and conversations is very important.

Try to share with your family and your spouse. Keep the lines of communication open. One thing to remember is that you will still need and maybe crave adult conversation. When everyone calls about the baby, be sure to share that you are well and discuss your plans or other details of your life.

All nap times are not to be spent fixing bottles or cleaning. At some point each day you need to do something purely for you: read a book, paint your toes, write a poem, talk on the phone, work on your dream notebook, or plan for the next phase of your life.

Share your thoughts. Be honest about what is on your mind. Stay focused on keeping your thoughts together. It is a fact that women lose themselves in their children and then years later, they have no sense of identity. They have experienced mid-life crisis, divorces after the children leave, or other severe medical conditions.

Keep your thoughts sharp. Keep your conversation sharp. Know that your thoughts still matter and are very important to your mental health and being a great parent.

Week Thirty — Saturday
Your Feelings are Important, Too

Similar to your thoughts, your feelings are important, maybe even more so than your thoughts. Your feelings drive your thoughts. Be prepared to be honest about your feelings with yourself, your spouse, your friends, family and others.

Your feelings and emotions may become blurred or overlapped but don't submit to the notion that there is something wrong with you or that your feelings are not valid. Please share your feelings, as well as your needs with those around you. They need to know that you are well. They need to dialogue with you about what your feelings are. I do not suggest that you look to them for validation. They will not validate your feelings. They may hurt your feelings but your feelings, your needs and emotions are all valid. You need to realize that and make sure that you are not seeking the approval of others about that.

When your feelings are hard to communicate or are not being received well, may I suggest you write them down or seek counseling. Most people do not receive that well but therapy is about your health, not the perception of others. Invariably, when you go to therapy, people may distance themselves. However, when a woman murders her husband and/or children or others, then they ask why didn't you talk to us or seek therapy. It is about YOU – not anyone else.

Be wise rather than worried about others. Be true to your feelings and your gut instincts. Follow your heart. Keep an open communication line with God.

Your feelings concern God the most.

WEEK THIRTY-ONE
BIRTH & ITS COMPLEXITIES

Twenty-five weeks ago, you were celebrating and excited. Now you may still be excited but you are not addressing the actual arrival. Childbirth is a daily occurrence around the globe, whether in the plush hospital in Houston, Texas or on the red clay in a hut in a third world country. You are not likely to create any milestones but your birth experience will be special.

It is about now that you have considered a birth plan. You have heard that birth involves pain. You are sure that you want to avoid that, but I am certain that there is not a way to avoid that pain. I wish there was a way.

Now we have to deal with reality. What is the plan to handle the pain? Do you and your spouse agree? Will you need a backup plan?

During this week we will also talk about the history of childbirth pains. Birth is complex and the pain that it produces is also complex. If you haven't already gone to the class, then when you go you will contemplate several scenarios. One of those scenarios is pain medication versus none. Pain medication usually refers to the epidural, where you are administered an injection in your back near your spine. As a result you don't feel anything from the waist down until several hours later. Other medicines are administered differently and are used in different situations.

The backup plan is for when your situation changes and a different medicine may be required rather than optional. You also want to consider your pain threshold and the possible side effects. You may want to consult your physician, do some internet research and ask your family, friends and co-workers what they did about pain. Everyone deals with this and each woman may have more than one story based on the number of children she has.

Consider the following pages carefully. You are deciding on something that affects your experiences. I thought that my experiences were going to be same with both children but I was wrong. They were as different as night and day. I will never forget them nor do I regret them. I cannot possibly figure how the experience could've been different.

Sunday	Eve and the Sentence We Endure Genesis
Monday	Is Redemption Possible? Eve's Reaction to God's Sentence Genesis
Tuesday	The List They Give You at the Hospital
Wednesday	Pain Medication: The Game Plan
Thursday	My Personal Choice & Testimony for Child One
Friday	My Personal Choice & Testimony for Child Two
Saturday	What is Best for the Baby

Week Thirty-One — Sunday
Eve and the Sentence We Endure
Genesis

Eve sinned. She disobeyed God. She was the first one to sin. Because of her sin, we were promised pain during childbirth. Eve was created in the image of God from one of Adam's ribs. He created Eve as a companion and helpmate for Adam. Adam was in charge of Eve and the whole Earth and everything in it.

Eve sinned. There was no going back. There was not forgiveness without consequence. While God forgave them both, Eve earned herself and the rest of us pain during childbirth. There is no way to avoid the pain. You can get pain medication but you still know that the pain exists.

Why would God sentence us to that type of pain when she broke the rules, not us? I have several theories, one of which is we would've eventually earned it personally. I sin daily. I don't always intend to but I do. Secondly, God's instructions were simple, clear and concise. "Don't eat from the Tree of Life." Eve had other choices about what she could eat. She made a choice. God disciplines us for our good. Does this pain stop us – no, absolutely not. Is it supposed to get our attention, yes, absolutely. That pain is God's reminder that He is still God. We owe Him our obedience and attention and respect.

Eve "got us in trouble," but would we have done it on our own. He could've just disciplined Eve but Eve's offense was severe enough to deem that type of discipline.

I wonder what would have happened if Eve hadn't sinned?

Week Thirty-One — Monday
Is Redemption Possible? Eve's Reaction to God's Sentence
Genesis

Yes, Eve did. Yes, we also are disciplined for Eve's transgression. Can we ask for forgiveness for Eve and be relieved from this consequence? Sure we could ask but why would God do that now?

What did Eve do to increase God's anger? She persuaded Adam to sin with her. Don't you hate when you get into trouble but it wasn't your idea? Don't you hate it when you are disciplined because someone else's plan didn't work and you get in trouble? I didn't like that at all. I think that the person whose idea it is should be more severely punished. However in this case, God judges that impact. In Adam's case, he was in trouble because he was the leader. She got disciplined because she persuaded Adam to sin.

Eve didn't ask for forgiveness as reported by the Bible. I would've had to ask for His forgiveness. Nothing else in the Bible really accounts for what she does after that. I am certain that in some way she reconciled with God. God blessed her with children. God blessed her children's children. God continued to bless her descendants. While the Bible doesn't say that she asked, I am certain that He forgave her.

Eve had to be committed to God at this point and more focused than before. She was not prepared to face God's wrath at that level again. She grew up spiritually in that hour when she and Adam had to answer to God for their actions.

Makes me wonder how we can be better prepared for the times when God is about to increase our spirituality through our own actions.

How can we learn to accept our callings, be obedient, and take our spiritual places?

Week Thirty-One — Tuesday
The List They Give You at the Hospital

The list looks like this: I added:

mirror	massager	Bible
music	lotion	favorite scriptures
focal point		other favorite stuff
movies		
disk player		
tennis ball		
phone list		
exercise ball		
lip balm		
socks – non-slip		

Whatever I have left off the original list, I brought everything on the list inclusive of what I added. I think that them supplying a list was great and thoughtful. Having never had a baby, I appreciated the list. I brought everything on it because I didn't know which will help me have a better birth experience. Even if you don't know what to do with it or how it's going to help, bring it. It is better to have it and not need, than need it and not have it.

In short, the list is based on experience. Use this information to your advantage. If you don't understand how something could be instrumental in childbirth, ask. They will help you. Keep this list close to you in case you need to reference it for the next child as well.

Week Thirty-One — Wednesday
Pain Medication: The Game Plan

We spoke earlier about pain medication options. There are several options to consider. One is Demerol. This is a mild pain reliever. There are others along this same line. The next level up is the epidural. When pain medication is offered this is usually what is being referred to. This medication requires an anesthesiologist. There is a procedure where this medicine is placed near your spine. It prevents you from feeling anything from the waist down. After several hours it wears off and you are able to feel your faculties. Hopefully childbirth has already happened by this point.

Now, with every medication, there are possible side effects, things that could go wrong but don't. Precautionary disclosure warning against possible adverse effects for both mother and baby.

I urge you to consider carefully any decisions you make regarding medicines of any kind. Ask the questions and do the research to make the right decisions. Be educated. Be wise. Be considerate. Be knowledgeable. Be resourceful. Seek actual mothers who used what you are considering.

Don't be afraid to share you concerns with your doctor. They need to know so that you are in total agreement about what is expected and desired.

Week Thirty-One — Thursday
My Personal Choice & Testimony for Child One

In the class I always refer to, my husband and I decided to have our child by natural methods meaning: NO PAIN MEDICATION! Yes, read those words again. We had heard the concerns about the aftereffects of the medicine on the mother and the child. In addition, I had to decide that I was up for the challenge. I had to decide how much pain I could tolerate. I saw his mouth moving but at the end of the day, the 5 lb. 9 oz. infant came out my body. I really got the final say. I went for natural.

As you know, I brought everything off the list. I used the majority of the items, but especially the exercise ball. Sitting on that ball helped prepare my muscles for the birth. My doctor broke my water himself. I sat on that ball for twenty minutes and my daughter crowned. Sounds scary but not so much. I was able to get back on the table and call the doctor all before delivering my darling daughter.

I was in labor from 8:00 p.m. to 10:21 a.m. the next day. I had one dose of Demerol which helped me sleep, but was later informed that it prolongs the labor. I was dilating at a slow pace but at the time I still had the "water" so she was not motivated to come out. But about 35 minutes after he broke my "water," she was out. I was proud of my strength and my courage. We brag about this birth. We consider the entire experience a total blessing. I was grateful that she didn't come while I was on that ball. It really helped.

Week Thirty-One — Friday
My Personal Choice & Testimony for Child Two

The second birth was quite far from my wildest dreams and certainly my imagination. Again we reflected on our daughter's birth and said we would do it all again the same way. I packed that entire bag. I didn't use a single item, well maybe a few things.

My "water" broke at my sister's home, 30 minutes from the hospital. When we arrived, the baby seemed distressed. I wasn't allowed to walk as I had with our daughter. I could only lay on one side. The nurse was new. I was miserable! I couldn't use my ball. I wasn't dilating very quickly. This was a concern because of the "water" missing.

After a while of more misery, I asked to see my doctor. I called his service from my personal cell phone because they would not call for me. He was already in the hospital with other deliveries. We consulted. He offered the epidural. I refused. More misery. A few hours later, he came back and checked my progress.

The baby was presenting face first, meaning he was trying to come out with his face first rather than the head. The doctor said two words. The lights went up completely and four people walked in. They came to prepare me for the Cesarean Section and administer the anesthesia. I was completely surprised and overwhelmed and immediately cried. The doctor tried to reassure me that this was best for baby. My main concern is this baby. The anesthesia team was forced to graciously accept my husband's presence during the epidural administration.

Our son was delivered minutes later. Relief came over me. I could rest and relax.

I am proud of that birth. God really did what He does: Our baby was happy, healthy and distress free. I really am proud of his birth. I am able to share a great testimony where the outcome was better than I could've requested.

Week Thirty-One — Saturday
What is Best for the Baby

The bottom line is what is best for the baby is the <u>most</u> important person to consider. Your health is equally important but that baby is inside and we can't see if she is okay or if the umbilical cord is cutting off the circulation to some part of the body. That baby can't knock on your uterus and say help. Time is of the essence when a baby is in distress.

What is best for baby? When I was presented with the Cesarean plan, I was crushed but that was pride and ego that could be mended. If I lost that baby, then I would've had to work to be mended. Especially if it was because I refused what was best for my baby.

What is best for baby? When I was presented with the Cesarean plan, I didn't have a plan. I never considered what would happen in this situation. I was overwhelmed. I consented with a fright. My doctor stayed for what would normally be preparation time to talk to me about the rest of what this meant because he knew that this was going to make the rest go better.

What is best for baby? When I was presented the epidural portion of the Cesarean plan, I demanded my husband be there for me to lean on, rather than the staff. I needed him for support: emotionally and spiritually. They allowed him with reservation but the other problem was they had to do what was best for baby too. Time is of the essence.

What is best for baby? Do that and only that.

WEEK THIRTY-TWO
BIBLICAL PARENTS

God created and ordained parenting. God gives directives to parents about what to do, what to name, how and when to discipline and when you will be blessed with children. God chooses parents. God promised certain blessings, some are in the form of children. God gifts you to parent. God gives us the lives of several parents, whose lives have changed as parents. They are not perfect, even though they are Biblical. As parents, we all have our trials and triumphs. These parents lead the way with lessons about God's expectations. You may find yourself in these examples or someone you know. Realizing that parenthood is God ordained, and knowing that God communicated directly with these parents, there were still some obedience issues.

We are the same parents that they are: anxious, impatient, strategic and victorious. Simultaneously. Parents are driven by successful events. Those events range from successful births to academics to spiritual leadership. By Gage's definition, success is a result of being in God's will. In other words, He allowed this event to be successful so this was His will. While this may not stand the absolute test of time, I do have substantial evidence supporting my claim.

Parents make mistakes and miracles on a daily basis. When you error, forgive yourself, apologize and move forward. Do not wallow in either miracle or mistake. You cannot afford to spend time basking because you will miss the defense at the other end of the court, a basketball analogy. What happens is that we will miss some details if we are focusing that last outcome.

Be a PARENT. There are some people who have children who do not parent. Be strong, decisive, meek and humble. Parenting is hard work and requires perseverance and patience and engagement. Successful parents rely on God's wisdom, strength, guidance and His word.

Last note on parenting. Parenting is a full-time, round the clock, thankless, researching job that pays in huge smiles, laughter, colds, and love. Parenting does not stop when they leave home. Parenting stops when one of you dies, not before. Keep parenting.

Sunday	The Parent Who Laughs Genesis 21:1-7
Monday	Parent With Faith Genesis 22:1-19
Tuesday	Parenting With God's Favor Genesis 17:5-6
Wednesday	Parent With Trust Genesis 9:1, 8, 11
Thursday	Parent as Protector Genesis 21:11
Friday	Parenting Requires Resourcefulness 1 Kings 17:12-16; Matthew 14:13-21
Saturday	Parenting With Love John 3:16

271

Week Thirty-Two — Sunday
The Parent who Laughs
Genesis 21:1-7

[6]Sarah said, "God has brought me laughter, and everyone who hears about this will laugh with me."
Genesis 21:6

God was gracious and blessed Sarah with a son after she was anxious and other offenses. When God blessed her with Isaac, she laughed. God renewed her faith and hope and the ability to laugh.

God through children does renew your laughter. You will laugh at them, with them, and at yourself. It is a great time to remember to laugh. As good parents, you have to have a sense of humor.

As a parent, you have many opportunities to laugh and laugh loudly. At your children and at yourself. Laughter really increases your life span and reminds you that you are human. Life is too serious not to laugh. If you are a serious person, then this will be quite an awakening for you. Your children will say phrases that will make you laugh but could've angered you. They will do stunts that will make you throw your head back. They will influence you to enjoy life. They cause you to pause and reevaluate you priorities.

The parent who laughs enjoys successful parenthood. The parent who laughs recognizes that life is too short to be so serious. The parent who laughs has fun and shares with her children how to do the same.

The parent who laughs shares a special bond with her children. The parent who laughs will know more about her children and possesses their respect and love. Children of parents who laugh seek advice from their parents before they make a mistake because they don't feel that the judgments they would otherwise fear will come.

Parents who laugh are funner.

Week Thirty-Two — Monday
Parents with Faith
Genesis 22:1-19

[1]Some time later God tested Abraham. He said to him, "Abraham." "Here I am," he replied. [2]Then God said, "Take your son, your only son, Isaac, whom you love, and go to the region of Moriah. Sacrifice him there as a burnt offering on one of the mountains I will tell you about."

Genesis 22:1-2

Abraham has been asked to sacrifice the promise fulfilled by God, Isaac. Abraham goes without questioning God or telling Sarah. God tests his faith in God. God tests our love for Him as well. God tests our faith as well. God gifts us with children and spouses but He still wants to know that He is first as well as we still have faith and believe in Him.

Could you have been Abraham, Sarah or Mary? Sometimes I can see it. Other times I know not. As parents, our faith is tested on different levels. You send your child to school with the faith that the teachers are doing their jobs and investing in your child. You have to believe that they are safe when they are away from you. Your faith is challenged if something happens to your child.

God wants us to seek Him and have faith in Him rather than the individuals in whose care we may leave them. God expects us to trust Him rather than individuals. Faith is believing in what is hoped for without any tangible evidence. Faith is following God with obedience, not knowing or doubting the outcome. God will provide. Faith expects God to show up in your personal situation and do only what God calls: the abundant, the miraculous and the unconventional. Faith requires constant communication with God. Keeping focused on God, His word and His promises. God is truly amazing. He requires our faith in Him and His track record. Parent with faith that his plan is perfect.

Week Thirty-Two — Tuesday
Parenting with God's Favor
Genesis 17:5-6

[5]No longer will you be called Abram; your name will be Abraham for I have made you a father of many nations. [6]I will make you fruitful; I will make nations of you, and kings will come from you.

Genesis 17:5-6

Abraham had God's attention. But more importantly, God had Abraham's attention. When God called him, he answers here I am. God knows where he is and God calls him to let him know that as well. God keeps account of us and knows where we are and what we are doing.

Abraham defines the realm of God's favor: how far reaching it is and how all encompassing it is. Abraham is the example of what God will and won't do and what His will for each of us encompasses.

Parents find favor with God. Parenting moves us closer to God. You are the steward of a child's life. You need God now more than ever. You seek Him and your circumstances become more favorable. God has compassion over your situation. He opens your heart to feel some things. He opens your ears to hear Him. He opens your mind to understand more. He gifts your situation with favor when He blesses you out of the "blue."

Favor is a gift of unexpected measure when your situation needs it the most. Favor is when you have thrown up your hands finally after all of "your" solutions and efforts and you give it over to God. He fixes it within moments and you thank Him rather than saying what took You so long.

Favor is the undeserved measure of God which He gives generously because without it we would surely fail. Favor is the bridge in my life when I say that I can't but He says that I am the Great I am and can do all things.

Favor is what we receive when we give our whole selves to Him.

Week Thirty-Two — Wednesday
Parent with Trust
Genesis 9:1, 8, 11

[1]Then God blessed Noah and his sons, saying to them, "Be fruitful and increase in number and fill the earth." [8]Then God said to Noah and to his sons with him: "I establish my covenant with you: Never again will all life be cut off by the waters of a flood; never again will there be a flood to destroy the Earth."

Genesis 9:1, 8

Considering that God chose Noah and his sons to live beyond the flood, that Noah lived to be 950 years old and was 10 generations before Abraham, trust is required to parent. When allocating trust, I am referring to us trusting God and God trusting us.

What can God trust you with? His gifting you with children. He trusts you. God trusted Noah to build an ark, to gather two animals of each species and prepare to live through a flood that destroyed all the people in the world. God trusted Noah. Then God made Noah some promises.

Do we deserve His trust? Do we deserve his covenants and promises? No, we don't deserve it but he gives it us anyway. God does not owe us anything. He promised Noah that there would never be a flood of that magnitude again. Noah is not alive to hold God accountable for that. God could change his mind and probably should but doesn't.

I, on the other hand, would not want to be held at that level of accountability. God trusts me anyway. He gave me two wonderful children that He is trusting that I will do my job and do my best and seek Him in all situations. When I don't do my job, He doesn't fire me. He still trusts me. We have to do what He requires of us. We have to be trustworthy. We have to trust God, fully and completely and all the time.

Trust is hard but is required.

Week Thirty-Two — Thursday
Parent as Protector
Genesis 21:11

[11]The matter distressed Abraham greatly because it concerned his son.

Genesis 21:11

When my children are at stake, I am a different person. I am focused and driven and Abraham is a great example of a concerned parent. Abraham tried not to show favoritism between his sons but that was not possible for various reasons. At any rate, Abraham was concerned about his care.

As a parent, your child will experience misfortune, hurt, harm and danger. Your natural response is to protect your child, whether they are right or wrong. Certainly, to someone who does not parent, this may seem over the top but not so to a parent. Protecting my children is my top priority. I protect them from animals, other children, adults, and any things that hurt them or bring them harm. I defend them and fight for them. I am their number one fan and their advocate. They know that their mother is not going to let anyone mistreat them in any manner.

My daughter broke her arm when she was 5 years old. I went to pick her up right away. When I arrived to pick her up, her arm was worse than I imagined or was notified. I raced her to the doctor. She was in pain. Her pain hurt me. I called back to the school and let them know that I needed a complete report on what happened. It is my job to make sure that she receives the best of everything. In this case, she was afforded the best experience because the school nurse didn't give an accurate account of what happened.

When my children are at stake, I am a driven person and focused and resourceful. They need to know that I am their advocate. I protect them at all costs.

Abraham is a great example. Parenting requires protecting them from those that mean them harm or ill-will. Sometimes this happens in the most unlikely places. Be alert.

Week Thirty-Two — Friday
Parenting Requires Resourcefulness
1 Kings 17:12-16; Matthew 14:13-21

[14]For this is what the Lord, the God of Israel, says: 'the jar of flour will not be used and the jug of oil will not run dry until the day the Lord gives rain on the land.' [20]They all ate and were satisfied, and the disciples picked up twelve basketfuls of broken pieces that were left over.

1 Kings 17:14; Matthew 14:20

When Jesus fed the 5000 men plus women and children with five fish and two loaves, it was labeled a miracle. When we do that as a parent, we call it parenting. Any impossibility we overcome is a parenting requirement.

Parenting 36 years ago and now is very different. We have the internet and many other resources available to help our parenting efforts. However, coupled with the guidance of God and whatever tools you have, we can all be successful parents.

Great parents are resourceful. The widow had given up but God is faithful to us and sent Elijah for her to serve. While she was helping Elijah, she and her son were cared for, even to revive the son from death. The Lord provides.

The moms that I know are resourceful. We work more than one job. We research the internet for information our kids need. We clip coupons. We save money. We shop sales. We sacrifice for our children to have what we want them to have. We are resourceful. We do the creative and the imaginative so that we can give our children what they need and what we want them to have.

Resourcefulness includes career changes and budget changes. Parenting is a lifestyle change considering you have to share your life, yourself, your space and your resources with a person who comes here completely needy and naked and loveable, demanding your attention on an on-call basis. By the way, when they don't seem to need you, you find yourself staring at them while they are asleep.

Resourceful: the widow and Jesus set the example: don't give up and stay focused on the goals.

277

Week Thirty-Two — Saturday
Parenting with Love
John 3:16

[16] "For God so loved the world that He gave His one and only son, that whoever believes in Him shall not perish but have eternal life."

John 3:16

Love is a verb. Children require your time and attention. This is their measure of how much they are loved. When my daughter was two years old, she said to me to put my pen down and clap for her. She needed my time and attention. She requires my time and attention now. She knew that I loved her.

Love is a verb. Love is what you do and how you do it and when you do it. Love is keeping your promises. Love is shared and warm. I know that I am loved when my parents are concerned about me.

Love means that Abraham sent a servant to find Isaac a wife. Love means that we sacrifice our careers or lifestyle to do our best for our children.

God gave us His son. That act of unselfish love creates an unbelievable story and example of love. Consider who He chose to carry Jesus. God chose someone he could trust. Mary showed her love for Jesus by obedience to God through her care for Jesus. As you consider the love you have for your child, do you have a Mary type love? Mary witnessed her son's miracles, death, burial and resurrection. She is the "perfect" mother.

All great leaders and celebrities and activists have parents. Who will your child be? What will your child achieve? What will your child accomplish? How will you love your child? Love is a verb. How will you love your child? Will that be sufficient in meeting their needs? How will they know that you love them?

Love is a verb. What you do is heard better than the words coming out of your mouth.

WEEK THIRTY-THREE
BIBLICAL PARENTS

The hardest job you'll ever have is and it is also the most rewarding of all the jobs you'll ever have. God created parenting, all of the expectations of parenting, along with the responsibilities, rewards, privileges, pains, and sacrifices. God ordained parenthood and continues to instruct parents on how to do what He gifts us to do. God empowers us to parent through His extraordinary omnipresence, grace and forgiveness. Biblical parents make mistakes, too, and great sacrifices. Also, Biblical parents have access to the Lord's guidance and submit to His leadership. We have hardships as parents but we have victories and miracles. The book of Genesis provides countless examples of parenthood, some for us to follow and some for us to avoid. The lessons presented and learned in parenting are both subtle and obvious.

When you see your child for the very first time, you have then truly experienced God's touch and His warm embrace. I could hear His voice so much clearer when I had my daughter and He really showed up and out when I birthed my son.

Biblical parents lead their families the way God requests. Biblical parents learn and grow spiritually as parents from God, mentor parents, their children and their triumphs and mistakes.

Biblical parents seek mentorship from other Biblical parents. Biblical parents pray for their children and are committed to their spiritual growth and relationship. When I studied Catholicism, I discovered that the religion requires the parent to raise their child as a Catholic. While this may be an unspoken rule in other faiths, in Catholicism this is a rule that if not followed, there may be judgement for the parents. The point is that as Biblical parents, there should be certain commitments, practices and guidelines that we need to follow and implement in our homes and as a part of our parenting.

Biblical parenting also has standards. There is an additional level of accountability because we have access to God who has gifted us to be parents and the tools He provides. God expects us to be Biblical parents. When we have problems, we seek Him.

Sunday	Parenting as a Student Deuteronomy 4:9; Proverbs 22:6
Monday	Parenting with Conviction Psalm 51:10
Tuesday	Parenting with Commitment 1 Kings 8:61; 2 Chronicles 16:9a
Wednesday	Parenting with Wisdom Proverbs 31:26; Psalm 111:10; James 1:5
Thursday	Parenting with Pride Genesis 21:8
Friday	Parenting with Leadership Proverbs 23:13; Isaiah 11:6
Saturday	Parenting with a Legacy Genesis 17:6; Deuteronomy 4:9

279

Week Thirty-Three — Sunday
Parenting as a Student
Deuteronomy 4:9; Proverbs 22:6

[9]Only be careful, and watch yourselves closely so that you do not forget the things your eyes have seen or let them slip from your heart as long as you live. Teach them to your children and to their children after them. [6]Train up a child in the way he should go, and when he is old he will not turn from it.

Deuteronomy 4:9; Proverbs 22:6

Parenting requires you to be an avid and attentive learner. God teaches you many lessons through your children. You are not smarter than God, sometimes your child and a fifth grader. You should be available to learn. Your further growth and knowledge is one of the reasons that God gifted you to have children. When you are not flexible to learning, then your effectiveness as a parent is challenged.

The hit game show, "Are You Smarter Than a Fifth Grader?" debuted in 2007, hosting guests who try to answer questions from first to fifth grade for money. While watching this show, I have learned and been reminded of what I learned as a child. The show asks questions about spelling, culture, science, math and other topics. There are times when I know the answers and times when I consider going back to school. This is when I realize that I need to pay attention to everything that my child learns and says. They are sponges at this age. When I am paying attention, I learn a lot. I have two children so multiply that times two.

Never assume that once you have done this once, you know enough to put your parenting on autopilot. You have so much to learn about this new person, her likes, his dislikes, the different meanings of the tones of their voices, and what they like to eat.

You are like most of us, will encounter times when what you learn will overwhelm you and your spouse and your family. You will be a lifelong student of your child and parenthood. You have so much to learn and re-learn as a parent. Your child will ask you questions to which you don't have the answer. Years ago, parents had to know it all and rely on the latest version of the encyclopedia. Now, you can say let's research that on the internet and both of you can have an answer within moments.

Keep an open mind. Remember it is okay if you don't know it all. Your child will respect you more if you tell them the truth rather than making up an answer to appease them.

You are also the student. I learned the most about myself.

Week Thirty-Three — Monday
Parenting with Conviction
Psalm 51:10

[10]Create in me a pure heart, O God, and renew a steadfast spirit within me.

Psalm 51:10

Gage's definition of conviction is holding strong on the reins of what you say and do, equally for yourself and the child. Conviction is the difference between having rules versus being ruled. If you are convicted, then you are less likely to be convinced to do something contrary to that initial decision. This doesn't mean that you can't change your mind or be persuaded that there is not a better way. It does mean that you have a curfew and you hold firm to curfew no matter what other parents are doing. Conviction does mean that you use you upbringing to decide on how you will raise your child. Conviction means taking a stand for your house rules, even when your family, including your spouse, challenges your rules and tries to persuade you to relax that rule.

We have a firm car seat and seatbelt rule. I have to let my sister and father-in-law know that if they cannot follow our rules for the safety of our children then our children cannot be a passenger with them. Those words were hard to say but when I consider the possible consequences of their actions, I have to take a stand.

As you are steadfast and convicted, remember to guard their eyes. Protect them from what will damage their purity through what they see. Children see actions of others that they are never able to articulate. They are not able to get answers because they cannot explain the feelings that they felt.

The scripture speaks of the renewal process and you will need that process daily in order to remain firm in the parenting course you have chosen.

Remember your calling.

Remember your charge.

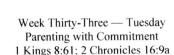

Onedia N. Gage

Week Thirty-Three — Tuesday
Parenting with Commitment
1 Kings 8:61; 2 Chronicles 16:9a

[61]But your hearts must be fully committed to the Lord our God, to live by His decrees and obey His commands, at this time. [a]For the eyes of the Lord, range throughout the earth to strengthen those whose hearts are fully committed to Him.

1 Kings 8:61; 2 Chronicles 16:9a

Commitment to God is critical. These children are not to become your replacement gods. God completely expects you to remain committed to Him as you promised you would be when you propositioned Him to give you these children.

1 Samuel 1:10-11 reads: "In bitterness of soul Hannah wept much and prayed to the Lord." And she made a vow, saying, "O Lord Almighty, if you will only look upon your servant's misery and remember me, and not forget your servant but give her a son, then I will give him to the Lord for all the days of his life, and no razor will ever be used on his head."

1 Samuel 1:20 reads: "So in the course of time Hannah conceived and gave birth to a son. She named him Samuel, saying, "Because I asked the Lord for him."

Is this your story? In some odd fashion, it is all of our stories. Each woman has her own story. Some get pregnant immediately. Others adopt. There are some women the Lord has blessed after she made some promises. If this is not your story, consider if you had been in Hannah's situation. Would this be your story? Act like it is. Keep your commitment to God. Be fully committed to God from the heart.

Because of your complete commitment to God, He will strengthen you so that you can continue to be committed to Him. Just like you, that child is on this Earth to do God's will. Your commitment to God remains critical. You are your child's example of what commitment to God looks like and means. They learn to trust, believe and commit because of what we do – what they see, not what we say.

Hannah kept her word. God blessed him to lead a nation.

Week Thirty-Three — Wednesday
Parenting with Wisdom
Proverbs 31:26; Psalm 111:10; James 1:5

[26]She speaks with wisdom, and faithful instruction is on her tongue. [10]The fear of the Lord is the beginning of wisdom;
[5]If any of you lacks wisdom, he should ask God, who gives generously to all without finding fault, and it will be given to him.

Proverbs 31:26; Psalm 111:10; James 1:5

Parenting is hard. After several years at it, I continue to ask God for wisdom at this stage. Each level and age is different and the requirements are different. The teacher will come when the student is ready.

Wisdom is more than knowledge or experience. Growth stimulates wisdom. I have some of the same knowledge I have always had but I use it differently now because of wisdom. As you look back over your life, there are different scenarios where you have made different decisions based on your knowledge, your previous experience and your mere wisdom.

Wisdom creates the opportunity for us to make a difference in the lives of our children. Wisdom is doing it differently and with better results than in previous situations. There may have been a time in your life when you said when I am a parent I will do this differently. This could be from all the candy that you could eat to a better neighborhood or a life without harm done to a child.

Wisdom occurs when we listen to God and we are in tune with the Holy Spirit. Wisdom can be requested from God. God will reveal your steps to you as you requested. Your wisdom impacts your family and their growth and their blessings. The children are blessed based on the parents' actions.

Wisdom is free. Wisdom for those smart enough to ask for it. Wisdom is for us now, not when we are old and burdened.

Ask for wisdom. Receive that wisdom. Act and speak wisely. Pass that wisdom on.

Week Thirty-Three — Thursday
Parenting with Pride
Genesis 21:8

[8]The child grew and was weaned, and on the day Isaac was weaned, Abraham held a great feast.

Genesis 21:8

Parenthood produces pride. Like it or not. Planned or surprise. Parents are proud. When the child is born, dads give away cigars and call everyone in their telephone directories, whether electronic or paper. Abraham sets the stage by hosting a feast when Isaac is weaned. We may never celebrate that publicly but we do celebrate other similar events.

Parents are proud. Check them for photos, either on paper or electronically formatted. If you ask the parent how the child is doing, the parent shares the unsolicited, yet highly attractive photographs. At some point, you will do this too. You will throw elaborate parties and events for your children. You will buy gifts they ask for but don't exactly need. You are a proud parent. But not so proud that you forget that God did this. He blessed you to conceive. He blessed you to carry the baby to term. He blessed you to have a delivery that brings Him glory. He blessed you to be the steward and guardian of His servant. He blessed you. He is proud of His creation. He is proud.

You will be proud. Remember that God doesn't need you to do what He has planned. He chose you to be the vehicle for his message.

Parenthood produces pride. Parent with pride. Be proud to parent your child. Take pride in the family's appearance. Take pride in the family's image. Be proud of what God has blessed you to do and be a part of.

Monitor your pride. Pride got Lucifer kicked out of heaven. Don't let pride influence you to do something foolish. Parenthood produces pride. Wisdom produces balance.

Week Thirty-Three — Friday
Parenting with Leadership
Proverbs 23:13; Isaiah 11:6

[13]Do not withhold discipline from a child if you punish him with the rod, he will not die. [6b]and a little child will lead them.

Proverbs 23:13; Isaiah 11:6

Leaders breed leaders. Excuse-makers breed the same. Laborers breed laborers. Big thinkers breed bigger thinkers. How do you lead a child to excellence? This is a question that many parents ask even after they have done some work.

Leaders are groomed by seeing their parents as leaders. Nannies and babysitters do not model or teach leadership. Leaders are groomed based on time spent.

Spend time with your child. Talk about life situations, sharing with her how you would handle that situation or circumstance. Your children admire you already. They already feel that you are the best parent. Honestly, they don't know any other parent so you are the best. You reinforce that "best" title by spending time and giving attention to them.

Leaders speak to children with respect and care. Leaders set the clear expectations for their lives. Leaders coach to success and does not condemn them for choices we don't agree. Coaching includes redirection, a mild tone, and a forgiving spirit.

Leaders train leadership through praise and practice. Leaders lead from the front. Leaders distinguish themselves by the work that they do which supports the words that they speak. Leadership is a decision that we make as parents. Leadership is firm and decisive. Leadership does not waiver or cause confusion.

Leadership is compassionate and kind. Leadership forces you to address your own areas of weakness and fears and areas you avoid.

Leadership produces growth. Leading a young person propels growth at a different level and introduces an increased level of accountability.

Leaders build leaders. Iron sharpens iron.

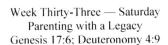

Week Thirty-Three — Saturday
Parenting with a Legacy
Genesis 17:6; Deuteronomy 4:9

[6]I will make you very fruitful; I will make nations of you, and kings will come from you.

Genesis 17:6

My personal dreams and goals leave a legacy for my children. You are holding my legacy for my children in your hand. My desire to own other businesses offers them an inheritance and a career, and preserves their lifestyle. My goals are for me but the results of that effort is the legacy I leave for them.

As I succeed, their ability to develop excuses falls away. I am the first in my family to earn a master's degree. I will be the first to aspire for a Ph.D. or other doctoral degree. I shared this with Hillary when she was five years old. She tells other people that she will earn her doctorate. A legacy is what you have done that leaves material evidence for your family. A legacy is what you expect of them. Sororities and fraternities have an unofficial legacy clause: as a member, my offspring have automatic admittance. In business it is nepotism. In life, it is called parenting.

Noah is the dad of all dads. His sons witnessed his legacy and lived his legacy and lived as a result of his legacy. Abraham entered into covenant with God. This covenant of circumcision is in effect today.

What will your legacy be? How will you manifest that legacy? What will your children do to further grow your legacy into a legacy of their own? How will it remain a family icon for hundreds of years?

God's power is strong enough to manifest such a legacy within you and your family.

What will your legacy be?

When will you start?

WEEK THIRTY FOUR
COMPLEX FAMILY DISCREPANCIES

Every family has complexities. We all have family members we are not proud of. For all applicable reasons, all family members do not get along. Families are complex entities. Members have their favorite members. The family history is sometimes sordid and often members are not completely clear about what happened at all. The Bible seems to be no different. We will discuss some families who are true leaders among their peers, but have some family issues.

Our purpose of covering them and their issues is to discuss how you and your spouse handle family issues. We are also going to investigate how certain situations could be different. We will discuss family secrets and family lies.

As the matriarch and patriarch, this is the time to break old, bad habits and create new traditions. At the same time, you can decide how family issues are handled rather than resort to the lies and the cover up. Family discrepancies are the foundation for who your child will become and how your child will handle life issues and conflict.

As we investigate the families of Abraham and Sarah, Isaac and Rebekah, Jacob, Leah and Rachel, Noah and his sons, Abraham and Keturah, and Abraham and Haggar, we will consider what they did right, wrong and how to apply these principles to our families.

Generational curses also exist and it is our job to end these curses and patterns through examples and prayer. Communication and forgiveness are keys to ending generational curses and patterns. Honesty plays a role; however, families tend not to be honest.

The most embarrassing event as an adult is being told you have additional family members and you find out from a stranger. Then when said adult asks or confronts her family she receives less than the anticipated truth from her family. The family acts as if they would never have to face these issues. The family stills try to work around the truth. Make a pact with you spouse and family to tell the truth and reveal the family secrets. Figure out how to get past the generational curses. The enemy wishes the secrets remain secrets. When the truth is revealed, the family thrives.

Sunday:	Banishing Anxiety Genesis 16
Monday:	God's Promises Are Real Genesis 17:19; 21:1-3
Tuesday:	The Promise is Fulfilled Genesis 24:4
Wednesday:	Family Traditions Enforced/A Breach of Trust Genesis 29:26-27
Thursday:	A Man of Honor Genesis 29: 28-30; 29:11
Friday:	Blended Families Genesis 25:1-11
Saturday:	Then He Trusts You & The Children He Gifts Genesis 6, 7, 8, & 9; Genesis 9: 1, 8, 11

Week Thirty-Four — Sunday
Anxiety Birthed Ishmael/Banishing Anxiety
Genesis 16

Lack of faith + your time = anxiety. Sarah used this equation to introduce anxiety in her own family history and legacy. She was in a hurry for a child defined as God's blessings. We could put our name in the blank on issues, maybe not that exact issue. I introduced anxiety about my daughter's education. The biggest mistake we make is that we want what we want when we want it. Our timing is not God's timing. Because He has the master plan and He knows the outcome of our mistakes and anxieties. He is in charge of the timing of all that we experience.

Anxiety birthed Ishmael and the after effects of that were unexpected and heart breaking. Our actions which result from anxiety lead to additional troubles. For Sarah, she didn't expect to despise Hagar. She still hadn't birthed a child at that time. Abraham had to bless his son regardless of how Sarah felt. The Lord blessed Haggar, Ishmael, Sarah, Isaac and Abraham despite how Sarah acted.

Your anxiety may not block your blessings, but your blessings may be delayed or presented differently based on your own behavior.

Prayer and supplication banishes anxiety. When you feel yourself interfering with God's work, pray. This may be hard initially, but your strength as a Christian is evident when you are able to be still and stay out of God's way.

The effects of our anxiety are far reaching. The work that God wanted to do through Abraham took a turn and possibly took longer because of the anxiety. Abraham lived with blessing Ishmail in spite of Sarah's attitude.

The anxiety that births our "Ishmail's" can be reminded by communion with God.

Week Thirty-Four — Monday
God Promised Isaac — God Promises Are Real
Genesis 17: 19; 21: 1-3

[1]Now the Lord was gracious to Sarah as he had said, and the Lord did for Sarah what he had promised. [2]Sarah became pregnant and bore a son to Abraham in his old age, at the very time God had promised him. [3]Abraham gave the name Isaac to the son Sarah bore him.

Genesis 21:1-3

When God promises anything, He delivers. Ironically, even you cannot cancel the plans God has for you that include His promises. Sarah was disappointed in the fact that she hadn't had a baby. God reminded Abraham that Sarah would parent based on the covenant they entered based on circumcision.

Isaac is born. God fulfilled His promise. Sarah realizes motherhood. Sarah is vindictive as well and has Abraham send Hager and Ishmael away.

God's promises are real. He fulfills them on His time and when He does, there should be no mistake about who gets the glory. God doesn't owe us anything further. He is not obligated to fulfill those promises. Based on our behavior, we don't deserve anything.

Isaac is blessed with nations, full blessings for his future based on God's covenant with Abraham. God also tested Abraham with Isaac asking Abraham to sacrifice Isaac. The Lord sent a ram instead. God was well pleased when Abraham didn't hesitate because of his love for God. God is first to Abraham. The ram was sacrificed. Isaac lived a long, blessed and fruitful life.

Hebrews 11: 1 reads "Now faith is the substance of things hoped for, the evidence of things not seen."Abraham's faith inspires us to move in faith rather than fear, move in faith rather than foolishness, and act based on faith, rather than actions resulting from anxiety.

You will receive based on your ability to believe. Isaac arrived as promised and received more blessings than they ever imagined.

God keeps His word. He fulfills His promises.

Week Thirty-Four — Tuesday
The Promise is Fulfilled
Genesis 24:4

[4]but will go to my country and my own relatives and get a wife for my son Isaac.

Genesis 24:4

Abraham sent his servant to find a wife for Isaac, who is to be a leader among his family and of this great nation. Isaac is living on the inheritance and legacy of his father, Abraham, who is blessed and highly favored by God. As a couple, you may want to address how you will handle their future. I tease my husband that I am seeking my son's wife. Arranged marriages are not a part of this culture now. Abraham did not want Isaac to marry a Canaanite woman, so he arranged for a wife for Isaac.

Our children are conditioned to do what they see, rather what they know, but have no evidence or experience to support. What they do based on what they have seen?

Isaac was a blessing to Abraham. Abraham was not going to jeopardize the promises of God by letting Isaac do something foolish.

This is our job as well. When God fulfills the promises, we are not to squander and/or let our children go astray. While an arranged marriage is not the answer, the proper training is the answer and is required. What are you going to do? What are your plans? What do your prayers contain?

Abraham taught Isaac to act like the promise he is and we should do the same. Isaac marries Rebekkah and they lived to see the move of God's work and His promises come to life. Could Isaac find a wife without assistance? Maybe, but would she have been exactly what God had in mind?

God is going to do what He plans in spite of ourselves. His promises are real.

Week Thirty-Four — Wednesday
Family Traditions Enforced
Genesis 29:26-27

[26]Laban replied, "It is not our custom here to give the younger daughter in marriage before the older one. [27]Finish this daughter's Bridal week; then we will give you the younger one also, in return for another seven years of work."

Genesis 29:26-27

What are your family's traditions? How are they upheld? Do they have to be enforced? Laban should've been honest initially rather than waiting until after the time Jacob already served. This exists in other families as well. How you handle it is what distinguishes your family from others.

My niece mentioned that I was getting married before my sister. I never considered this to be a problem or concern. My family has traditions and I am working hard to build our own and keep the ones we have. How do you influence your child(ren) to keep the traditions in place? They need to know what the tradition is. They need to participate in making the tradition happen. They need to be able to add something to the tradition.

Laban didn't want to dishonor his oldest daughter so he did what he thought a best for the family. Extreme? Maybe so. Parenting requires some extreme measures sometimes – nothing illegal, by any means, but extreme at the same time.

As parents we have to plan to execute family traditions to family standard. Laban suffered from lack of planning. Remember Jacob served him from for seven years for Rachel's hand. Proper planning usually prevents poor performances. Most of my family's traditions are centered around eating. Recently I have been hosting some big holidays, such as Thanksgiving and Christmas. Because I was entrusted with such holidays, I wanted to own my complete china pattern. In 2007, I completed my china pattern. When I served my 83-year old grandmother on china, I was proud to have carried out the tradition. She was proud because she has passed on the tradition in such a fashion that effort and pride went into maintaining the tradition each year.

Week Thirty-Four — Thursday
A Man of Honor
Genesis 29:11, 28-30

[11]Then Jacob kissed Rachel and began to weep aloud. [28]And Jacob did so. He finished the week with Leah, and then Laban gave him his daughter Rachel to be his wife. [29]Laban gave his servant girl Bilhah to his daughter Rachel as her maidservant. [30]Jacob lay with Rachel also, and he loved Rachel more than Leah. And he worked for Laban another seven years.

Genesis 29:11, 28-30

Jacob's passion for Rachel was clear. At their first kiss, he wept. He pledged seven years of labor for her hand in marriage. He then gave an additional seven years for her hand. Rachel meant that much to him.

Did Isaac teach Jacob how to be honorable in this manner? Did Isaac show Jacob how to be honorable in this manner? Certainly, Jacob is an honorable man. How do we as parents show our children to be honorable? Spend time with them and show and share the honorable parent you are.

Expecting them to be honorable requires accountability. We have to be honorable.

At three-years old, Nehemiah told my husband that he wanted to throw something out of the window. My husband told him no and that throwing stuff out of the window was wrong. Nehemiah told his father that he just wanted to do it one time. His father said no again. Nehemiah returned with, "Daddy, you did it one time."

He was gently reminded that they are watching his every move. When we consider what we do, we need to remember that they can see and hear what we do and say. As a responsible parent, we can no longer use our parent's old saying of, "do as I say not as I do."

Do not say anything that you would not like to come out of your baby's mouth – no matter how old. They are star reporters at an early age. They are depending on you for the difference between right and wrong. They only know what you show them and tell them. Your actions as a parent must be distinguishable as different from those of the world.

Honorable is both learned through listening, seeing, and experience. This learning occurs from several stages of life and of course over time. Remember exactly how you decide you would parent is how your child decides they will or will not parent.

Honor is a choice.

Week Thirty-Four — Friday
(With No Strings Attached) Blended Families
Genesis 25: 1-11

[1]Abraham took another wife, whose name was Keturah. [2]She bore hime Zimran, Joksan, Medan, Midian, Ishbak, and Shuah. [3]Jokshan was the father of Dedan; the descendants of Dedan were the Asshurities, the Letushities and the Leummites. [4]The sons of Midian were Ephan, Epher, Hanoch, Abida and Eldaah. All these were descendants of Keturah. [5]Abraham left everything he owned to Isaac. [6]But when he was still living, he gave gifts to the sons of his concubines and sent them away from his son Isaac to the land of the east. [7]Altogether , Abraham lived a hundred and seventy-five years. [8]Then Abraham breathed his last and dies at a good old age, an old man and full of years; and he was gathered to his people. [9]His sons Isaac and Ishmeal buried him in the cave of Machpelah near Mamre, in the field of Ephron of Zohar the Hittite, [10]the field Araham had bought from Hittities. There Abraham was buried with his wife Sarah. [11]After Abraham's death, God blessed his son Isaac, who then lived near Beer Luhai Roi.

Genesis 25: 1-11

Abraham remarries. Abraham and Keturah have more children. Abraham further extended his blended family. How do you manage blended family? How do you manage extended family? Abraham managed pretty well. He gifted parts of his estate to his additional children, including Ishmael. When Abraham died, Isaac inherited Abraham's entire estate.

One of my friends has a blended family. Each member of the family presents a different level of difficulty when dealing with the family differences. The add-on effects of natural family plus blended family add some additional pressure on the couple and their marriage.

If you are a blended family, I suggest that you and your spouse develop some additional ground rules relative specifically to the children and their respective other parents. Such rules would include communicating with the new couple appropriately, respect for the other spouse, the other parent(s) following the house rules of the couple, and other rules which would not add pressure to the marriage or interfere with the upbringing of the children.

Agreeing on how the children should be raised introduces lots of conversation for new couples, but it has an extra level of concern when additional parents are involved.

As a blended family, family meetings are a great way to hear all views and reach a consensus on how to raise the children of blended family. Family meetings also facilitate communication and create livable circumstances that make life easier. In this case the children are the most important people.

293

Week Thirty-Four — Saturday
When He Trusts You and The Children He Gifts
Genesis 9: 1, 8, 11

[1]Then God blessed Noah and his sons, saying to them, "Be fruitful and increase in number and fill the earth. [8]Then God said to Noah and to his sons with him. [11]I establish my covenant with you: Never again will all life be cut off by the waters of a flood; never again will there be a flood to destroy the earth.

Genesis 9: 1, 8, 11

Noah was a righteous man as defined by God, the ultimate authority on righteousness. This is a high title for anyone so when God told Noah to build an Ark. God entrusted Noah to take his family and two of each animal on this ark because God would be making s flood soon. God had it rain for 40 days: God also explained to Noah how upset He was with the world because of their sins and lack of respect for God. God trusted Noah and his family. God trusted Noah to build the ark, care for his family and the animals, then to repopulate the earth.

Can I be trusted with that love and responsibility? Can you be trusted with the plans God has for you? Can we be trusted with the responsibility God gives us? God knows who can be trusted with what He has planned for us. When He gives us an assignment, we have already demonstrated our trustworthiness. He just waits on our obedience and completion of our assignments. When we complete this assignment, then He receives the praise, honor and glory.

The second most important after God's trust for Noah is that because of Noah's righteousness, his sons reaped the benefit and the heavenly legacy God had reserved for them. Noah's sons saw God's awesome promises fulfilled through their father. When you as a parent are successful and you children know that your success is a blessing from God, they will be influenced to believe more deeply in God because they will seek a more intimate relationship with God. Noah's boys grew spiritually by leaps and bounds because they experienced their father's exercise of faith. Because of their father's legacy, their testimonies were also made great.

How will your legacy and testimony influence your child?

WEEK THIRTY-FIVE
CHILDREN OF THE BIBLE

When you read about children, your reality is surreal. Each person came from a woman – a parent. As a parent, we cannot possibly imagine or plan all the things that your child will see, accomplish or achieve in their lifetime. You have no idea if your child will be the 55th President of the United States or a teacher or travel with Cirque de Soliel. Our children are exceptional creatures who are blessed by God based on what He has planned for them as well as how He blessed them based on the promises He has made to us as parents. Similar to the covenant God made with Abraham, God has a covenant with us as parents.

The children of the Bible we will discuss this week are extraordinary and resilient and unbelievable. These children are exactly how our children are. Our children are extraordinary who are made by God and will do what He says, and no, it won't make since to you sometimes. Our children are resilient. They rise above the "stuff" which sinks us and stifles us and stalls us and stops us. They don't respond like us. They do not quit. They are creative when seeking solutions. Our children are unbelievable. They do things we won't do and sometimes hoped that they would never do. They do what they want to do. They do the socially questionable. They are inquisitive. They are thoughtful. They believe. They have faith. They are our children.

Children teach us life lessons. They teach us those lessons we have forgotten, ignored, avoided, and missed. They remind us to live breath, and laugh. They teach us to laugh at ourselves, to clap at the really important time – times that happen daily. They remind us to live in the moment.

Children are a mirror of us, if only we had the courage to do what we are truly called to do.

We will discuss Joseph, his brothers, Cain, Able, Ruth, the Prodigal Son, his brother, and his father and how to parent these children. We are encouraged by their stories to remain focused as parents, to continue to seek God's face for our lives and our children's lives, to remember we are stewards of their lives – God is really the author of their stories. We are their Earthly guidance. God is their heavenly Father.

Sunday:	The Whole Story Revealed: Joseph Chosen Genesis 37: 28, 36; 45: 3-9
Monday:	If You Could, Would You Change Your Mind? Genesis 37: 3-5, 8, 11, 31-36
Tuesday:	Jealousy to the Highest Power Genesis 4: 1-16
Wednesday:	Where You Go, I will Go Ruth
Thursday:	A Model Father: A True Role Model Luke 15: 11, 20b, 22-24, 31-32
Friday:	Wisdom Develops Over Time Luke 15: 12-20a, 21
Saturday:	Can't See the Forest Because of the Trees Luke 15: 25-30

Week Thirty-Five — Sunday
The Whole Story Revealed: Joseph Chosen
Genesis 37:3, 36; 45: 3-9

[3]Now Israel loved Joseph more than any of his other sons, because he had been born to him in his old age; and he made a richly ornamented robe for him. [36]Meanwhile, the Midianites sold Joseph in Egypt to Potiphar, one of Pharaoh's officials, the captain of the guard. [3]Joseph said to his brothers, "I am Joseph! Is my father still living?" But his brothers were not able to answer him because they were terrified at his presence. [4]Then Joseph said to his brothers, "Come close to me." When they had done so, he said, "I am your brother Joseph, the one you sold into Egypt!" [5]And now, do not be distressed and do not be angry with yourself for selling me here, because I was to save lives that God sent me ahead of you. [6]For two years now there has been famine in the land, and for the next five years there will not be plowing and reaping. 7But God sent me ahead of you to preserve for you a remnant on earth and to save your lives by great deliverance. [8]"So then, it was not you who sent me here, but God. He made me father to Pharaoh, lord of his entire household and ruler of all Egypt. [9]Now hurry back to my father and say to him, "This is what your son Joseph says: God has made me lord of all Egypt. Come down to me; don't delay.

Genesis 37:3, 36; 45: 3-9

As a child, I reflect on the harm God kept me from and the success He blessed me with, I know Joseph's story. Do you know Joseph's Story? How does that relate to your story? As a parent, we want the best for our children. As a parent, you dread part one of Joseph's story but consider the outcome of Joseph's testimony.

Joseph's attitude is awesome. During this time, Joseph experiences God's hand with great affection. Joseph is sold by his own brothers then becomes a King in the position to save his family from famine. He matures as a man and a Christian. He is truly a vessel for God. He knows and delivers the distinction of love as a leader.

Compare Joseph's story to how we may have handled it. Not the same results. How would we have acted toward the brothers who sold us and the father who never looked for us? We would not have responded the same. Joseph never asked them for anything. He embraced them as if nothing ever happened. Consider the milestone that maybe accomplished in that same fashion for our children.

Joseph profoundly announces that this was God's plan. Joseph credited his whole life and all the experience to God and to his brothers. His spiritual maturity is remarkable. This spiritual maturity is so profound that he realized all the dreams that God gave him became true. He shared the dreams with his brothers because of love for them but also spiritual immaturity. When the dreams came true and he realized leadership by God's plan and ordination, Joseph had achieved his calling. Children do eventually reach the level God desired for them. That requires our prayer, love, time and attention for each of our children. Our children may not accomplish the "things" that we have dreamed for them, but they will do what God has desired for them. None of us can stand in the way of what God as planned for us.

Joseph is the outstanding example for that. What the devil intended for Joseph's desires worked into God's plan for Joseph's prosperity.

I failed to mention that this all started with Joseph talking and because Joseph was his daddy's favorite and he was blessed and highly favored by God.

Week Thirty-Five — Monday
If You Could, Would You Change Your Mind?
Genesis 37: 3-5, 8, 11, 31-36

[3]Now Israel loved Joseph more than any other sons because he had been born to him in his old age; and he made a richly ornamented robe for him. [4]When his brothers saw that their father loved him more than any of them, they hated him and could not speak a kind word to him. [5]Joseph had a dream, and when he told it to his brothers, they hated him all the more. [8]His brothers said to him, "Do you intend to reign over us? Will you actually rule us? And they hated him all the more because of his dreams and what he had said. His brothers were jealous of him but his father kept the matter in mind. [31]Then they got Joseph's robe, slaughtered a goat and dipped the robe in the blood. [32]They took the ornamented robe back to their father and said, "We found this. Examine it to see whether it is your son's robe." [33]He recognized it and said, "It is my son's robe! Some ferocious animal has devoured him. Joseph has surely been torn to pieces." [34]Then Jacob tore his clothes, put on sackcloth and mourned for his son many days. [35]All his sons and daughters came to comfort him, but he refused to be comforted. "No," he said, "in the morning will I go down to the grave to my son." So his father wept for him. [36]Meanwhile, the Midianites sold Joseph in Egypt to Potiphar, one of Pharaoh's officials, the captain of the guard.

Genesis 37: 3-5, 8, 11, 31-36

Joseph's brothers did a horrible act to him. And why? Jealousy took over and tried to sabotage God's plan. Joseph's brothers had a chance to be reconciled to the father but never did. Joseph's brothers could've accepted whatever he said and continued with their business. They are great examples if what hatred and jealousy will do to a family. Likewise, they are even greater examples if the reaping and sowing principles. As well because they treated him so badly, God put them in a position to need him. Hypothetically speaking if you were Joseph's sibling, would you change your behavior before you know the actual outcome? Not many people can say they would.

As a parent, I find myself monitoring the behavior between my children. I tell them that they need to treat each other kindly and with love. I recently reminded them that they only have each other. They need to depend on each other, not fight each other and confide in one another. I feel that need an interdependent relationship. I also do not show favoritism or compare them to one another. The favoritism is harmful to the spirit if the child who is not favored; the essence of that spirit can never be completely recovered. The comparison also shows that one is better than the other. The comparison also does not value the talents of the other child. These are ways that can build a great relationship with your children.

As a parent, we never know what we will face. I respect the way Joseph's dad handled the event. However, he didn't seem to see what he did to strain the relationship.

As a parent, we endure many tests and trials but we have to give our 110% each time. I find that there are times when I don't feel like it but I try in spite of to give them my 110%. They need my 110% because I am their source for information, love, respect, and most of the life lessons they need.

Week Thirty-Five — Tuesday
Jealousy To The Highest Power
Genesis 4: 1-16

[1]Adam lay with his wife Eve, and she became pregnant and gave birth to Cain. She said, "With the help of the Lord I have brought forth a man." [2]Later she gave birth to his brother Abel. Now Abel kept flocks, and Cain worked the soil. [3]In the course of time Cain brought some of he fruits of the soil as an offering to the Lord. [4]But Abel brought fat portions from some of the firstborn of his flock. The Lord looked with favor on Abel and his offering, [5]but on Cain and his offering he did not look with favor. So Cain was very angry, and his face was downcast. [6]Then the Lord said to Cain, "Why are you angry? Why is your face downcast? [7]If you do what is right will you not be accepted? But if you do not do what is right, sin is crouching at your door; it desires to have you, but you must master it." [8]Now Cain said to his brother Abel, "Let's go out to the field." And while they were in the field, Cain attacked his brother Abel and killed him. [9]Then the Lord said to Cain, "Where is your brother Abel?" "I don't know," he replied. "Am I my brothers Keeper?" [10]The Lord said, "hat you have done? Listen! You brother's blood cries out to me from the ground. [11]Now you are under a curse and driven from the ground, which opened its mouth to receive your brother's blood from your hand. [12]When you work the ground, it will no longer yield its crops for you. You will be a restless wanderer on the earth. [13]Cain said to the Lord, "My punishment is more than I can bear. [14]Today you are driving me from the land, and I will be hidden from your presence, I will be a restless wanderer on the earth, and whoever finds me will kill me." [15]But the Lord said to him, "Not so, if anyone kills Cain, he will suffer vengeance seven times over." Then the Lord put a mark on Cain so that no one who found him would kill him. [16]So Cain went out from the Lord's presence and lived in the land of Nod, east of Eden.

Genesis 4: 1-16

The story of Cain and Abel has been told over and over. Usually feelings of anger and fear follow the hearing of that story. Consider your own attitude and feelings – of you feeling unwanted and second, you are capable of exactly the same actions. When God told him that his brother's blood was calling him from the ground, he was devastated.

We as humans think that we are above the jealousy that influences us to bring harm to another individual. This however is very far from the truth. There are cases daily of death and injury. But more personally is hurting each other's feelings. This is done by attacking the character of another through our words and deeds and intentions.

Jealousy is a deep emotion that presents itself the most interesting times, when one least expects it. Teaching children how to address jealousy is a lesson that will repeatedly need reinforcing based on the new environments that she will experience during her lifetime. Parents manage sibling rivalry. Parents control the nature of the relationship between siblings by how the parents teach them to relate and hold them accountable for their relationship. When we manage jealously properly as a child, we manage it as adults when issues present themselves.

"Keeping up with the Jones'" is a cliché that is articulated, however still holds validity in that people still compare themselves and their assets to others. "Trying to do better than the Jones'" seems to be the new cliché. Families are trying to out do one another? Is anyone trying to compete about healthy relationships and happy children and healthy bodies? Not so much. Be the Jones' with a healthy body, relationship and children. Jealousy can be controlled with the appropriate attitude and perspective. Accentuating your own assets and talents should occupy all of your time and leave no time for jealousy or the reaction that jealousy yields.

Prohibiting this behavior for our children is critical for their growth and development.

Week Thirty-Five — Wednesday
Where You Go, I Will Go
Ruth 1: 16

[16]But Ruth replied, "Don't urge me to leave you or to turn back from you. Where you go I will go, and where you stay I will stay. Your people will be my people and your God my God.

Ruth 1:16

Wisdom is not easily shared. The Bible says that if you ask for wisdom, God will give you wisdom. Naomi had wisdom. Ruth is also wise. Naomi lost her husband and her two sons and was left with two daughters-in-law. Naomi wanted to send them both back to their families after her sons died. Ruth told her they weren't going back home. Instead, Ruth opted to stay with Naomi. Ruth insisted that she would follow Naomi wherever she went.

Naomi conceded and let Ruth stay. Naomi could not sink into the depression she had planned and anticipated. Ruth forces Naomi to address her needs as well as Ruth's. They journey together from Moab to Bethlehem. When they arrive to Bethlehem, they met Boaz. Naomi advised Ruth on how to get Boaz's attention. Boaz wanted her and made provisions for her care while she was in the fields gathering. Eventually Ruth and Boaz were together. Ruth's wisdom gained the trust and respect of Naomi. Boaz was attracted to Ruth's wisdom as well.

Wisdom births compassion and love and awareness. When we share our lives and our time with our children, they grow. When we share our lives and our time with our children, we grow. Ruth renewed Naomi's hope while Naomi imparted wisdom. We have a song that we sing that states, "I love you, I love you, I love you and where you go I'll follow. I will follow you wherever you may go." Ruth stated these words to Naomi. We say this to each other as a family.

Ruth recognized wisdom in Naomi and recognized that they needed each other. Ruth gained a husband and maintained a mother-in-law.

Our daughters and sons may have a Ruth and Boaz experience. We focus on their surroundings and are in tune to the Holy Spirit for guidance for them.

Be prepared to tell your children the truth. Be willing to help them with their issues and needs. Be honest with yourself about your past and how it relates to their future.

299

Week Thirty-Five — Thursday
A Model Father: A True Role Model
Luke 15: 11, 20b, 22-24, 31-32

[11]Jesus continued: "There was a man who had two sons." [20b]But while he was still a long way of, his father saw him and was filled with compassion for him; he ran to his son, threw his arms around him and kissed him. [22]"But the father said to the servants, 'Quick! Bring the best robe and put it on him. Put a ring on his finger and sandals on his feet. [23]Bring the fattened calf and kill it. Let's have a feast and celebrate. [24]For this son of mine was dead and is alive again; he was lost and is found.' So the began to celebrate." [31]"My son,' the father said, 'you are always with me, and everything I have is yours. [32]But we have to celebrate and be glad, because this brother of yours was dead and is alive again; he was lost and is found"

Luke 15: 11, 20B, 22-24, 31-32

The story of the lost or prodigal son is the parable where one son asks for his portion of his father's inheritance, then leaves, squanders the inheritance and returns home.

Dad is the role model. Before you say what you would do, let's look at what this dad did.

Dad had an inheritance to give his sons. He was prepared to give his sons his residual wealth. He worked so that they were able to reap the financial benefit of his labor. When we consider our lives, how will we live in our latter days? Will we take care of ourselves or will our children take care of us because we didn't prepare? Are we savers or spenders? Do we have enough planned for retirement? Do we have a college plan? Dad was a financial role model. He encouraged working, saving and planning.

Dad gave him the portion of the inheritance and was okay. He shared his wealth and wisdom. He didn't argue with his son. He gave him some money and sent him on his way. The father never said a bad word. He never spoke unkindly about the son. He kept working, saving, planning, and living. He never worried. He kept nurturing his older son. He kept sharing his wisdom. The older son kept focused on his father's teaching, becoming wiser. Dad taught him to let God retain control, to keep focus on your goals and work while you wait. Another lesson he shares with us is to relish in God's peace. God provides him a peace that has the option to use rather than an obligation. We worry because we don't access His peace.

The other lesson that dad lends is forgiveness, love and joy. He received his son from a long way off. He started the process a long time before the son arrived. He was excited upon sight of the son. He rallied the others around him as well. Then he ordered them to shower him with gifts: a robe and jewelry. The Dad was compassionate, forgiving, loving, and welcoming. Dad did not shut him out. He treated his sons with dignity. He received him as God receives us.

Week Thirty-Five — Friday
Wisdom Develops Over Time
Luke 15: 12-20a, 21

[12]The younger said to his father, 'Father, give me my share of the estate.' So he divided his property between them. [13]"Not long after that, the younger son got together all he had, set off for a distant country and there squandered his wealth in wild living. [14]After he had spent everything, there was a severe famine in that whole country, and he began to be in need. [15]So he went and hired himself out to a citizen of that country, who sent him to his fields to feed pigs. [16]He longed to fill his stomach with the pods that the pigs were eating, but no one gave him anything. [17]When he came to his senses, he said, 'How many of my father's hired men have food to spare, and here I am starving to death! [18]I will set out and go back to my father and say to him: Father, I have sinned against heaven and against you. [19]I am no longer worthy to be called your son; make me like one of your hired men.' [20a]So he got up and went to his father. [21]"The son said to him, 'Father, I have sinned against heaven and against you. I am no longer worthy to be called your son.'

Luke 15: 12-20a, 21

If my son tells me that he needs his inheritance and that he will be leaving, I am sure that laughter will be inevitable. First of all I, I would have to have an inheritance to give him in order for this to be a viable option. After the laughter, I then would be asking what will he be using the funds for then I would like to know where he is going. After all of that, I probably would be saying, "No!"

I am in fact not that parent and many of us are not. However, this man is the parent who is sharing his wisdom about what to do when your child behaves out of character. All of us will experience this "out of character" experience at least once. So what does a wise parent do?

This parent gave him a portion of his estate and sent him happily on his way. The dad did not worry or fret or express fear. The parent did not seem angry or concerned. Why was this? Does God's wisdom offer the opportunity to do this and move on with life, as we know it? Never miss the inheritance? Never grieved the absence?

Is it God's grace that keeps us as parents when our children venture to unsafe territories and foreign lands where hurt, harm and danger can overcome them? Does God only trust the parents who can place this situation in his hand and it does not seem like he ever shed a tear? Does the wisdom that is required get fully exercised leading up to this point? So then the son comes back, the parent is wiser than I, accepts the son back without question. The dad hosted a party for the son, brought him a robe and restored him to son "status" immediately although the son returned to work as a servant.

Wisdom is key to parenting. If we ask then He said He would give wisdom to each of us. Finally, the father was thankful that wisdom developed in his son. Wise enough to return to the teaching they know.

Week Thirty-Five — Saturday
Can's See the Forest Because of the Trees
Luke 15: 25-30

[25]"Meanwhile, the older son was in the field. When he came near the house, he heard music and dancing. [26]So he called one of his servants and asked him what was going on. [27]'Your brother has come,' he replied. 'and your father has killed the fattened calf because he has him back safe and sound.'" [28]The older became angry and refused to go in. So his father went out and pleaded with him. [29]But he answered his father, 'Look! All these years I've been slaving for you and never disobeyed your orders. Yet you never gave me even a young goat so I could celebrate with my friends. [30]But when this son of yours who has squandered your property with prostitutes comes home, you kill a fattened calf for him!

Luke 15: 25-30

The son who stayed with his dad was offended that his dad treated his brother just like he never left home. The son was angry. He addresses his father and learned a valuable lesson.

The son is not impacted by the brother's return. The son has lost nothing by his brother's return. Siblings feel this way. The older son is jealous of the younger one because he didn't think of leaving (based on his understanding of the upbringing), he doesn't feel confident enough to leave, (was that an option), and he didn't expect his brother's return or his father's excitement upon the return.

Instead of being excited about his brother's safe return, he is upset about what the brother deserves versus what he deserves. He lets this interrupt his blessing. The brother safely returns. That is the blessing.

Everything else is inconsequential. We as humans are subject to these same feelings. As a parent, we need to manage ourselves. As a parent, we lead our children. We do not know what actually happen between the father and the son who stayed but it doesn't mean that they discussed the son's departure. I decided they didn't talk about it because when the prodigal son returned, the son was surprised at the dad's reaction.

As a parent we have time and the opportunity to lead, educate, and share with our children all that we need and want them to know. We sometimes miss this opportunity to share and we still expect the same results as if we spoke to them. The son missed the whole picture because he was focused on the division of assets or something else inconsequential. As we parent we need to share with them how to be optimistic and to get excited about a blessing.

I had a poem as a child about a child learning based on what they see and experience. If you want a child to have faith, show love and not complaining, they have to be exposed to faith, love and optimism and positive thinking.

There are incredible responsibilities for parents. There is a race to educate and train great children. How do these parents do it? As a parent trying to parent great children, we will discuss some great children and the parents of those great children. What are the qualities of the parents and children who are great? How do you groom a President, a leader, a motivator, an anointed one and a history maker? Consider the life and lifestyle of the family who the President of the United States. Consider the life and lifestyle of leaders who create other leaders. Consider the life and lifestyle of families who are not leaders who create leaders.

At first consideration the characteristics includes integrity, honor, honesty, respect, discipline, work ethic, self-control, and leadership. The most important consideration is God is the key factor in each life. Other considerations include motivation, desire, and goal driven.

Quite important is love for your child regardless of what they become. Children spell love: TIME. Try to avoid the myth of purchase power. I substituted in two schools a few years ago and the students were different socio-economically, but they were the same academically. One group didn't drive cars to school. The other group drove Hummers and BMW's and other luxury vehicles to school. The problem is that they want their parent's time rather than the stuff the parents provide.

What kind of time do these "great" parents spend with their parents? What kinds of activities do these families do together? What kind of student do they need to be to be considered "great"? Did they make conscious decisions about avoiding drugs, alcohol, pregnancy, and other distractions as a teen so that they could be great? Do they understand how to avoid events that they will regret later?

As a final note, even when a child or parent does something that may challenge their potential greatness there is still an opportunity to keep the greatness course. Some of my hero's have bad incidents and they still have reached greatness. While the media may not forgive and some family may delay their forgiveness, but God forgives upon request all the time.

Sunday:	Jesse: the Father of David 1 Samuel 16: 11
Monday:	David 1 Samuel 16: 7, 12-13
Tuesday:	Elizabeth and Zechariah Luke 1: 5-25
Wednesday:	John the Baptist Luke 1: 66, 76-80
Thursday:	Mary and Joseph Luke 1: 26-38
Friday:	Jesus Luke 2: 42-43, 49-52
Saturday:	Paul Acts 9

303

Week Thirty-Six — Sunday
Jesse: The Father of David
1 Samuel 16: 11

[11]So he asked Jesse, "Are these all the sons you have?" "There is still the youngest," Jesse answered, "but he is tending the sheep." Samuel said, "Send for him; we will not sit down until he arrives."

1 Samuel 16: 11

When Samuel visits Jesse, this is an awesome event in his life. Jesse's son is about to be anointed by God to be King. How does that make Jesse feel? How would that make you feel as a parent?

This could be considered the report card: parent and spiritually. Imagine what it's like to be the parent of someone who is considered great and historically popular; a profound leader. What kind of parenting is required to parent with that stature? While the Bible doesn't explicitly describe that parent, there are references to that parent in several places in the Bible.

Looking at Jesse's demeanor, I consider Jesse as meek, mild, leader, and visionary. Jesse passed these characteristics onto David. Jesse demonstrates meekness, care, concern, and leadership to his sons through their work in the fields and at home.

Consider how Jesse addresses Samuel. Read 1 Samuel 16: 1-13. Jesse is also patient and humble. Jesse passes these characteristics onto his sons. David has the benefit of his dad and his brother's experience to make his decisions. Jesse has to be focused on God and the spirit of God so that he can be in tune to what God needs. As Jesse does this, he models for his eight sons God's expectations of a man chosen by God.

Perseverance is required to great parenting of great individuals. What an awesome call on your life: to be the parent of the next President of the United States or the next teacher of the year or the scientist who discovers a cure for cancer or the police officer who stops hundreds of people from being massacred or the poet laureate or the Nobel Peace Prize winner or the National Child Advocate. Behave as a parent of someone great because your child is great. Your child has the same greatness potential based on what we do as patents, no matter what the socio-economic status is.

Be a great parent. Raise great children.

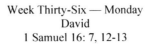

Week Thirty-Six — Monday
David
1 Samuel 16: 7, 12-13

[7]"But the Lord said to Samuel, "Do no consider his appearance or his eight for I have rejected him. The Lord does not look at the things man look at. Man looks at the outward appearance, but the Lord looks at the heart." [12b]Then the Lord said, "Rise and anoint him; he is the one."

1 Samuel 16: 7, 12b

David was selected to be King. Anointed by God as King is an awesome assignment. David has been called a man after God's own heart. David truly has a heart for God. Why would God choose a child? God shares with Samuel that He considers the heart of a man.

God selects youngest of eight to serve as King. God picks David because He knows He can trust David. My question is how did David earn the name man after God's own heart: compassion, love, diligence, perseverance, forgiveness, and honesty. David exhibited these characteristics through deeds and actions and attitudes.

BUT DAVID SINNED. Yes, he did but he is honest and asks for forgiveness and is obedient to God's command for restoration.

In all of David's accomplishments, David acknowledges and seeks God for guidance. David is truly submitted to God. When we serve God, this is His expectation. Further, David is eager to please God. David tries to reject his fleshly desires and submit to God's will as often as possible.

David is the definition of what God will do when we are humbly submitted. David's lineage creates Jesus. This is certainly a connection to greatness. Who will out lineage birth? This is a hard question to answer but completely worth preparing for.

Jesse used some basic principles to prepare David for greatness. The list while not comprehensive, certainly in order of priority includes discipline, wisdom, compassion and faith.

David demonstrated that he was excellent shepherd by keeping close watch over all of his flock. He had complete understanding of his role by not losing any sheep, but instead by searching for the lost one. David was comfortable with who God called him to be by knowing slaying Goliath was a job he could do but with Gods guidance and faith rejecting Saul's armor and other equipment.

David mentioned in his role even when pushed and tempted to do otherwise. David did what God called him to do even when his own brothers ridiculed him. David knew to seek wise counsel from his father.

Week Thirty-Six — Tuesday
Elizabeth and Zechariah
Luke 1: 5-25

[11]Then an angel of the Lord appeared to him, standing at the right side of the altar of incense. [12]When Zechariah saw him, he was startled and was gripped with fear. [13]But the angel said to him: "Do not be afraid, Zechariah; your prayer has been heard. Your wife Elizabeth will bear you a son, and you are to give him the name John. [14]He will be a joy and delight to you, and many will rejoice because if his birth, [15]for he will be great in the sight of the Lord. He is never to take wine or other fermented drink, and he will be filled with the Holy Spirit even from birth. [16]Many if the people of Israel will he bring back to the Lord their God. [17]And he will go on before the Lord, in the spirit and power of Elijah, to turn the hearts of the fathers to their children and the disobedient to the wisdom of the righteous – to make ready a people prepared for the Lord." [18]Zechariah asked the angel, "How can I be sure of this? I am an old man and my wife is well along in years." [19]The angel answered, "I am Gabriel, I stand in the presence of God, and I have been sent to speak to you and to tell you this good news. [20]And now you will come true at their proper time." [21]Meanwhile, the people were waiting for Zechariah and wondering why he stayed so long in the temple. [22]When he came out, he could not speak to them. They realized he had seen a vision in the temple, for he kept making signs to them but remained unable to speak. [23]When his time of service was completed he returned home. [24]After his wife Elizabeth became pregnant and for five months remained in seclusion. [25]"The Lord has done this for me," she said. "In these days he has shown his favor and taken away my disgrace among the people."

Luke 1:11-25

Elizabeth had been barren and her husband, Zechariah, was told that she would birth a child to be called John. Zechariah did not believe the angel who visited him so he was made unable to speak until the birth of the baby. God chose Elizabeth and Zechariah to birth greatness. The angel told Zechariah all that would be expected of John and what would contribute to the Christian faith.

What if you knew what God has planned for your child? How would you behave? Would you only expose the child to activities related to God's plan? The angel visited Zechariah explained John, "will be great in the sight of the Lord" (v. 15). We are not quite that fortunate. When God showed me Nehemiah's name I was not clear about exactly what He had planned for him.

In response to those questions, I would exercise tunnel vision about his upbringing since I knew exactly what He had planned. Let's examine "tunnel-vision parenting." It is not an official parenting style or a Biblical term, but I'll assume the responsibility for the concept. Gage defines "tunnel-vision parenting" as parenting with God as the sole focus and the sole purpose. I do believe that this God-centered parenting style is what God has in mind for us. This is a positive parenting focus that can be used when God did not send the angel to tell you exactly what He has planned.

The additional lesson is when the angel visits you, believe what the angel says. In order to be the parents of someone great, God has to trust you. God trusted Elizabeth and Zechariah. Even though Zechariah originally questioned God's ability to transform a barren woman to fertile one, God still trusted them to parent John in such a manner God had planned. How can we use their example to parent great?

306

Week Thirty-Six — Wednesday
John the Baptist
Luke 1:66, 76-80

[76]And you, my child, will be called a prophet of the Most High; for you will go on before the Lord to prepare the way for Him

Luke 1:76

John, you will prepare the way for Jesus Christ. What a job; what an awesome responsibility and calling on your life. God trusted John to share salvation with a land that had no idea how their lives were about to change. John was born filled with the Holy Spirit. Even when he was in the womb, he leaped for joy (Luke 1:44). God is in the details. Only God could time the pregnancies, births and circumstances, and Zechariah's silence to show that He is God and capable of everything He desires.

John stayed in the desert after birth and was presented in public during the fifteenth year of Tiberius Caesar's reign. Isaiah foretold of his birth and role. Now as this becomes flesh, John is preaching, baptizing and sharing Jesus' coming. John is aware that Jesus is also being prepared to preach and save lives. John baptized Jesus.

John was born of the Holy Spirit which is accompanied by wisdom and knowledge. John's parents are wise and spirit filled as well. Zechariah, while initially questioning the possibility, used his several silent months prior to John's birth as time to become closer to God while preparing for his son.

John had an audience to minister. He reached several hundred souls with his message as well as baptizing them. As he is delivering his message, he rebukes the evil governor, Herod, and is put in prison. Jailed for Jesus—the first of many.

Are we willing to be John—modern day with no modifications? Are we willing to be the parents of John? When we consider John's role and responsibilities, it is no small feat to accomplish in light of what John achieved. John as a disciple and paid the ultimate cost with his life (Matthew 14:1-2).

John the Baptist was a pioneer for Jesus. John the Baptist was not a disciple. Because John was in prison, he didn't get to minister with Jesus as one might have thought.

When God hands out an assignment, He creates the entire activity especially the outcome.

Week Thirty-Six — Thursday
Mary and Joseph
Luke 1:26-38

[37]For nothing is impossible with God.

Luke 1:37

God is the definition of perfect timing. Here is a young couple who are about to be married. Mary is a virgin. Joseph is also honorable. Two model citizens. An angel visits Joseph and tells him that Mary is with child and they have never had intercourse. Joseph was prepared to put her away silently. She was confused because she was a loyal and faithful servant to God.

Why had He chosen them? Could He have trusted you? With that level of responsibility? Mary carried our Lord and Savior, Jesus Christ inside of her womb. Could you be trusted with such a responsibility? I often wonder and I would say no—which is why I wasn't selected. God selected Mary because of her faith and commitment to Him. Sometimes I am not committed to God. If you are honest, you are selfish too. God cannot, will not use us when we are selfish.

Mary and Joseph did what great people do: obey God, love and fellowship with God and seek godly guidance. Mary went to see Elizabeth as wisdom and support. They discussed the glory of God.

Joseph didn't have anyone to visit. He was concerned about his image and still wanted to protect Mary. When the angel visits Joseph (Matthew 1:18-25), he is clear about his role. Mary had her own visit. She had similar concerns. In order to make the right decisions, we have to be filled with the Holy Spirit. We have to seek the Holy Spirit and God's guidance.

As a couple, it is easy to be swayed into disobedience, disbelief, selfishness and lack of focus. Trying to be a godly couple requires both persons to be completely centered on God and able to hear from Him.

How many times have we missed God's calling and assignment because we missed the message or doubted the messanger? It happens all the time. One of my favorite songs says, "He told me to go left, but I went right." We do the opposite and wrong thing everyday in some way.

I ask myself all the time: can God select me for the next big assignment? I laugh at myself because He trusts me all the time with something and I fail. Why would He trust me with the birth of Jesus?

308

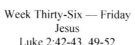

Week Thirty-Six — Friday
Jesus
Luke 2:42-43, 49-52

[51b]But his mother treasured all these things in her heart.

Luke 2:51b

A great child! Your child saves your life and the lives of all other sinners in the world. What a fact. Your child heals the blind, heals the sick, makes women whole again, aids the crippled and raises your own brother from the dead. Other children have done great things. My children will grow up to do great things. But Jesus did great things AND DID NOT SIN FOR 33 YEARS.

He was born to a virgin, an engaged virgin. Jesus was a special child. Jesus stayed at the temple in Jerusalem to sit at the feet of teachers. Only wisdom seeks wisdom and education.

Jesus was born to save the world. He taught and preached while He waited to save us. He saved, repaired, prepared and resolved lives while He was alive. He had a unique calling on His life. He was accountable to God first then His earthly parents. He understood that relationship at early age. Even though His parents knew His purpose, they still seemed unprepared sometimes for His greatness and amazed at the response of others.

Why are we amazed at our children's achievements? What kind of child was Jesus? I imagine that Mary did not have to ask Him to clean His room or other such chores.

What is it like to have to hold your parents accountable just like other Christians? (Luke 8:21)

His mother finally got the point. Mary Magdelene, His aunt, sometimes needed help fully comprehending that she was in the midst of Christ. She often needed reassuring and reminding as many of us do. We need help getting it. Jesus has a way of being subtle and poetic. I refer to it as a metaphorical misunderstanding. Jesus is making a point and we take days, months, years, or even decades fully understanding His message. We miss the message because our hearts are not pure. Jesus expects us to behave a certain way. We disobey—sometimes knowingly. We consider our own desires before we ask what would Jesus want me to do.

Jesus is GREAT! We were made in His image.

Week Thirty-Six — Saturday
Paul
Acts 9; Acts 13:9

[17]Then Ananias went to the house and entered it. Placing his hands on Saul, he said, "Brother Saul, the Lord—Jesus, who appeared to you on the road as you were coming here—has sent me so that you may see again and be filled with the Holy Spirit."

Acts 9:17

Saul was certainly a trouble maker. Then the Lord transformed his life. That is your testimony. That is my testimony. I was a trouble maker and could make small parts of hell rise and shake but you may never know how or when or why. I was a covert sinner. You may have been as well. Saul was an overt sinner. In Acts, Saul's conversion is described. The chapter opens with "Meanwhile, Saul was breathing out murderous threats against the Lord's disciples." (Acts 9:1a).

The tongue possesses mighty power—life and death power. I reckon with this all the time. I have "murdered" a spirit or two with a harsh tongue. In some ways, I had the same transformation. God took the tongue the devil could use for evil and turned it around for His use and His edification. Saul became a minister for God, for Christ. Saul converted into Paul, the <u>minister</u> of the New Testament. Paul's conversion was absolutely powerful and amazing and great. Don't say what God can or cannot or will or will not do. God uses who He chooses. He does so everyday.

The other facet of greatness is a transformation moment. Saul could've rejected it or denied or what we do: self-doubt. We let our own sin sink us into blessing rejection. WE talk ourselves out of blessings. We talk ourselves out of conversion or transformation because we do not <u>feel</u> worthy to do what God called us to do. We let others mock us into believing that He has not forgiven us for that sin. We treat our children like this because we are treated like this. We are standing in the way of each other's greatness!

Paul is the author of fourteen of the twenty-seven books of the New Testament. God does put Paul to work. Paul is preaching in a few chapters and authors the very next book in the Bible, Romans, which covers spiritual renewal.

God does not use the critical, judgmental, and harsh and unforgiving guidelines that we use when measuring greatness. God examines our hearts and then equips us for the greatness He has planned for us. We are not great without His plans and the execution of those plans.

Paul is GREAT. And humble.

WEEK THIRTY-SEVEN
WHAT KIND OF PARENT WOULD JESUS BE?

Jesus Christ was not a parent. Although unfortunate, He was not a parent but would have made a great parent. His character, attitude, and demeanor lends itself well to parenting. He is a also patient and kind and honest. Jesus would make a great parent. Using Him as an example, how can I be a great parent? I personally could use some tweaking of my parenting skills. Parenting gets complicated when issues are added such as financial, or marital or anything that keeps you from focusing on your parenting.

Child abuse is horrible but the actual child abuse takes place with majority women, Caucasian, ages 29-34, and middle class. The majority of the audience of this book fits the description of the average child abuser.

Why does that woman abuse her child? My best guess is based on my volunteer experience, she is overwhelmed with her life and all that her life entails. She doesn't have any help. Family doesn't live close. She and her husband haven't been on a date in months. She doesn't feel good about herself and she is too busy to know it. Take your life, add a child or two, add expenses to a budget that was already stretched, issues with employment, and stir, then you fit the description.

Parenting requires focus on the child. Jesus focused on us individually and collectively. When we are parenting, we have to prioritize what is most important between children and life. The children are the most important, if we forget or get distracted.

Jesus is a profound example of parenting. He knew how to discipline with love and compassion. Parenting at the level God's prescribes requires love, forgiveness, intercessory, obedience, instruction, spiritual knowledge, and disciplinarian. Parenting also requires compassion, time, attention, research, resourcefulness. God demands your best investment in His children. We are the steward of His children. We need to consider what God has designed for that child and your family. That child carries on your great name. They may make your name great.

Parenting is the key to their success in life. How you treat them is how they expect to be treated in the world. As parents, we have full control of their self-image and self-esteem.

Sunday	Loving John 15:9-14, 17
Monday	Forgiving Luke 23:34; Matthew 18:21-22
Tuesday	Intercessor Matthew 6:9-13; 26-36
Wednesday	Obedient Mark 14:35-36
Thursday	Teacher John 7:16-17
Friday	Spiritual Luke 2:46-47, 49
Saturday	Disciplinarian Luke 8:24b

Week Thirty-Seven — Sunday
Jesus Would be a Loving Parent
John 15:9-14, 17

[9] "As the Father has loved Me, so have I loved you. Now remain in My love. [13]Greater love has no one than this, that he lay down his life for his friends.

John 15:9, 13

Jesus had made the ultimate sacrifice. He died for all of our sins. He forgave those that ridiculed Him. He died for those who meant Him harm. He approached God on behalf of those who persecuted Him to have them forgiven. As a parent, Jesus would have transferred those same characteristics that He exhibited daily. Jesus loves without judgment. Jesus loves us in spite of ourselves, our sinful selves. Parents are judgmental and critical and overbearing and protective and possessive. Jesus demonstrates His love for us through His presence, deeds, teaching, wisdom, and service.

Jesus would chastise us gently. He would teach us so that we would not be chastised as often. He would influence our obedience. He would be easy to follow as a leader parent. Jesus seeks to understand rather than to be understood. Jesus used every miracle as a teachable moment. He would parent that way too.

Jesus would have the popular house, where all of the children came after school and on weekends. Jesus would sit around and talk to us about issues and scenarios we are experiencing. Jesus would be the parent who would volunteer at school and bring His child lunch on Fridays.

Jesus would love at a significantly different level because He is omnipotent, what regular parents need to help them along their parenting journey. Jesus loves deeply and would transfer that love to a child. Likewise, He would teach that same depth of love.

Jesus is the example of the greatest love because of the sacrifice He made to die for us.

Jesus is our ultimate parenting example for love.

Week Thirty-Seven — Monday
Jesus Would be a Forgiving Parent
Luke 23:34a; Matthew 18:21-22

[34a]Jesus said, "Father, forgive them for they know not what they are doing."

Luke 23:34a

Even on the cross at the brink of death, Jesus is asking for forgiveness to those who wronged Him. He intercedes on their behalf in an effort to save their sorry lives. And mine. Ours.

Jesus would be a forgiving parent. Jesus forgives and corrects with such mercy. As a parent, we benefit from His forgiveness. We also benefit from forgiving our children. Forgiveness frees you up from hate, lack of love, lack of engagement, and lack of trust.

The Bible says that we are to forgive seven times seventy. This is not a literal translation. This means to continue to forgive without limits. Jesus forgives like this. He made us in His image but we don't forgive in His image. We forgive based on pride, experience and benefit. We consider ourselves and those benefits first before we forgive to the benefits of others.

Forgiveness is not optional. Jesus forgives even those who persecute Him. We do not believe we should forgive if we believe we are justified. Wouldn't you agree that we do this? Because we do withhold our forgiveness, God can withhold our forgiveness from us.

What does forgiveness cost? It costs pride. I have to give up my pride when I forgive. This requires work for me. It costs God forgiving me, which is more valuable than my pride. It costs love. When two or more people are not more forgiving, then they cannot love one another. Love that is not reproducible but needed. When love is at a sacrifice then time spent is effected.

Forgiveness is critical for personal growth and maturity. Lack of forgiveness stalls your growth and maturity. Forgiveness is essential to the relationship between people regardless of who those people are. As a parent, forgiveness is an essential to quality parenting.

313

Week Thirty-Seven — Tuesday
Jesus is Our Intercessor as Parent
Matthew 6:9-13; 26:36

[36]Then Jesus went with His disciples to a place called Gethsemane, and he said to them, "Sit here while I go over there and pray."

Matthew 26:36

As I use my sanctified imagination, I would hope that when Jesus returned from His many recounted prayer sessions that the disciples inquired about the contents of Jesus' prayer.

As a child I was SUPER inquisitive so I know that I would ask Jesus, "Did You pray for me?" I would also expect an answer in the affirmative.

My mother prays for me, as I would expect her to. I have asked her for what do you pray. She prays for wisdom, knowledge, great decision making, favor, and financial stability. She prays for my sister and her children and grandchildren. She prays for my children and my marriage.

As a parent, you and your spouse should pray for your children daily. You are to INTERCEDE on their behalf. You are to seek forgiveness for their past. You are to pray for what they will face daily. You are to pray for their future. You are to pray for their day, that the paths they travel be safe and they are fruitful in their endeavors. You are to pray for their spouses and friends. You are to pray for their education and careers. You are to seek guidance for their future and their needs.

You are to pray for them daily before they rise. While they are sleeping, you are to seek God's face for your children. Jesus asked God for everything. Jesus shared with God EXACTLY what He needed.

You are an intercessor for your child. You need to remember your role. Just like Jesus intercedes on your behalf, you intercede on the behalf of your children. Your intercession penetrates the heart and mind and soul of their very being. Intercedes on their behalf.

Week Thirty-Seven — Wednesday
Jesus Shows Us Obedience
Mark 14:35-36

[36] "Abba, Father," He said, "Everything is possible for You. Take this cup from Me. Yet not what I will, but what You will."

Mark 14:36

Jesus made the ultimate sacrifice. He died so that we may have life and have it more abundantly. When God told Jesus what He wanted Him to do, that Jesus would live for 33 years, sin-free but at the end of His earthly life He would die for my sins, Jesus said, "Yes, Sir."

Jesus watched God's plan and will for His life unfold. He walks us through each phase and each parable for use in our life. Jesus has God's bestowed powers but couldn't pass God's will.

Jesus is a lead by example leader. As a parent, I sometime lack this quality. Jesus asked to take this responsibility away. Then He totally submitted and surrendered to God. He told God that He will submit to God's will.

I need to do more of this. Jesus shows us obedient behavior modeling. He showed us how to be obedient and He shows us how to model obedient behavior.

God requires parents to be obedient as well. We are not exempt from obedience. Obedience shows God we love Him. When our children are obedient, they respect and love us. Parents often neglect the obedience because we are on a power trip. Parents are the ultimate authority in a child's life second to God. Sometimes we take the "authority" of our role too far. We extend and embellish our realm. We are not God to them. We have to obey God for their lives.

We are simply a steward of God's workmanship: "our children." As a steward, we are judged by God about how well we are handling our assignment. In order for that to workout, we have to be obedient and use Jesus as our leader and example.

Negotiation is not applicable while obedient.

Week Thirty-Seven — Thursday
Jesus Is Our Teacher
John 7:16-17

[16]Jesus answered, "My teaching is not my own. It comes from Him who sent Me. [17]If anyone chooses to do God's will, He will find out whether My teaching come from God or whether I speak on my own."

John 7:16-17

I love math. I teach math. I tutor math. I advocate math. I love math because it is objective. Other subjects are subjective. I can prove a math problem to others who don't speak English and vice versa. God's word is the same way: His word can be proven and will be proven. When I teach, I am seen as the expert. I have been given credit for extensive knowledge in certain subject matters. I have been invited to speak in front of incredible audiences. These invitations have been great and the time is awesome. However, when I give false information then I sacrifice my "expert" designation.

Jesus suggests that we test His teachings through living according to God's word. When we live according to His word, then certain things happen. Jesus' teaching can be measured against a standard: God.

As a parent, we are expected to be an "expert" teacher. When we are wrong, we have to be honest. When we don't know, we need to say so. When we promise to find out information, then find it and relay that information.

As a parent, we are the first teacher. We are responsible for all the information that they intake whether they get it from us or not. We are responsible for their learning, education, and development. Jesus only authorized certain persons to teach. Jesus trained the teachers personally as disciples. His guidelines for teachers are clear.

Further, Paul states that teachers are accountable at a higher level. As a parent, we are responsible for their knowledge intake. We have to be selective about who pours into their lives at all levels. We are accountable for this. In addition, we are their ADVOCATE. We hold those educational contributors accountable as well.

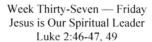

Week Thirty-Seven — Friday
Jesus is Our Spiritual Leader
Luke 2:46-47, 49

[46]After three days they found Him in the temple courts, sitting among the teachers, listening to them and asking them questions. [49] "Why were you searching for Me?" He asked. "Didn't you know I had to be in My Father's House?"

Luke 2:46, 49

Effective parenting requires mutual accountability. Jesus sets the tone for spiritual leadership in our lives. Husbands, you are personally responsible for that spiritual leadership in our homes. Wives, you are to support his leadership. Husbands, your family is looking to you to set the agenda and follow-up on your plan. Husbands, do know that this role is heavily accountable and least appreciated but the most spirtitually rewarded. Spiritual leadership requires a plan that influences growth, development and progress.

Husbands insure that regular prayer and Bible study and church attendance and ministry involvement. He leads these activities by scheduling prayer and following through. He may not lead Bible study but he insures that his family attends Bible study regularly. He supports and encourages authentic ministry participation. He \also participates in ministry opportunities.

The husband as the spiritual leader insures that his family is fed spiritually through all available means. Regular church attendance and fellowship with a local church is required for a healthy life. The wife enhances the relationship when the couple is spiritually aligned.

Jesus was about His Father's business at an early age. He committed to be the Jesus God called Him to be. Jesus provides an example for us to follow for spiritual guidance and leadership.

317

Week Thirty-Seven — Saturday
Jesus As the Disciplinarian Parents
Luke 8:24b

[24b]He got up and rebuked the wind and the raging waters: the storm subsided, and all was calm.

Luke 8:24b

Jesus disciplines us because He loves us. I discipline my children because I love them. Whatever method you choose, your children respect you for discipline. Discipline is administered because of and with love. Discipline is also timely—not held as retaliation or used to reduce the child's esteem. Further, discipline corrects behavior and is not related to them personally or their feelings or future.

Jesus' discipline is complete POWER. He calmed the winds and raging waters with His voice. Even the winds obey Him—that's the power of His discipline.

Discipline requires consistency. Jesus models consistency. He disciplines us based on what we need for discipline. He does not discipline us the same. We are motivated by different entities. The consistency is key for the discipline to be effective.

These factors apply to our discipline: consistency, applicable, and timeliness. When I consider discipline, I ask myself is this an appropriate response for the "offense" or is this an attention stunt. I acknowledge that something inappropriate happened. I consider how many times this may have occurred before this offense. I decide whether the effects are lasting or fleeting. Lasting effects deem more severe discipline than fleeting effects.

Why did Jesus calm the storm? He taught several lessons: (1) Jesus possesses all power, (2) HIS POWER is far-reaching, (3) He reminded the disciples that faith in Jesus is required to be an effective disciple, and, (4) He uses anyone or any situation to demonstrate His point.

Consistent discipline delivers effective parenting.

WEEK THIRTY-EIGHT
PARENTING EFFECTIVELY

Jesus effectively influences and assists us to parent. When we consider the sacrifice Jesus made for us to have life. To live on the veil of His mercy, grace, and forgiveness, He shows us how to give those benefits to our children. He teaches us to lead, to offer compassion, to serve, to comfort, to counsel, to provide, and to be faithful as parents. As a leader and example of what Jesus will do, we had to focus on His actions and His ATTITUDE. As parents, your GREAT attitude makes the difference. Your attitude determines your child's attitude. The cliché of the "apple does not fall far from the tree" holds especially true here. Your response to a situation heavily influences how the child responds to what he/se faces. When I am optimistic and positive, my children respond the same way. When I am not, they respond the same way. In so many ways, I control their response and their behavior with my behavior and responses.

Jesus shows us how to respond and react through how He treated those closest to Him: His disciples. As parents, we have to impart knowledge and wisdom to our children. I know this is the most difficult part of what we do because we have to find time to do it! In our current culture and economy, we have to work two jobs to maintain these "Dream" lifestyles. We work 60-80 hours per week per person to do this maintenance. So this begs the question: "WHO IS WATCHING THE CHILDREN?"

I have a friend who is the mother of three girls and stepmother to two boys. When she quit her job during the third pregnancy, my first thought was 'why would she do that?' But after more consideration, I know that she made the BEST decision. In order for her to work, she took the children to daycare. She was spending her entire paycheck on the daycare, so she was working for someone to watch her children. She decided that spending time with them was more important than working.

I have another friend who responds, "It's not my day to watch them", when she is asked where someone is. When she first said it to me I laughed. One day, I made a choice to pickup my child and return to work with her. It was my day to WATCH her. Spending time with our children is how they learn what we need them to know. It is your turn to spend QUALITY time with your children.

Sunday:	Compassionate as Parent John 11: 35
Monday:	Leader as Parent John 6: 1-2
Tuesday:	Comforter as Parent John 16: 33; Isaiah 66: 13; Matthew 11:28, 30
Wednesday:	Servant as Parent John 13: 5-17
Thursday:	Faithful as Parent Hebrews 11: 6
Friday:	Counselor as Parent Isaiah 9: 6
Saturday :	Provider as Parent John 6: 11-13

319

Week Thirty-Eight — Sunday
Compassionate as Parent
John 11:35

[35]Jesus wept.

John 11:35

Jesus wept. Jesus expressed emotion. Jesus shared His feelings with others. Did your parents talk to you? My father was absent. My mother tried to talk some – sometimes. If you are in your 30's, you can relate. People stop talking when they become parents. I think that the responsibility and the changes influence that. We should talk to our children A LOT! We should be sharing our feelings with them. When we share, they understand what is important and they feel free to share with us. When we do not talk and share, our children get their information from other adults and mostly children, who know less that our children. YOU ARE THE SOURCE.

I am emotional. I am moved to tears often. I am secure when I cry. My children have seen me cry. They are sensitive to my tears. They know that I am sensitive to their tears. They know that I do not judge their tears. They know that I embrace them when they cry.

Tears convey compassion. Jesus wept. What is the difference between weeping and crying? Weeping expresses a heavy burden – more serious then a cry. Jesus wept the death of Lazarus, His uncle. Although Jesus would later raise Lazarus from the dead, He still wept.

Children REQUIRE compassion. Compassion communicates care, concern and commitment. Listening, hugs, soothing, affirmations, reaffirmations, and general love delivers compassion.

A compassionate parent empowers a child and enhances her self-esteem, confirms her self-worth and assures her of your commitment to her.

COMPASSION IS REQUIRED.

Week Thirty-Eight — Monday
Leader as Parent
John 6: 2

[2]and a great crowd of people followed Him because they saw the miraculous signs he had performed in the sick.

John 6: 2

The people who FOLLOW you define your leadership. Jesus never announced the He was our LEADER. The disciples and other observes witnessed His LEADERSHIP.

How does He do that? Jesus did His job. He healed the sick, feed the hungry, and ministered to the broken. He did it un-assumedly, meaning He did it without expecting anything in return, including recognition.

As a parent, you are the leader by virtue of stewardship of those children, I read this definition of leader and always refer to it: "A leader has nothing to do with ability, but the inability to let things fall apart around you." A parent takes action so that the world doesn't fall apart around them and their family. There are times when I feel that similar miracle in my kitchen and checkbook.

Jesus led by example. Jesus did what He was suppose to do first, shared His expectations secondly and then He holds us accountably for doing His assignment, finally. Jesus expects us to lead by example. This is the hardest thing to do as a parent. My children challenge me about my word choices and my actions. As a leader, this will happen in any setting, however this is critical when raising kids because you are sharing their skills as a leader and their work ethic as a person.

Jesus shaped us to be forthright, honest, ethical, and confident. When you are in the presence of a leader, you should leave His presence full and eager to return.

Parenting at the leadership level requires self-respect, submission, and service. Parenting at the leadership level requires pride at past tense.

You are responsible for the knowledge and wisdom that your child possesses and what they lack as well, regardless of the source of the information. Your leadership is designed to be so powerful that your information is the source, not only for your children, but also to their friends and classmates. Leadership requires discipline. The leader has to be disciplined. Iron sharpens iron. Sharp parents produce sharp children.

Week Thirty-Eight — Tuesday
Comforter as Parent
John 16:33; Isaiah 66:13; Matthew 11:28, 30

[33]"I have told you these things, so that in me you may have peace. In this world you will have trouble. But take heart! I have overcome the world"
[13]As a mother comforts her child, so will I comfort you; and you will be comforted over Jerusalem."
[28] "Come to me. All you who are weary and burdened, and I will give you rest. [30] For my yoke is easy and my burden is light.

John 16:33; Isaiah 66:13; Matthew 11:28, 30

My daughter forces me to expand my ability to comfort her. She has also made me aware of the need for comfort. She further makes me address my own need for comfort. When you decide you need comfort, you face the fact that you are having a difficult time. It is not cool to admit that you need comfort or need help. You may think of it as a weakness or deficiency. Needing comfort is not the weakness that we think it is. Comfort from Jesus and the Holy Spirit. We need the Holy Spirit's comfort to endure the tough times, the anxiety and the weak moments.

As a parent, our children look to us to offer them that comfort. The challenges are knowing when to comfort and how to comfort. The challenge is getting it right.

My daughter bit her nails and sucked her thumb. Well I didn't know that was her source of comfort until I asked her to stop sucking her thumb. She was harassed by her teacher and others. I made a proposal that she stop the nail biting in exchange for nail polishes – unlimited. I also had to work on her daddy who bites his nails.

The thumb sucking has the audience held captive. Sucking her thumb comforts but has all who meet her annoyed. I let that go because she seeks that comfort, but does not know how to ask.

The last thing that brings her comfort is to sit in my lap. She climbs into my lap and that is her source of comfort. I have to settle down to appreciate that time. Comfort is important to each of us. We first have to know how to access it.

Week Thirty-Eight — Wednesday
Servant as Parent
John 13: 16

[16] I tell you the truth, no servant is greater than his master, nor is a messenger greater than the one who sent him.

John 13: 16

As a parent, you are the custodian and steward of these children. THE CHILDREN BELONG TO GOD. When God blesses us with children, God retains ownership thus parenthood. We serve God as parents. As parents, we are servants. God expects us to serve Him through:

(a) Loving the children
(b) Educating the children about God, Jesus and the Holy Spirit and all related spiritual education
(c) Education = book knowledge
(d) Provide food, shelter and clothes under God's provision and direction.
(e) Give Biblical and Christian direction
(f) Live a life which God is glorified, which pleases God
(g) Sharing how to live with faith
(h) Guiding them with Christ-centered disciples
(i) Emotionally feed the children
(j) Listening to them
(k) Teaching them to serve God

When we serve God through parenting we submit to God's leadership and guidance. Submitting to God's leadership means seeking His voice and consulting His word for how to guide His children.

Don't forget, you are His child too. He feels the same way about you as He feels about your baby.

God equips you to handle your calling as parent well. Use your imagination for how much God expects us to achieve as parents. We just need to do it. God is not accepting our excuses for poor results. As with your job/career, your 110% effort is expected. Also with your job, you are promoted based on your performance. God places children in our lives for two reasons: (1) to test how much He can trust us; and, (2) to use what He trusts you with to assist in the development of His design through the life of this child.

Yes, completely overwhelming and overwhelmed. This is your chance to see the fruits of great hard work and the results of divine intervention. God wants to know how you will depend on Him for proper parenting.

Parenting is service unto God.

Week Thirty-Eight — Thursday
Faithful as Parent
Hebrews 11: 6

[6] And without faith it is impossible to please God, because anyone who comes to Him must believe that He exists and that He rewards those who earnestly seek Him.

Hebrews 11: 6

A child exposes your faith and mostly the lack there of. There are days when many parents do not know how they are going to feed, clothe, shelter, keep the power on and love all at the same time. That may be you. Sometimes it has been me. I certainly consider the Lord's favor when I consider the mismatch between my bank account and bills. The Lord provides.

I have been viewed as resourceful on all levels in all walks of my life. I consider that a compliment. I use what I have to do what I need. I consider my resourcefulness a gift. I use it wisely and call it up when I need it. When our son was born, I was in training at a brokerage firm to sell mutual funds and life insurance. I also started a home-based business that was based on sales and recruiting. I wanted to stay available for my son so I had to make that business work. And I did. I became moderately successful and I replaced my previous salary within six months of this start-up.

I worked so I could be at home with my son when I wanted to rather than when I could base on a work schedule. My husband didn't understand or appreciate my effort and that didn't matter. I didn't really want to do the business and he didn't ask me if I wanted to do it. I did it anyway. I decided it was what I needed to do so I could do what I wanted to do: spend time with my children.

I had to exercise all the faith I had daily so that I could be successful in that business so that my income didn't burden my household. Although the Bible doesn't say that, that was my job, I did it and I did it with FAITH.

Parenting requires BOLD FAITH! No matter how much faith. The amount of a mustard seed will suffice but whatever the measure, BOLDNESS is required. Subtle faith will never do. Timid faith will not accomplish the goal. Mediocre faith will cause failure.

Parenting requires complete, BOLD, unwavering, resounding, and submissive faith. Your faith pleases God. God responds to your faith.

Week Thirty-Eight — Friday
Counselor as Parent
Isaiah 9: 6

[6] For to us a child is born, to us a Son is given, and the government will be on His shoulders. And He will be called Wonderful Counselor, Mighty God, Everlasting Father, Prince of Peace.

Isaiah 9: 6

"In Jesus' name, Amen." I end all of my prayers this way, like many Christians. Jesus shared with us that if we asked for anything in Jesus' name, it would be granted! When I seek His guidance and leadership, He counsels me. He counsels me when I ask and when I don't. He counsels me because I need help to the next step and level. He counsels me because I am frustrated and have had enough of my current situation. He counsels me because He loves me and cares for me. He counsels me because the Lord destined Him to and He has the power to counsel me. He counsels me when I am in need. He counsels me because He was gifted to do so.

A parent counsels a child the same way for the same reasons with love. Counsel is wise and sound advice. Counsel is legal and sometimes profound. Counsel solves problems, overcomes fears, extinguishes doubt and intimidates fear. Counsel is the conversation that a mother and daughter share when the daughter has her first "crush." Counsel is love through listening. Counsel is love through time.

At 3-years old, I told my mother and the doctor that I wasn't taking anymore allergy shots. The doctor probably thought that the three year old was operating without wise counsel. Sometimes we do not seek counsel. Our children will opt out of counsel as well sometimes. We do have to accept that however, we are designed to be ready to give wise counsel. Sometimes wise counsel is referring to another source, such as the Bible and professionals in that field.

"In Jesus' name, Amen." I call on Him even when I don't know I need counsel. He answers without judgment. Parents often counsel in judgment; judgment we couldn't possibly personally sustain. The rules of wise counsel: timely, non-judgmental, non-consequential and lovingly. Drop the "I told you so," and the "you need to listen to me."

"In Jesus' name, Amen."

325

Week Thirty-Eight — Saturday
Provider as Parent
John 6: 11-13

[11] Jesus then took the loaves, gave thanks, and distributed to those who were seated as much as they wanted. He did the same with the fish. [12] When they had all had enough to eat, he said to the disciples, "Gather the pieces that are left over. Let nothing be wasted." [13] So they gathered them and filled twelve baskets with the pieces of the five barley loaves left by those who had eaten.

John 6: 11-13

When God created Adam, He gave Adam a job. God provides for our children through the careers and talents with which He gifts us. When Christians recall miraculous, this is one of the first one that comes to mind, Jesus provides for something with so little.

Your ability to provide may be financially. There's move to it. When this miracle took place, Jesus also ministered to those same persons. As a church, we feed homeless persons, we help find shelter, and we offer them other resources. We do not minister to someone until they are physically full. The physical fullness makes the emotional and spiritual fullness comes shortly afterwards.

When you provide as a parent, it is the ENTIRE definition, not the financial portion alone.

Resourceful covers the financial provision.

I can teach them spiritually. When I need support spiritually, I have church members who support their growth. Spiritually, they need support but consistent exposure and reinforcement is the key to their spiritual fulfillment and growth.

The hardest provision I have to make for my children is the emotion shelter. Emotional provision is the hardest responsibility I have. Providing a safe space for full emotional disclosure is the job description. Most of us do not do this well because we personally do not have a safe place to fully disclose. When growing healthy emotional children, a child needs to feel safe about sharing how they feel. They also need quality time to share these feelings. Preparation for this area is key for a successful life.

WEEK THIRTY-NINE
RELAX

Around the time the baby is about to arrive, we start nesting meaning we clean and straighten and organize and fluff. We have this energy burst and become excited and we need to RELAX! We need to sit down and RELAX! After the baby arrives, RELAX will be a distant memory. Relax is defined however you decide. Relax for me is a manicure or pedicure or a nap or a message or a long drive or just QUIET.

As a mother, I have to schedule the Relax. I have to take my babies to the salon with me so I could get these things done. Those trips were far from relaxing. You may have to be creative about how this happens after the baby arrives, so do all you can now.

Encourage your spouse to Relax as well. Life changes completely when the baby is born. I have a cousin who told my husband when we married that he could kiss his golf good-bye. My husband didn't believe her. He knows better now. His time to play golf has severely diminished and the resources too.

Relax! Kick your feet up. Listen to all the songs on your iPod or MP3 player. Take time for yourself. Savor the nuances that you have personally taken for granted. Cherish waking up on your schedule rather than the schedule of a little one. Close your eyes and enjoy the silence. Stop scheduling things that don't involve RELAX!

Go sit with your friends, family and associates, which you have been promising all this time. Keep the moments fresh. Relax. Spend time with your spouse doing the things that you did when you met and dated. Read all of your magazines that you usually just skim, or never read at all.

Relax facilitates the refuel, the re-energizing and re-evaluate. If you appreciate the RELAX now, when you need to relax, it won't be foreign. Likewise, your appreciation will be great making the RELAX that valuable. When you are able to RELAX, you don't usually get overwhelmed. As a parent, you will face some difficult times. Knowing how to relax is critical for keeping a balanced household and life.

RELAX!

Sunday:	Enjoy each other Song of Solomon
Monday:	Enjoy Hot Meals
Tuesday:	Enjoy Warm Baths
Wednesday:	Enjoy Quiet Time
Thursday:	Enjoy Other People
Friday:	Enjoy a Clean House
Saturday:	Enjoy sleep

Week Thirty-Nine — Sunday
Enjoy Each Other

As a married couple, you have been intimate during cooking, quiet time, and bed time, just to name a few. The fact is that your creativity is about to be exercised – fully and completely. Enjoy this time together before the baby arrives. Talk to each other as often as possible. Talking as a couple changes as soon as the child starts talking.

Work hard to share time. This is critical to grow your marriage relationship. Often parents lose that marriage relationship because we forget the importance of our marriages. Keep your marriage and spouse secondary only to God.

Balance your life so that you do not neglect one another. Take time to understand and meet the needs of each other. This time should be used to maximize the relationship assuring the firm foundation of your marriage.

Your marriage will need maintenance. Establish regular date nights where you beg, borrow, or hire a babysitter, and have time with your spouse, ALONE. The date night is a time to reconnect with your spouse, laugh with your spouse and give your spouse your undivided attention. Enjoy your time with one another. When the child arrives, your time allocation changes greatly.

Spend the time the way you best enjoy. HAVE FUN! Go places together that are adult only or not child friendly. Go to movies and enjoy the time in the movies.

I realized that my marriage changed after my children arrived, meaning my marriage changed twice. The focus left us and was given to the children. We stopped focusing on each other and focused on our children, BAD IDEA. Your spouse is second to God only.

Neglecting your spouse for any reason will create dissension in your marriage. The resentment that builds doesn't show up until something terrible happens.

Please maintenance your marriage.

Week Thirty-Nine — Monday
Enjoy Hot Meals

My husband and I were out eating dinner one evening while I was expecting with Hillary, our first child. A couple stopped at our table and encouraged us to enjoy our hot meals. We laughed until they left, but realized that we hadn't thought of that. They were correct by the way.

ENJOY HOT MEALS! ENJOY ALL MEALS!

After the child arrives you are responsible for feeding that child. She gets hungry and is not aware of your hunger. I learned early in their lives to order their meal when I order my water. When their food arrives, I feed them and then order my food. I have started ordering salads so that some of this is overcome. I suggest a similar plan so that you can enjoy a meal out every now and then.

Also find all child friendly restaurants. Find out which restaurants offer "kids at free" nights. Keep in mind that you may consider some places crazy but you want to know these places. They will eventually know because they will have friends and be invited to birthday parties. I have friends who have stated that they will never go to certain kid-focused venues but they have had to abandon that stance because they have children.

As a help for you, please take care of the restroom trips before you are comfortable in your seat before anything arrives at your table, especially if you are out alone – the only adult and you are there with children. A lady once spoke to me and said to me, "Never leave your child with someone you don't know nor put your child in danger." Based on her wisdom, I strategize when I am everywhere.

A child changes your routine, inclusive of your names and lifestyles.

ENJOY YOUR MEALS!

Week Thirty-Nine — Tuesday
Enjoy Warm Baths

When my day was difficult when I was single, I would come home and take a long hot bath. When I would take that longer than normal bath, I could take my time and use all those products I purchase from Bath & Body Works. With a new baby, the long bath time does not happen as often, but the days are not easier. Now the long baths are further and further apart. We talked about the RELAX. The bath is one of my techniques. With the bath as risk, I have to deal with replacing the bath with something else. It is a process to establish a stress relieving mechanism. It is important to do this. Parenting can be overwhelming. That stress relief helps pass the overwhelming parts of parenting.

Enjoy any alone time that you have. Enjoy the hot baths or the hot chocolate or iced tea or whatever you do to take time to relax and unwind. Take time for self.

Parenting is hard work. Please plan time for this. It is hard for me as well, but I am certain to try to get in all my relaxation/me time. The list consists of my hair, toes, nails, body massage, and sleep.

So whatever you have to do to avoid being overwhelmed or stressed out remember what the airline attendant instructs us to do: "If there is a loss in cabin pressure, when the oxygen mask drops down, put your own mask on first, then help the child or dependant you are responsible for."

Help yourself so that you can help those who depend on you.

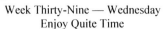

Week Thirty-Nine — Wednesday
Enjoy Quite Time

I love to sleep. I love to sleep-in. I love to sleep late. I love to take naps. I like to read. I like to write. I like to listen to music. None of these "likes" includes talking.

I do love to talk, don't misunderstand but when I want quiet, I want quiet.

As you child arrives and grows, quiet time is hard to achieve. Overall, after the child arrives, your quiet time takes place when they are asleep. Again, quiet time is the refuel. It is a time to spend with God, listen for His voice and direction. Our quiet time needs to be protected. At most costs.

In your quiet time, the following should be considered:

- Prayer time to pray over your family, each child individually and your spouse.
- Prayer time for yourself.
- Meditation on His word.
- Read His word.
- Journaling of the prayers and the answers.
- Quiet so I can hear from God.

What time is your established quiet time? What do you need to secure that time? How do you protect that time? How do you measure the value of that time?

How do you teach your children how to have quiet time? It is also important that they understand to respect your quiet time. Your spouse also needs to know to respect your quiet time. You and your spouse could schedule your quiet time together on a weekly basis.

Keep your time important so that you can be refueled.

Week Thirty-Nine — Thursday
Enjoy Other People

I gave up some relationships when I got married and lost more when I had children. BIG MISTAKE!
Iron sharpens iron! Keep yourself around people that will lift you, rather than bring you down, feed you with positive feedback and information, support your ideas no matter what happens and who you enjoy.

When you are around the people who you enjoy, then you are happier and are less likely to feel overwhelmed. You have a safe-haven of places where you can relax and share your life. Keep your friends and family close.

Have fun! Be a fun person! It's hard to do all the time. I lost my glowing laugh during the first seven years of my marriage and certainly after the second child. Stay in touch with people. MAKE THE EFFORT! It's worth it. I recently attended an event where people had not seen me in over a decade to more than sixteen years in some cases. I didn't realize that I missed that segment of my life. I cannot be an island. Nobody can survive alone. I know that I like to only depend on me. You need people.

I have had a Mary Kay business and we have weekly meetings. We would address why the meetings were important. "When you are up, the meetings need you. When you need to be up, you need the meetings."
People need each other. Enjoy other people! Stop avoiding the mom's groups, or social organizations or the church ministries. Stop avoiding people. Being around other people encourage you to feel better about yourself and stop feeling bad about your life and lifestyle. Remember that before you were married and had children, you lived a different life and while you may not be able to do all the same events but remember to maintain a life when you have friends and activities and things that are designated for adults.

Iron sharpens iron.

Week Thirty-Nine — Friday
Enjoy a Clean House

Your home may be showroom clean and detailed. Mine once was. I decided that once my home was out of hand, I left it there. I do not have any help. My children are learning to clean up after themselves. So when they are older, my home will return to showcase status.

I am learning to live simpler. I have learned to throw stuff away. I have learned to label what I keep. I have learned to keep only what I need. I have learned to share what I have and only buy what I am going to use. I had become a collector of stuff – things. A fetish is something that you have a strong affection for – Gage's interpretation.

I have several "fetishes" or collections: paper, writing instruments, purple stuff, and the other things I collect. The discipline for keeping these to a minimum is hard. These are the elements that keep me from keeping a clean house.

Keep in mind that you want to keep a clean house. A clean house insures a healthy child. Be careful with the chemicals you use around your baby. Your lungs and respiratory system have adjusted to those fumes so how you react to the chemicals and the baby's reactions will be different.

Now you clean your house weekly or bi-weekly or daily at your choice on your time schedule. Now you are on your baby's schedule. Understanding that when you clean your house it may not be as regular as before, however, remember not to neglect your child or time with your child. If your home is not "clean" when you have company, you should not feel guilty that your home is not spotless.

If your visitor is the 'white glove" or "the house inspector," then that visitor may need to help you clean. When they make a comment or a look, and then ask them to immediately help. Have specific things you need done, especially during your recovery time. Lastly, consider your budget and hire a maid to back you up with your cleaning efforts.

Week Thirty-Nine — Saturday
Enjoy Sleep!

SLEEP! I would love to sleep late on Saturday mornings. I define late as wake up on my own, rather than being awakened by a cry or a pat or a voice. This may never happen again, however I do try.

Sleep has never been the same since I have children. I remember one evening that I ate dinner and was in bed at 7 pm and slept until 7 am. I was pregnant at the time. When I was single, I slept into the morning because I would not get to bed until very late in the evening.

As a parent, now I wake up to voices, television, patting or feet. The "feet" happens when some child gets in my bed and falls asleep. I wake up because the feet are in my side, in my face or in my back.

Sleep when you can. When the baby is born, sleep when the baby sleeps. When the baby is sleep, this is not time to clean that closet or mop the floor or clean the fridge (the refrigerator). You need to rest. The rest keeps us from being overwhelmed. Child abuse occurs when the mother is overwhelmed. Have a plan for avoiding this. My strategy was calling friends or family members when I hadn't had enough rest. I was only overwhelmed once. I remember crying with no provocation. I was driving. I drove to my mother's house, gave her the baby and lay down. I slept for hours. Once I woke, I hugged my mother, thanked her and left.

There is no judgment for needing sleep or resting to relaxing or reading – some type of downtime, unrelated to cleaning or parenting.

SLEEP! SLEEP! SLEEP!

Enjoy SLEEP!

WEEK FORTY
SEVEN DAYS OF PRAYER

Start your seven days of prayer. Prayer summons power. God hears us when we pray. Seven days of prayer will fill you with His presence and guidance and instruction.

We have discussed completely that prayer is the communication that we need to be within God's will. Prayer is designed to face the issues we address as parents. Prayer is REQUIRED! Seven days of prayer influences your life, your marriage, your child(ren), and your circumstances.

Seven days of prayer can include your entire family or your extended family. Set a special time for prayer. At that agreed upon time, raise the prayer concerns. Pray for as long as God leads you and speaks to you.

From the days of prayer, you will access the power you need to keep focused on your child. The power of prayer keeps us from being overwhelmed. Pray as a couple. PRAY as a couple! Pray as a COUPLE! PRAY AS A COUPLE!

God has gifted you as a couple to be a couple, to have a child together, and have given you the stewardship of that child. You need to access God for your needs. He is waiting for you to ask in Jesus' name for what you need and your heart desires.

Pray for all things that you are thinking about and what you need and whatever overwhelms you and what scares you and what hurts you and what excites you. Pay about everything. I Thessalonians 5: 12 states, "Pray continually." All the time! Yes, when you break the tape closure for the diaper, PRAY! Nothing is too silly or too small for God.

Prayer accesses POWER! Prayer lifts your head! Prayer reintroduces the positive. Prayer reminds us that we are not alone.

Pray together. Fast together. Feel together. Prayer reminds us not to internalize, rather to verbalize to God and to each other what is happening. The communication is critical to maintaining healthy relationships.
You will need this POWER. PRAYER stimulates POWER. PRAYER summons POWER from above and within. God ANSWERS PRAYER!

Sunday: Pray for Health

Tuesday: Pray for Cohesion in Your Marriage

Wednesday: Pray for Guidance as a Parent

Thursday: Pray for Trust, Faith, and Confidence

Friday: Pray for God's Favor

Saturday: Pray for God's Peace

335

Week Forty — Sunday
Pray for Health

Your health is important. Your child's health is important. You get one body. You are the steward of that body. This means that we have to be conscious of what we eat, how we live and how we exercise or NOT.

Get to know your family's health history. TAKE THIS SERIOUSLY. I have history of diabetes in my family. I am careful about how I eat. I have to exercise. I maintain my weight. I get regular check-ups and blood work so that I know where I am. I do not want diabetes. I do not want that lifestyle. I lived through that as a child.

On the other hand, my husband does not consistently take care of his health. He is on the weight roller coaster. I have insisted that he take better care of himself. Many of us are in this situation. Health needs to be maintained so we need to be honest about our health. Honesty means that you are telling your spouse what your weaknesses are so that you can support each other. Now my husband is more honest and more focused on his health. Health can be hereditary. I am concerned about what health issues will be passed on to me from my lineage and likewise to my children.

Our health habits are contagious! My children love to exercise. They love outdoors. They love it because they see the inside of the gym four times each week. They eat healthy because we serve healthy food as often as possible. Fit families groom fit families. My children want to workout. They are active. They do watch television and play games, but not all the time. They initiate the outdoor activities.

You have one body. Use it well. Be healthy.

Week Forty — Monday
Pray for Cohesion (New or Renewed) in Your Marriage

Marriage is HARD. Adding children to your marriage increases the difficulty level of the marriage. Children demand you divide your time, responsibilities, and finances. These demands can cause strained cohesion in your marriage.

Pray for cohesion in your marriage. Your marriage needs PRAYER. Your marriage needs cohesion. This cohesion is what keeps you married. Cohesion keeps your marriage flourishing. Cohesion aligns your marriage with God's design for marriage, and specifically, your marriage.

Pray for your marriage. Pray for enhanced communication in your marriage. You are able to complete all of your thoughts at one point, now you may not be able to complete all your conversations.

Without cohesion, your marriage will struggle. Without communication, your marriage may falter. Without prayer, your marriage may fail. You need to save your marriage through prayer. Many marriages have failed after the children are born because the couple does not know how to transition with this life event.

This is also a great time to enlist the prayer of others. Your relationship will be challenged in various ways. Knowing this is the challenge is the best defense. When the "challenges" come you will not be surprised. I know that most of what happened in out marriage surprised my husband in various ways. We were surprised by different situations.

Pray for aligned thoughts and actions between you and your spouse. Our children and most children probably test us. He will ask my husband for something and the response is no – not what he wanted to hear – so then he will ask me. I redirect him and remind him that "your dad said no" to let him know that we are on the same page.

Children will stretch the cohesion of your relationship.

Week Forty — Tuesday
Pray for Guidance as a Parent

Parenting is a difficult job, at best. Why we sign up for and ask to be here, I will always question. Children are gifts from God. He plants them where He plans to do His best work. Children change your life – all aspects. As adults, our adjustment time is slow. Where we need immediate transition, we are still on gradual changes.

Parents have rules and regulations imposed on them from all governments and outside persons, whether; the rules or expectations are realistic or not is not the issue. Parents need guidance and wisdom. Grandparents are usually key in this area. In the absence of grandparents, parents seek outside guidance.

Pray that all guidance you seek is Godly, Christ-centered and child-focused. The Bible says that if anyone asks wisdom, he will receive it.

As a parent, you will need answers, help and support. Guidance may come in the form of asking a nurse how high can the fever be or asking your sibling to come over for a few hours so that he can watch the child while you take an uninterrupted bath and a nap.

Each child is unique, so when their teeth come out or how they grow will be different and not worth talking about. However, asking how to address a particular problem, such as how to understand them emotionally, how to teach them to win and lose gracefully, and how to be patient with their progress or lack thereof, is worth discussing.

Seek God first. Then decide what successful parenting looks like. Then be advised not to judge. Also be careful when you complain about your children and her behavior.

My mother and I were visiting a family. My mother was talking about my teenage disobedience about being on the phone. We were going on and on. Eventually, the mother said that at least she wasn't on drugs. Her son had been on drugs, through several rehabilitation centers and was still unsuccessful, now as an adult. The mother had spent many sleepless nights worrying and wondering about his whereabouts and well being. Always remember that your situation could be worse. For someone else it is worse.

Week Forty — Wednesday
Pray for the Release if Fear, Anxiety and Doubt

Parenting can be scary. You are the steward of that child's life. You can do this. God is there with you through your parenting. Yes, there are things to fear about parenting. How do I feed this child? How do I care for this child? Who is going to care for my child while I a working? What happens if they fall and bleed? Who will be the pediatrician? What is a pediatrician? God gifted you with this child so He has prepared you and sent someone to help you. He may have sent others as well to help you.

God didn't give you spirit of fear. Where you feel fear approaching, seek God first. Seek His face and voice to cast away the fear. FEAR has been appropriately acronymed as False Evidence Appearing Real. When FEAR is overwhelming you and your situation, God considers what you do to seek Him. You are to seek Him when you have fear.

When we have anxiety, we are to lay our burdens on Jesus who gives us rest. "Be anxious for nothing, but in everything in prayer and supplication give your burden to Christ." Gage's version of the scripture. In short, give your anxieties to Christ. Cast your worries on Him. Easy to say? Yes. Easy to do? Not necessarily.

Pray for the ability to give over your worries, anxiety, fear, and any related doubt. Pray for your ability to leave your fear with God. Anxiety, fear and doubt introduce stress. Stress causes other issues. Pray for the release of fear, anxiety, and doubt. Pray for the relaxation that results from the release.

Pray.

Week Forty — Thursday
Pray for Trust, Faith, and Confidence

Parenting is a TEST of your trust, faith, and confidence. Trust is dedication to God – not your mate, not your family or friends or others, and not yourself. TRUST is limited to and focused on God, Jesus Christ and the Holy Spirit.

As parents. we are trusting God for guidance, wisdom and leadership. We are depending solely on HIM.
God will bring you through your parenting storms, whether they are slow drizzles or full category five hurricanes. Parents certainly need God.

I found myself trusting myself and other and often being disappointed when I trusted persons other than God. Keep in mind that God will send people to you to assist, provide, guide and share with you. However, your trust is only to be in the Lord.

Parenting is the test of your faith. Your faith will grow and expand exponentially. You will never move beyond the faith growth. Your faith will always deepen and broaden. Your faith offers you the opportunity to share your faith and your testimony with other parents. Your testimony will grow another parent's faith. Hebrews 11 addresses faith. Hebrews 11: 6 reads "without faith it is impossible to please God." The lady with the issue of blood touched the hem of Jesus' garment – just the hem and Jesus looked for her. He felt Himself transfer power to her. She was found and Jesus addresses her saying that her faith made her whole. YOUR FAITH MAKES YOU WHOLE! Confidence to do what God directs you to do. Where God guides, God provides.

God will enhance your confidence about what to do for His child. God will give you the confidence you need to execute the decisions you make for the children. God is a creator. He creates builders. He gives the builders the tools. He expects it to be used for His glory.

Pray.

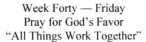

Week Forty — Friday
Pray for God's Favor
"All Things Work Together"

We are on the sixth day of prayer for today. We are asking for God's favor. We are asking for God's favor with full faith and confidence that God will deliver.

God's favor is the unexplainable positive events, thoughts and occurrences that we experience. Favor is unexplained and UNMERITED! Favor is often UNDESERVED!

Pray for favor – mercy, grace.

Pray for the unforeseen issues which God transfers to a blessing. Pray for the impossible in your life to work out for your good. The Lord uses your worst moments to bless you and show up on your behalf. The events in your life are designed to glorify HIM. I remember when Nehemiah was two he jumped off of a table at "daycare" and hurt his head. When I got the call, he was bleeding. I raced to his school to pick him up from there to go to the Texas Children's Hospital. This gash in his head is not bothering him at all, but I am anxious. Once in the care area, the doctor comes in and suggests a staple and I immediately wanted to go with the stitch. We have a short debate about the difference. Finally, she comes to place his one stitch. The nurse who accompanied was the true blessing. Because Nehemiah had eaten, he was not supposed to have anesthesia. He has just eaten. In addition, they didn't normally do stitches. The nurse helped the doctor with my request. We did a stitch with local anesthesia. The nurse has full conversation with Nehemiah about his favorite movie "Cars." She knew every character and most of the scenes. Nehemiah was completely comfortable. As s matter of fact, they were still comparing notes when the stitch was completed.

Nehemiah was cared for and my needs were met. The doctor learned some new things.

God placed the nurse. He sent the exact nurse who would do exactly what she did. That is on exhibit of God's favor. Nehemiah never cried. That is favor from God.

341

Week Forty — Saturday
Pray for God's Peace
"Which Transcends All Understanding"

"Jesus loves me this I know for the Bible tells me so. Little ones to Him belong they are weak but He is strong. Yes, Jesus loves me. Yes, Jesus loves me. Yes, Jesus loves me for the Bible tells me so." I sing this song to all babies. I started with mine.

After one verse of this song, the baby is calm and you are able to think, assess and act on the baby's behalf. "Jesus loves me" is a powerful song that brings peace That song has quieted and disciplined many storms.

You need to know how to access His peace. This song is a start. His peace is paramount. Your storms require His peace.

You will often not understand His peace. When Jesus called Peter out on the water, I was jealous but why should I be. Jesus calls me and escorts me out on the water all the time. When I am somewhere I wished had been my idea but it was God's plan instead, that's God's peace.

He calls me out to the water daily. When He protects me, I am on the water. When I start and finish the projects He gifts me with, I am walking on water at His invitation.

Pray to hear His invitation. Pray to hear His voice. Pray to RELAX in His peace.

Don't be like Peter who got nervous when he should have been praising Him and celebrating Jesus for what He has gifted him with.

When God's Peace is at work, explanations do not happen. HIS PEACE is HIS PLAN. Let him take you out on the walk. Let Him make His plans come true and your dreams fulfilled. Do this and your testimony will be rich with His peace, faith, mercy, and favor.

His peace is powerful. Access to His peace is divine.

AFTERWORD

Dear Parent:

While writing this, my children grew and my marriage changed several times. **As We Grow Together** has three important connotations: (1) as we grow together closer to Christ personally, (2) as we grow closer together as mother and child and as the father develops a bond with the child, and, (3) as we grow closer together as a couple.

It is my sincere prayer that this has blessed your relationships with God, Jesus and the Holy Spirit, as well as your mate, your child(ren) and family. Growth is all about relationships. When we enhance our relationships, we elevate others above ourselves.

Please let the Holy Spirit be your guide as you make decisions for your child. There are decisions that are not permanent, so that a mistake does not have long term effects. On the other hand, long term effects of decision require study and prayer and wise counsel.

It is my prayer that we have established some foundational Biblical principles that will be accessed as you and your child grow. I know this does not cover every issue that you will encounter, however, you have new tools you can use to be an effective, Christian parent.

Congratulations on this journey. Be careful to not miss anything that could be considered special. Also keep in mind you establish the pace and routine your children experience.

In His name and because of His love,

Onedia N. Gage

ACKNOWLEDGEMENTS

What a Majestic God I serve! Your awesomeness overwhelms me. Thank you for loving me, forgiving me and planning my life. I apologize for interrupting my plans.

To my children, thank you for being yourselves. I love you and cherish our time together.

To my family and friends, thank you for your support and encouragement.

To my church family, thank you for your prayers and leadership.

To Mrs. Iris Jackson, thank you for typing such an overwhelming project.

To Mrs. Doris Broome, thank you for your insight and critique. Your opinion is truly appreciated.

To you, may these words impact your parenting and divulge the secrets of parenting others have chosen to keep to themselves.

About the Author

Minister Onedia N. Gage has been writing since age 13. She has written through each of her storms and her sunshine. The gift of writing is ever present in her life. She is often seen with a pad and pen. Rev. Gage is truly transparent in her writings and seeks to share her testimony with others. She

As We Grow Together Daily Devotional for Expectant Couples addresses Christian parenting. There is an accompanying **As We Grow Together Prayer Journal for Expectant Couples**.

The Blue Print, poetry that exposes her innermost thoughts, was developed over 15 years. She encourages the creativity in others and is starting a writing circle for those who write. She desires to turn what has previously been a hobby into full-time career.

In Purple Ink: Poetry for the Spirit captures the essence of the journey through pain and a reconciliation to God. The road away from pain is a complicated one so she offers this work to insure that you are not alone and certainly not forgotten.

The Measure of a Woman: The Details of Her Soul discloses the secrets and the nuances and the idiosyncrasies of a woman. **Measure** is bold and states clearly that we are more than conquerors and the journey of a woman will certainly show her worth.

On This Journey Daily Devotional for Young People covers issues young people struggle with daily. Because there is a shortage of resources which exist for the sole purpose of assisting our young people with biblical sources for worldly situations, Rev. Gage designed **OTJ** for that purpose. **On This Journey Prayer Journal for Young People** offers young people the opportunity to journal their prayers and concerns in a format comfortable for them.

She authored **Promises, Promises**, a novel, out a need for female heroines of her time.

Her life philosophy is three – fold: A) "What have you done today to invest in your future?" B) Reading is essential to your positive contribution to our community; and, C) "If not me, who? If not now, when?" She feels her time is best spent when youth benefit from her experiences.

Minister Gage was licensed June, 2009 at Wheeler Avenue Baptist Church. She is an active member of The Church Without Walls where she is on the clergy team, the women's ministry, has served with children's ministry and Vacation Bible School.

Because of her volunteerism with the Houston Area Urban League's NULITES, she was elected one of the youngest board members of the Houston Area Urban League. She is also a member of Zeta Phi Beta Sorority, Inc., National Council of Negro Women, Toastmasters, International, Top Ladies of Distinction, and "Sistah to Sistah," a literary review group.

Onedia N. Gage is a native Houstonian. She is a graduate of Kaplan University with a Masters in Business Administration, Lamar University with a Masters in Education in Education Administration, and University of Houston, central campus, with a Bachelor's of Science degree in Economics and a minor in African American Studies. She is a graduate of Bellaire Senior High School. She is currently pursuing her Ph. D. in Business Leadership and Masters of Arts in Christian Education.

She is has two beautiful children.

Please feel free to contact her at www.onediagage.com and Onediagage@onediagage.com.

INDEX

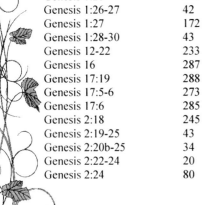

RESOURCES & TOOLS

www.biblegateway.com
www.lifeway.com
www.parenting.com

CPSIA information can be obtained at www.ICGtesting.com
Printed in the USA
LVOW07s2329171215

467085LV00001B/266/P

9 780980 100228